IMAGES
of America

PORT JERVIS

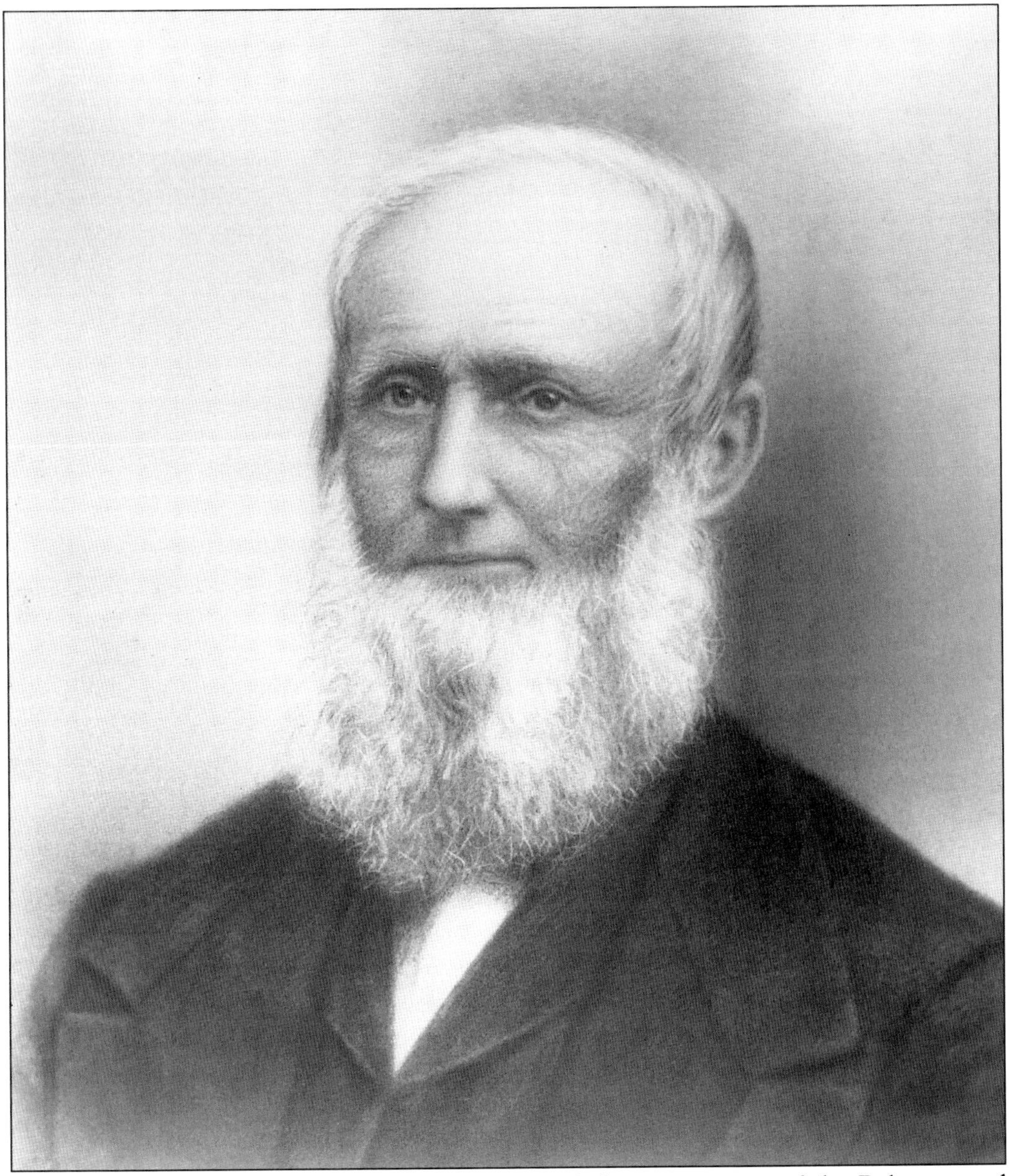

The namesake of the city, John B. Jervis, supervised the construction of the Delaware and Hudson (D & H) Canal and was responsible for having the Erie Railroad built down the Deerpark Mountain side of this valley and across the Neversink River. These two developments helped turn Port Jervis into a prosperous city. (Collection of the Minisink Valley Historical Society.)

IMAGES
of America

PORT JERVIS

Matthew M. Osterberg

ARCADIA
PUBLISHING

ISBN 978-0-7385-0900-6

Published by Arcadia Publishing
Charleston, South Carolina

Printed in the United States of America

Library of Congress Catalog Card Number: 2001090421

For all general information contact Arcadia Publishing at:
Telephone 843-853-2070
Fax 843-853-0044
E-mail sales@arcadiapublishing.com
For customer service and orders:
Toll-Free 1-888-313-2665

Visit us on the Internet at www.arcadiapublishing.com

This book is dedicated to my children, Stephanie and Michael, my parents, and my wife, Carol, and her family. It is families like hers that formed this city.

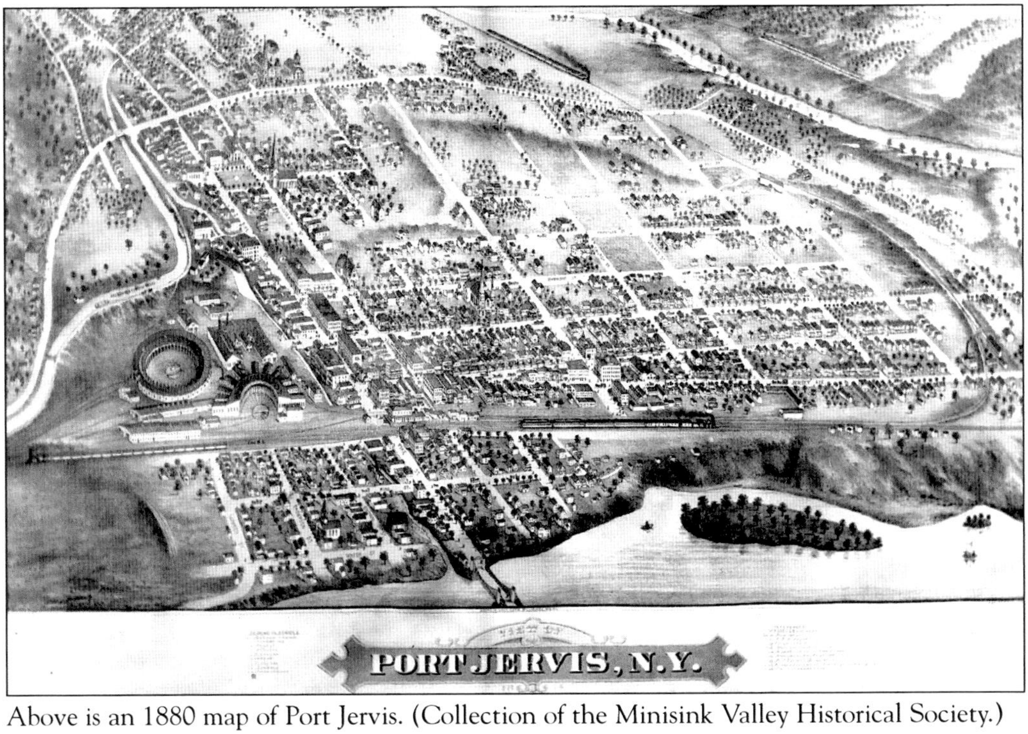

Above is an 1880 map of Port Jervis. (Collection of the Minisink Valley Historical Society.)

Contents

ACKNOWLEDGMENTS

There are many people and organizations to thank for helping me in the preparation of this book. I would like to begin by thanking my wife, Carol. She wrote many of the captions and kept me on course. I would also like to thank her family. Their unending love of this city and fond memories made compiling the information much easier. My wife's grandfather Jacob Caputo and others like him were instrumental in starting the Mount Carmel Society. Her grandparents Aurelio and Assunta Colaiaco ran a small candy store in the Acre. Her father, James Colaiaco Sr., entertained the people of Port Jervis with music; her mother, Fannie Caputo Colaiaco, volunteered her time for worthy causes; and her brother James Colaiaco Jr. is a local teacher. The men and women in Carol's family, and many others like them, are the kind, caring individuals who make up this community.

I thank the many groups and individuals who were generous in sharing their photographs, memories, time, and expertise to help create this book. A thank-you to Peter Osborne, for his guidance and for writing the introduction—he is an asset in every sense of the word to the city of Port Jervis; to the Minisink Valley Historical Society, for allowing me the use of its vast collection of photographs; and to Brian Lewis, whom I had just recently met and who was very excited about the book (I think he e-mailed me a thousand times with pictures and information for the text). A special thank-you to Lizanne Samuelson, Dan Dwyer, Jim Harrison, Will Hoppey, Ted Willers, Joe White, Fred White III, John and Tina Hess of Hess's General Store, Jane Connelly, Betty Collins, Dave Chant, Clara Hughson, Chris Farkelas, Norma Schadt, Sharon Lewis, Charles Gillinder and Gillinder Brothers Inc., Mike Latini Jr., the Mount Carmel Society, Dennis Gilpin, Ed Nikles Jr., Linda Brink, Darryl McKeeby, the Erie Depot, Jerry Walters and the Deerpark Dutch Reformed Church, Jerry Peill, and Dr. Frank Simpson.

I am very grateful to the individuals who wrote so extensively on Port Jervis. Their resources were invaluable in writing the captions for the photographs: *Port Jervis New York Diamond Jubilee 1907–1982; The Port Jervis Heritage Commission; Where the Rivers Meet: Golden Jubilee 1957; Stephen Crane: A Walking Tour; A Guide to the Region's Historical Markers; Coming of Age: The Chartering of the City of Port Jervis; A Family History: Eddy Farm; Orange County: A Journey through Time* (Orange/Ulster Board of Cooperative Educational Services); and *Coal Boats to Tidewater: The Story of the D & H Canal* (by Manvile B. Wakefield).

INTRODUCTION

When one speaks of Port Jervis, it is usually described as Orange County's smallest city, with a population of almost 10,000, retaining its quiet, unassuming charm and ways. However, Port Jervis today is only a ghost of the bustling city it was *c.* 1880–1925. During that time, the then village blossomed as a canal, railroad, and industrial center, so much so that it became a city in 1907. The town considered itself modern and took great pride in its affairs. It vied with Newburgh and Middletown, Orange County's other two cities, to be the leading urban area.

If there is one theme that runs through our city's history, it is that of transportation. Port Jervis has served as a crossroads in the region's transportation network. From earliest times, when the river was used to raft logs or when the Old Mine Road, America's first 100-mile road, was used by early European settlers, Port Jervis has been a transportation nexus. With the opening of the Delaware and Hudson Canal in the late 1820s, the village, named in honor of canal engineer John B. Jervis in 1826, began its meteoric rise as an economic center. The canal company laid out the original plan for the city, which was center was near present-day Canal and East Main Streets and the site of the canal's basins. As a result, the city developed as a major stop on the Delaware and Hudson Canal.

The canal was constructed to ship anthracite coal from the Moosic Mountains in the northeastern corner of Pennsylvania to the metropolitan New York City area and New England. After a run of 70 successful years, it fell victim to the railroad. But during the first half of the company's history, it dominated the region and its economy. Many of the village's most important businessmen got their start working on the canal, supplying the canal company with items or shipping local products.

The canal's impact on the local economy was eclipsed with the arrival of the first Erie train in December 1847. Much of our city's history has been defined by the Erie Railroad. The trains of the Erie stopped in Port Jervis, and it served as a division center between Jersey City, New Jersey, and Susquehanna, Pennsylvania. In 1922, 20 passenger trains passed through the city each day and six trains reached New York City before 10:30 a.m.

A brochure describes it as "the place where through trains changed their engines" because of its role as a mainline engine terminal, car shops, icing facilities, coach yard, fueling facilities, classification yard and a large freight yard.

By a 1922 estimate, at least 2,500 employees of the railroad lived in the Port Jervis area and worked in the shops. This was at a time when the decline in railroading was already becoming apparent to leaders in the community. Port Jervis was also a hotbed of union activity, as it was the meeting place of the Delaware and New York divisions. The unions started here were among the earliest formed across the entire system. It was said the payroll was over $125,000 per month in the first years of the 20th century.

The result of this excellent position in the transportation network has been economic growth that began in the 1850s and continued until the Depression. The city, at one time, was an industrial center with a variety of retail stores, glass houses, stove makers, five silk factories, some of which operated well into this century, five bottling works, six bakeries, two cigar factories, a silver plate factory, a saw factory, a tannery, a brewery, and glove, shirt, clothing, and shoe factories. Another benefit of being a transportation nexus is the interesting kinds of people who either lived here or used various transportation to get here. Stephen Crane and Zane Grey both come to mind, and any number of well-known architects came here to design buildings.

Port Jervis is a different city from what it was 100 years ago. Often people say they would like to have lived in another time because things were better. And, indeed, in many ways things were better in the bustling era of the late 19th and early 20th centuries. However, we are blessed in these times, although in many different ways. Each generation has its own challenges. This book focuses on a 90-year period in Port Jervis's history that lasted from c. 1880 until 1970. Many of the photographs in this book are from times that seem simpler and slower-paced.

The essence of history is remembering, and this delightful book is a perfect example of that old saying. There are almost 200 photographs included from public and private collections, many never before published. These pictures are of our families, our grandparents, their-grandparents, and their children. Many are prized possessions and are often all that remain. They bring back memories when we look at them.

The pictures, particularly the portraits, make us wonder what-was happening in people's lives at that moment. Were they thinking about a special occasion, like a wedding or social gathering, or were they preoccupied with something about their job? They look stiff, not like the lively people they probably were. The picture of Jacondo "Jake" Caputo, Frank Caputo, and Jake's brother-in-law Donato Callichio (all erect, handsome, and serious-looking) is a good example. The picture of the people standing on the open-air trolley car is another. How many of those boys might have gone off to World War I? How many young women became mothers in the decades that followed?

This book also reflects how much America has changed between the 1880s and today. We have long ago discarded trolleys, gaslights, and horses and buggies. In this day of declining volunteerism, we have forgotten how people used to volunteer for all kinds of things, whether it is the fire department, historical society, church or Mount Carmel Society. The political parades reveal how much more we used to pay attention to the burning issues of the day. Who today can remember the last political parade in the city of Port Jervis, where large banners were strung across the street?

That is not to say we do not live in better times—only different times. Port Jervis is a small city whose population is again about 10,000 for the first time in decades. It is a place where we still celebrate and remember Memorial Day, Veterans Day, Arbor Day and read the Declaration of Independence on the Fourth of July. We have a wonderful firemen's parade that lasts for hours, a community Christmas tree, and a Halloween parade. In many ways, Port Jervis carries forward traditions many people grew up with in decades past. It is a town where one can still raise a family.

As we look back on this the 94th anniversary of the creation of the city in 1907, we need to aspire to lofty goals, as our forefathers did in the early years of this century. We should aspire to greatness and capitalize on our geographic position—and use the wealth created by that to make our city an even better one.

Our historical society is proud to be a part of this book, and we are pleased with the work of Carol and Matt Osterberg. They have done a wonderful job in capturing the flavor of our community, remembering our history, and helping us preserve our heritage. We also see this as a way of helping to create a basis for our future, by remembering our past. We hope you enjoy this wonderful journey through our past.

Please go to our Web page at www.minisink.org to learn more about the Minisink Valley Historical Society.

—Peter Osborne

One

GETTING AROUND

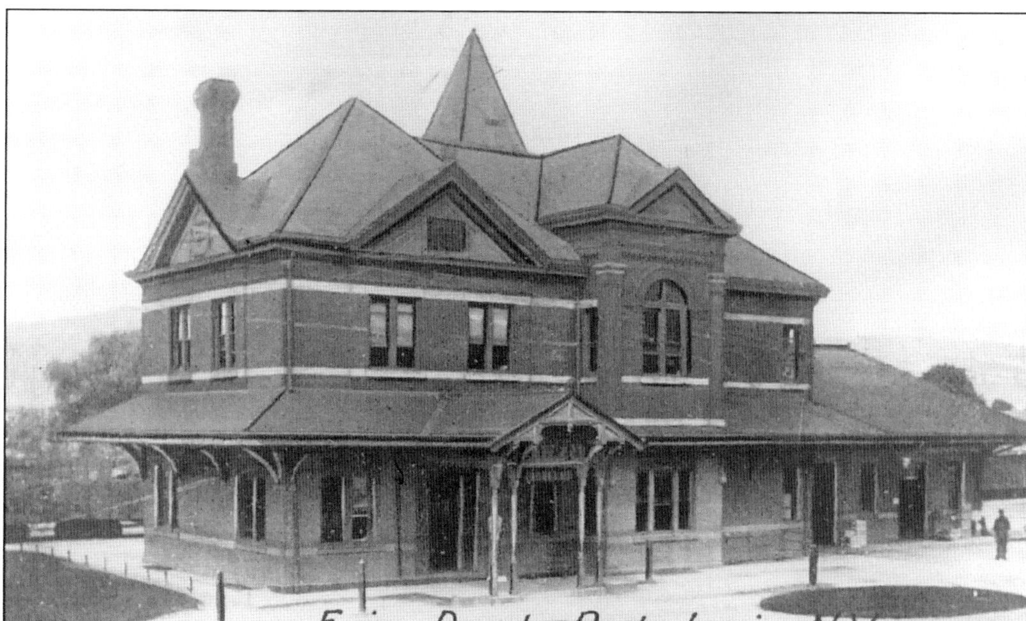

The current Erie Depot on Jersey Avenue opened for passenger and freight service on February 2, 1892. When the depot opened its doors, newspapers described the building as "a decided ornament to Port Jervis." Today the Erie Depot, after extensive interior renovation, is a home to many small shops and offices and is still a jewel to the city. (Collection of the Minisink Valley Historical Society.)

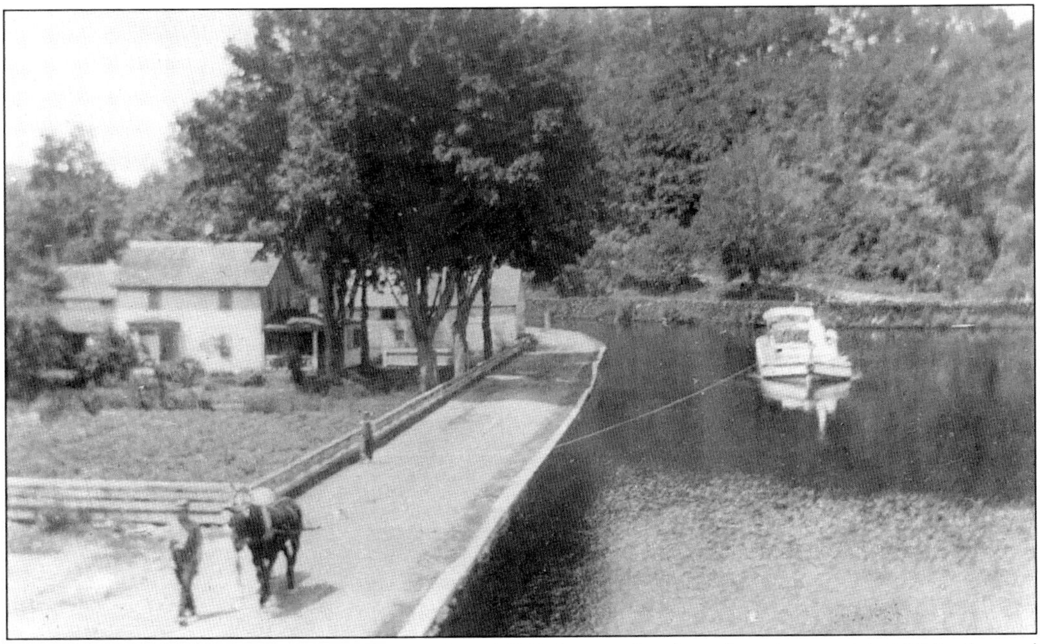

Construction of the D & H Canal started in 1825. It was dug four feet deep, with 108 locks and numerous basins, dams, canals, and aqueducts. It opened in 1828 and extended for more than 110 miles from Honesdale, Pennsylvania, to Kingston, New York. The construction of the canal included the operation of a gravity railroad from Carbondale, Pennsylvania, to Honesdale. In this area, the canal went through Sparrowbush, Port Jervis, Cuddebackville, Huguenot, and Westbrookville. Remnants of the canal can be seen today throughout the area. The photograph dates from *c*. 1890s. (Collection of the Minisink Valley Historical Society.)

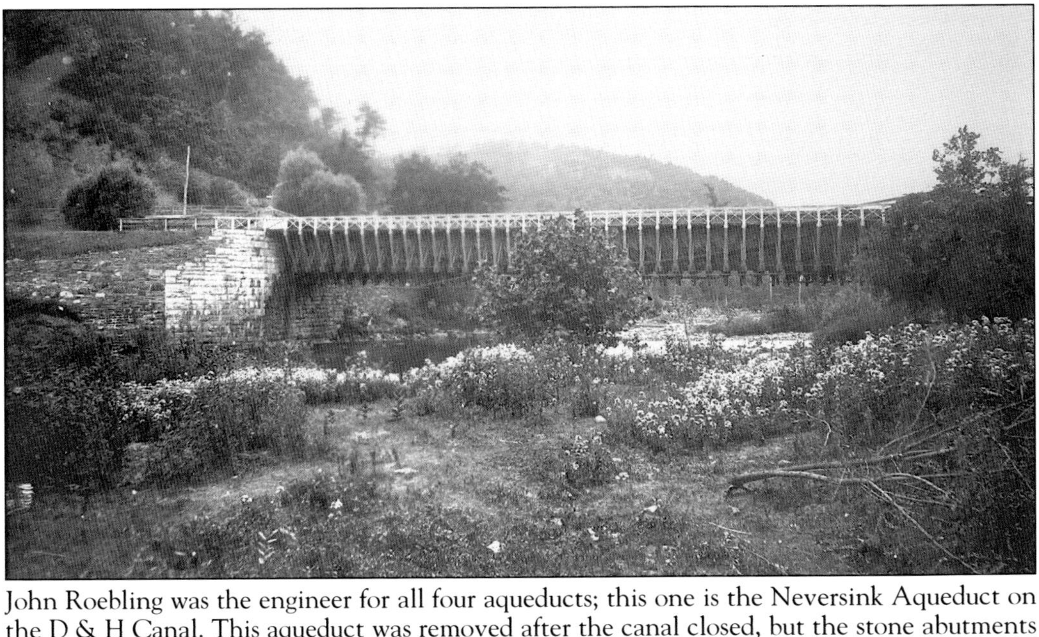

John Roebling was the engineer for all four aqueducts; this one is the Neversink Aqueduct on the D & H Canal. This aqueduct was removed after the canal closed, but the stone abutments can be seen near the Neversink Museum in Cuddebackville. (Collection of the Minisink Valley Historical Society.)

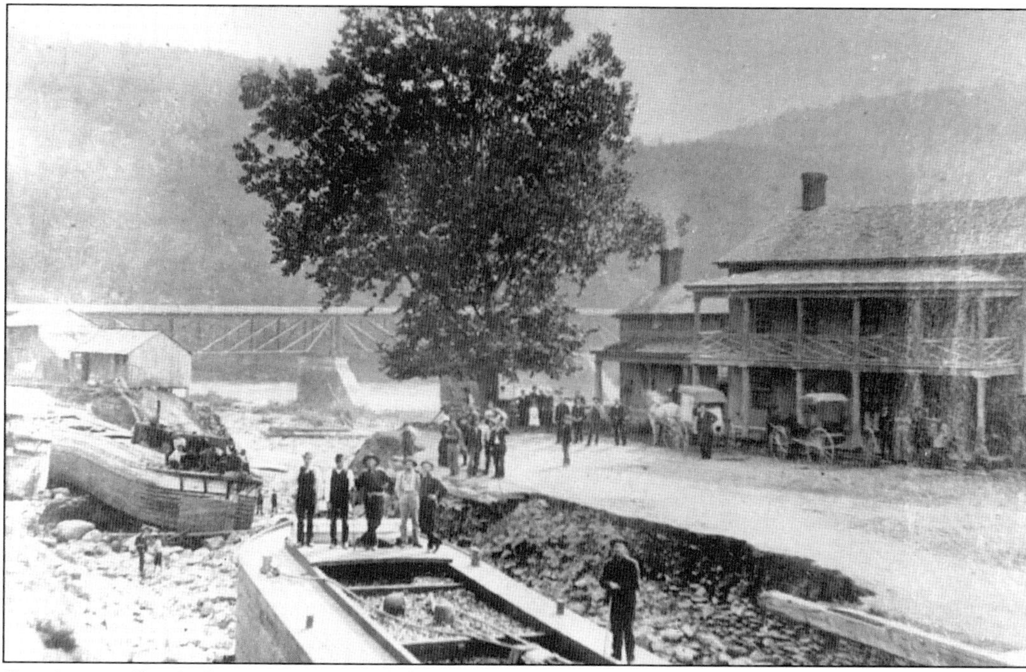

On August 5, 1885, a storm caused the canal to empty into the Delaware River. Repairs were made in the Bolton Basin area of Sparrowbush. The building to the right is the Simpson Hotel. (Collection of the Minisink Valley Historical Society.)

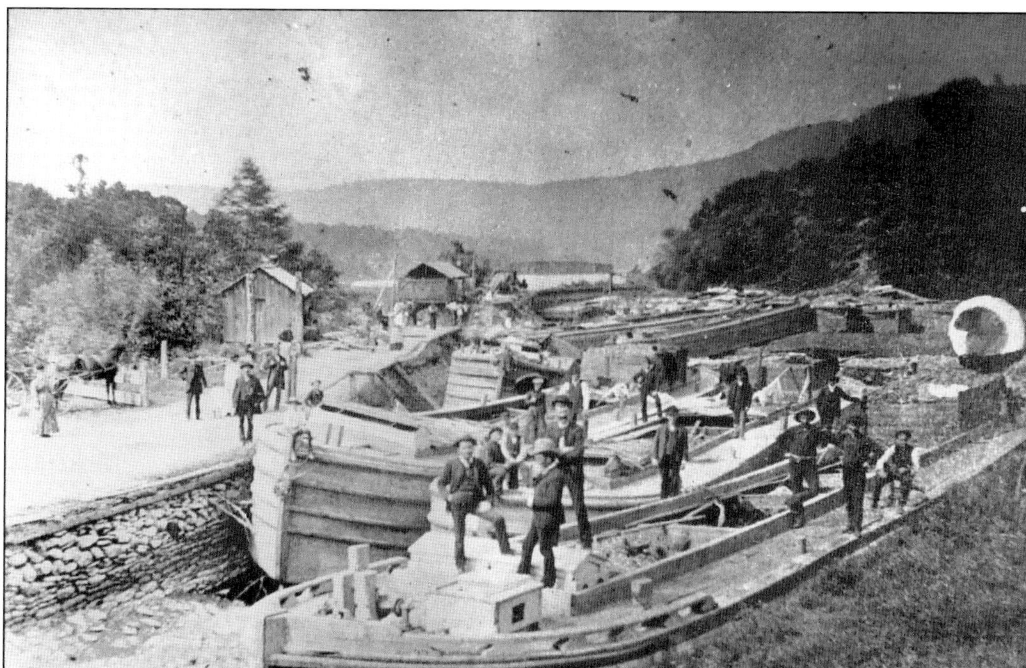

The No. 2 railroad bridge can be seen in the distance crossing over to Pennsylvania in this view of the break at Bolton Basin in Sparrowbush. (Collection of the Minisink Valley Historical Society.)

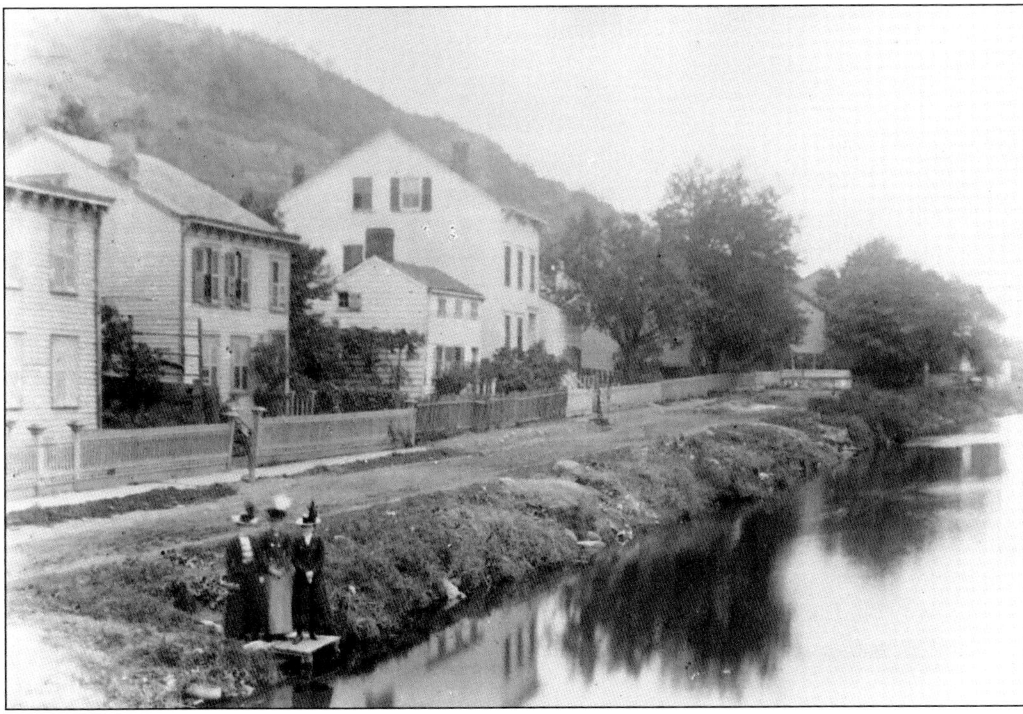

The canal came directly through Port Jervis. This is the scene of the canal near Grandview Avenue. In the wintertime, the canal was a favorite spot for ice-skating. (Collection of the Minisink Valley Historical Society.)

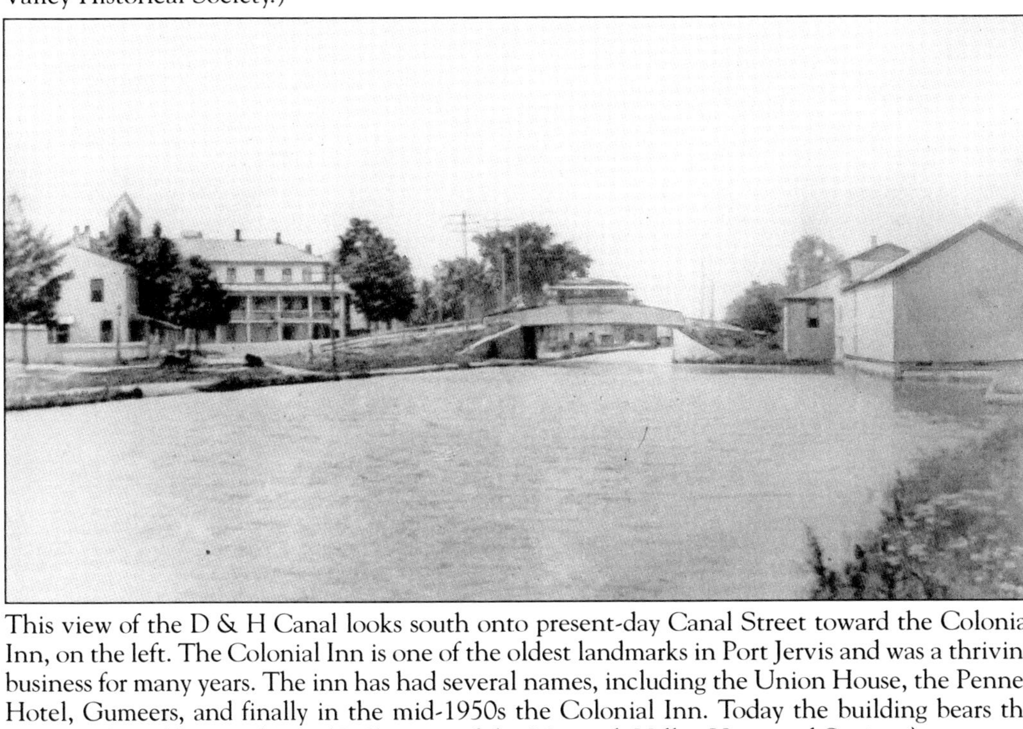

This view of the D & H Canal looks south onto present-day Canal Street toward the Colonial Inn, on the left. The Colonial Inn is one of the oldest landmarks in Port Jervis and was a thriving business for many years. The inn has had several names, including the Union House, the Penney Hotel, Gumeers, and finally in the mid-1950s the Colonial Inn. Today the building bears the name of the Olde Canal Inn. (Collection of the Minisink Valley Historical Society.)

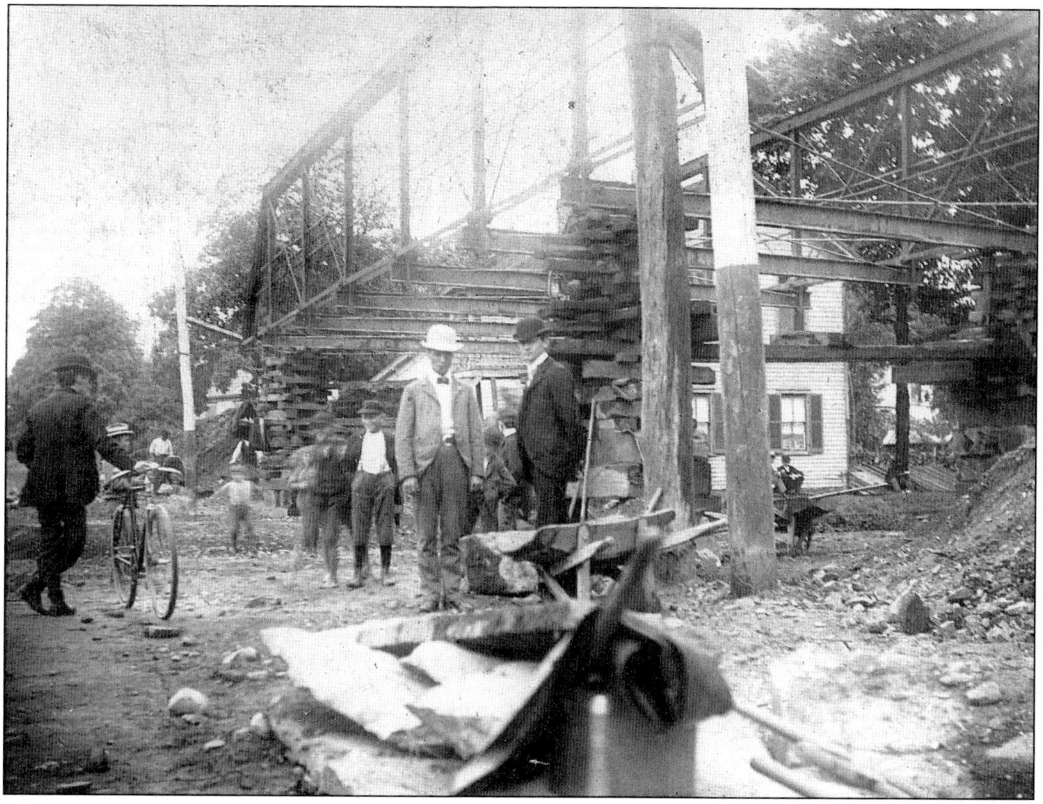

The canal was commonly called "the ditch." This is the *c.* 1880s construction of a bridge over the canal near Orange Street. This bridge is known as the "Brooklyn Bridge." (Collection of the Minisink Valley Historical Society.)

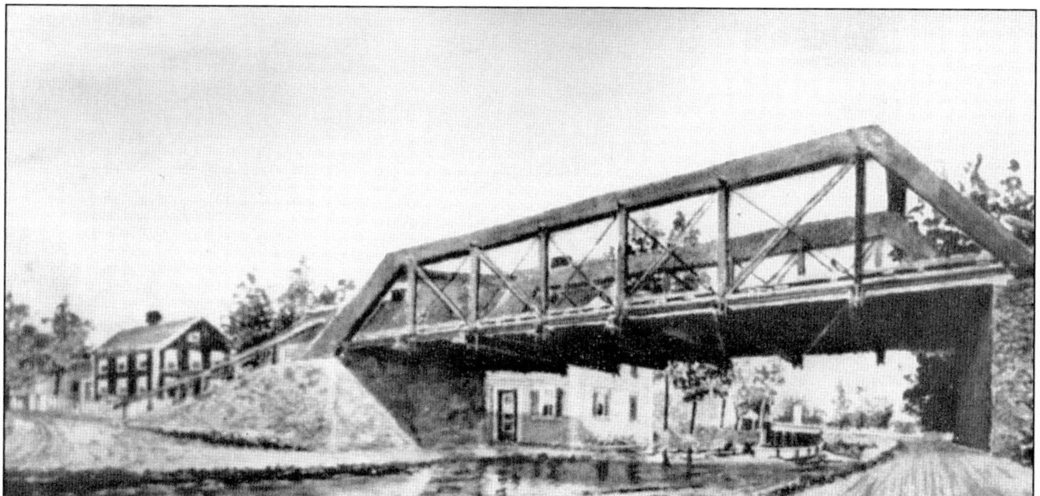

The completed "Brooklyn Bridge" is shown over the canal in Port Jervis. (Collection of the Minisink Valley Historical Society.)

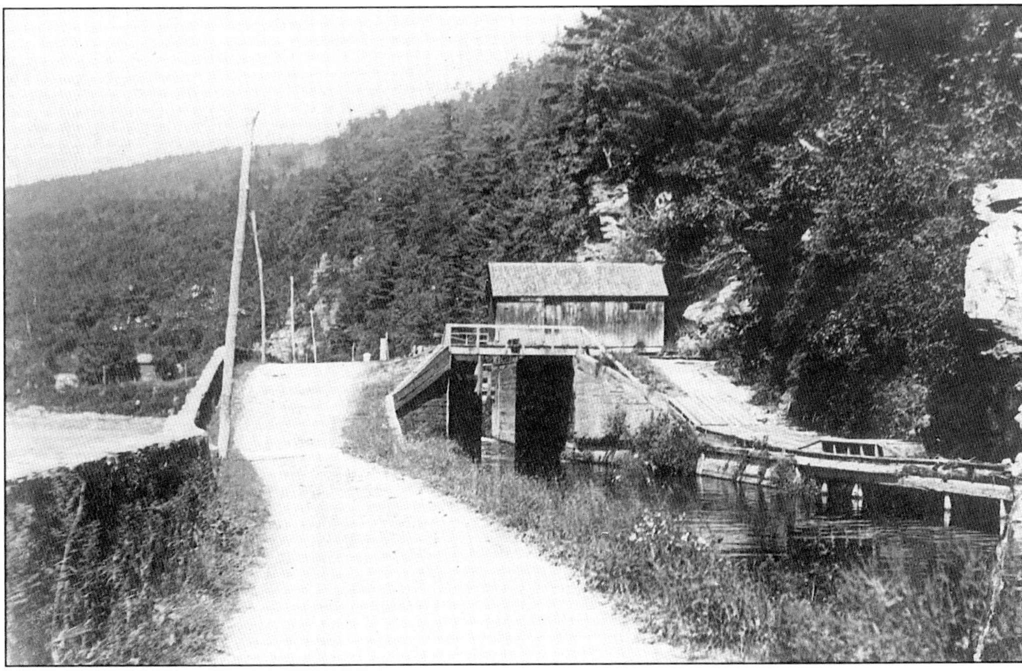

This c. 1890 photograph shows lock No. 57 at the Hawk's Nest near Port Jervis. Stores and hotels developed at the many locks along the D & H Canal. (Courtesy of Robbie Smith.)

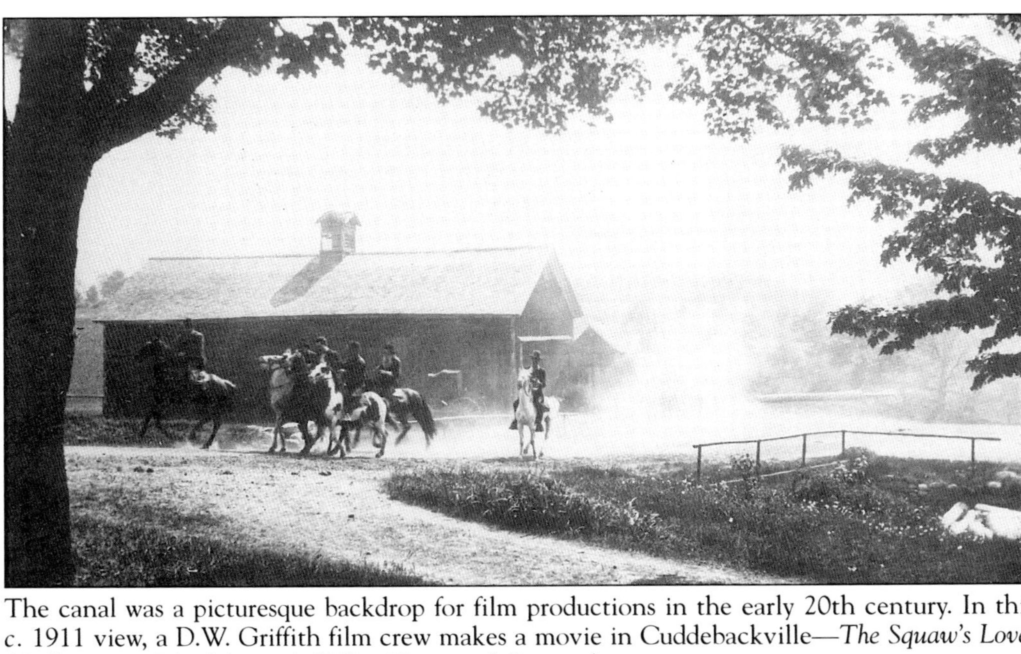

The canal was a picturesque backdrop for film productions in the early 20th century. In this c. 1911 view, a D.W. Griffith film crew makes a movie in Cuddebackville—*The Squaw's Love*. (Collection of the Minisink Valley Historical Society.)

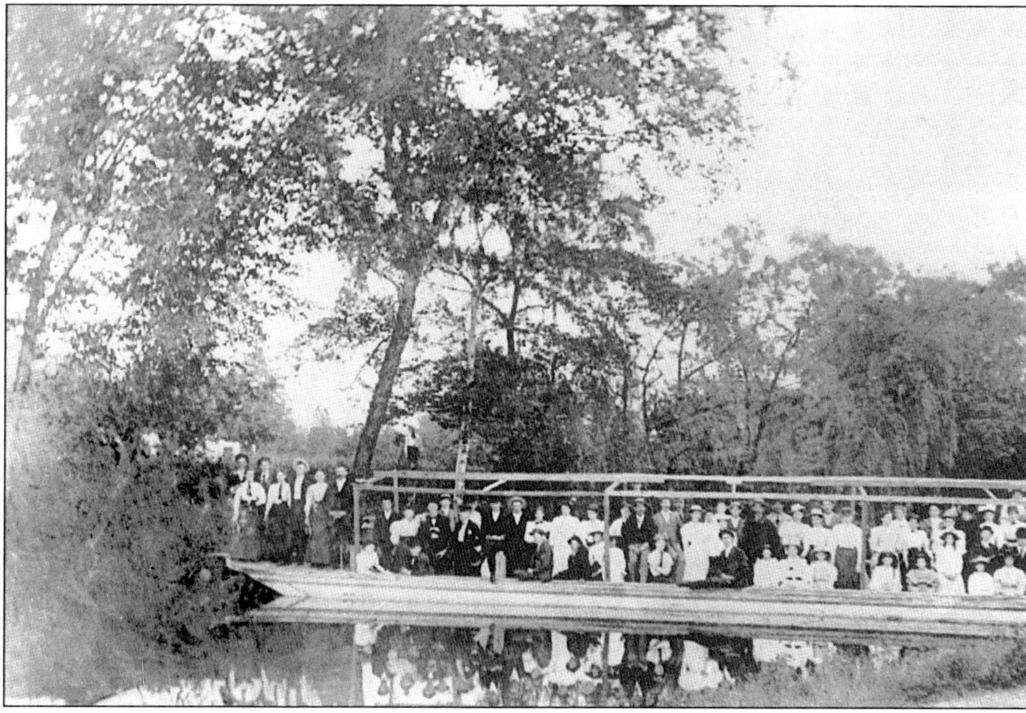

The D & H Canal was used not only for business purposes but also for groups, such as this Sunday school class enjoying a trek down the canal in Cuddebackville in the 1890s. (Collection of the Minisink Valley Historical Society.)

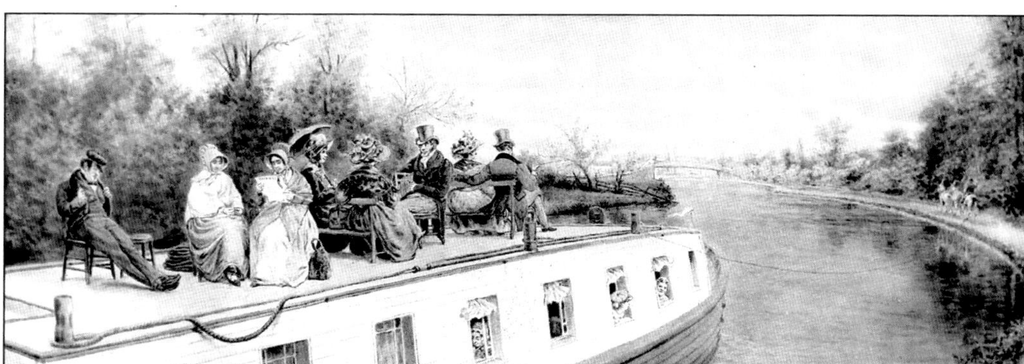

By the late 1890s, only 440 boats used the canal annually, down from as many as 1,600 15 years earlier. Packet boats were used for passenger travel along the canal. One of the most luxurious of these was called the *Fashion*, which could accommodate up to 100 passengers and had a saloon, dining room furnished with fine furnishings, and carpeting. It cost each passenger 5¢ to board—meals were extra. By 1898, the canal ceased all operations, and the railroad took over the mode of commercial transportation. (Collection of the Minisink Valley Historical Society.)

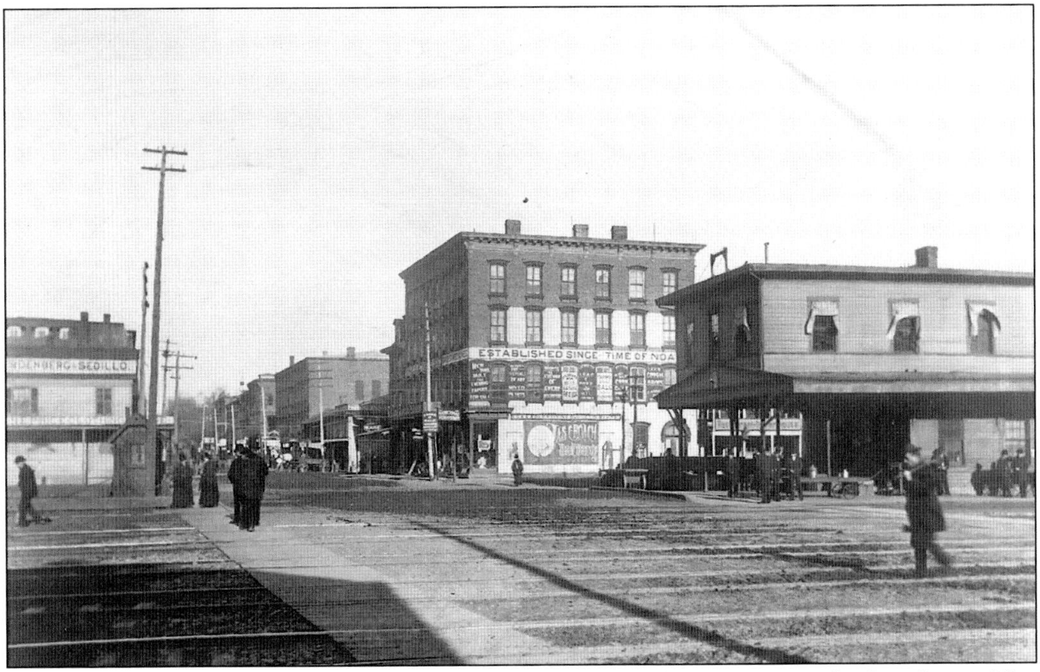

The Erie Railroad began service on December 31, 1847, marking a new era for Port Jervis. The first Erie Railroad Station, built in 1850, consisted of just a shed, but it met the needs of the six daily trains arriving at and departing from the station. Later, the station on the right was built between the eastbound and westbound tracks. (Courtesy of Robbie Smith.)

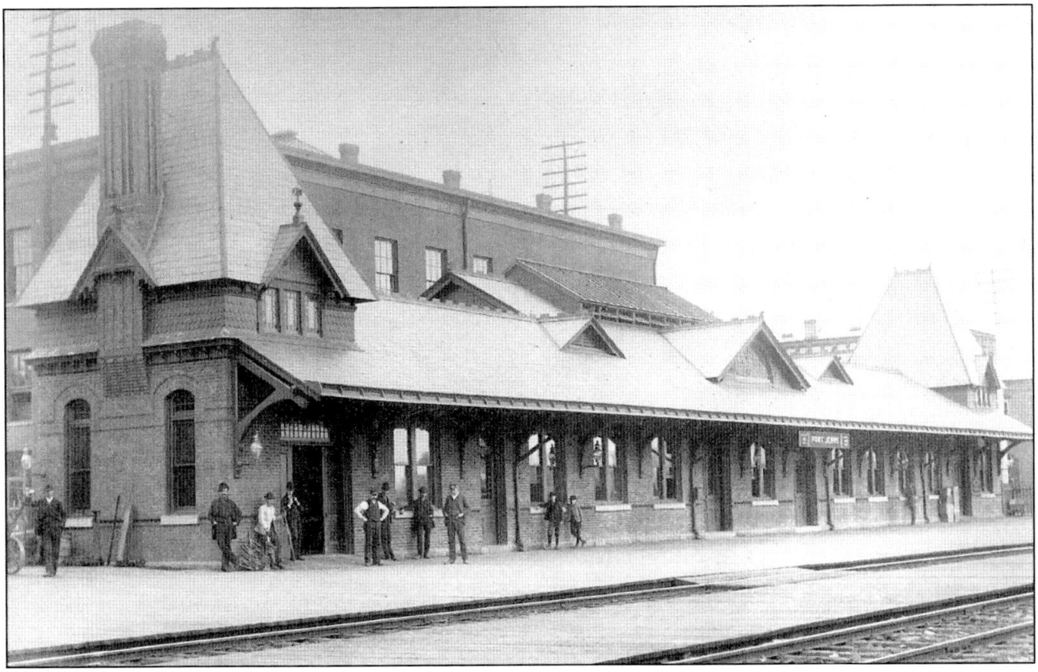

The second Erie Railroad Station, constructed of brick and stone on Jersey Avenue, opened on July 8, 1889. Unfortunately, the building was destroyed by fire only 18 months later on December 26, 1890. (Collection of Minisink Valley Historical Society.)

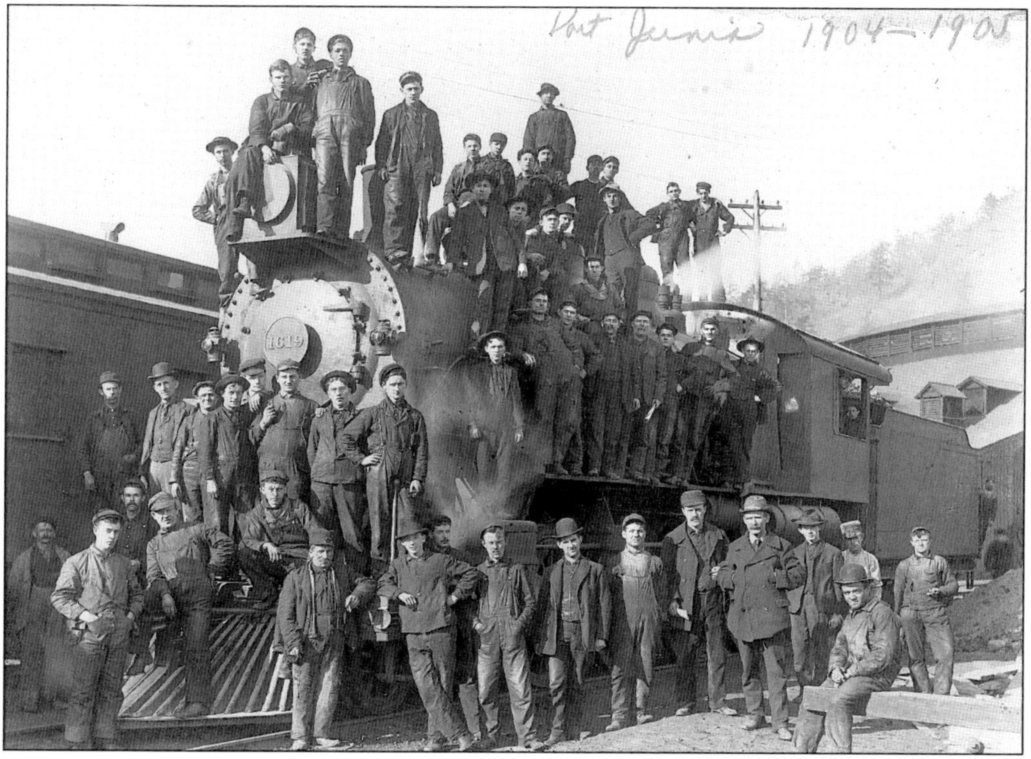

At one time, there were more than 2,500 people working for the railroad. Many came from all over Europe during the early part of the 20th century to establish a new life in America. (Collection of the Minisink Valley Historical Society.)

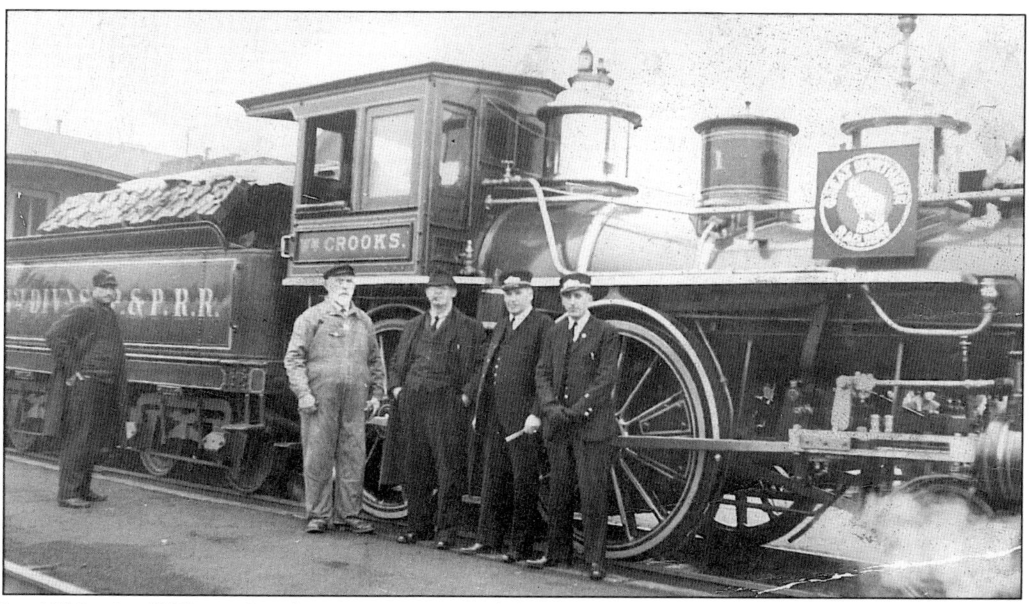

In 1939, the *William Crooks* steam engine of the Great Northern Railroad traveled through Port Jervis on its way to the 1939 World's Fair in New York City. Pictured on the far left is Jacob Caputo; on the far right is Joe Amato. (Courtesy of Clara Hughson.)

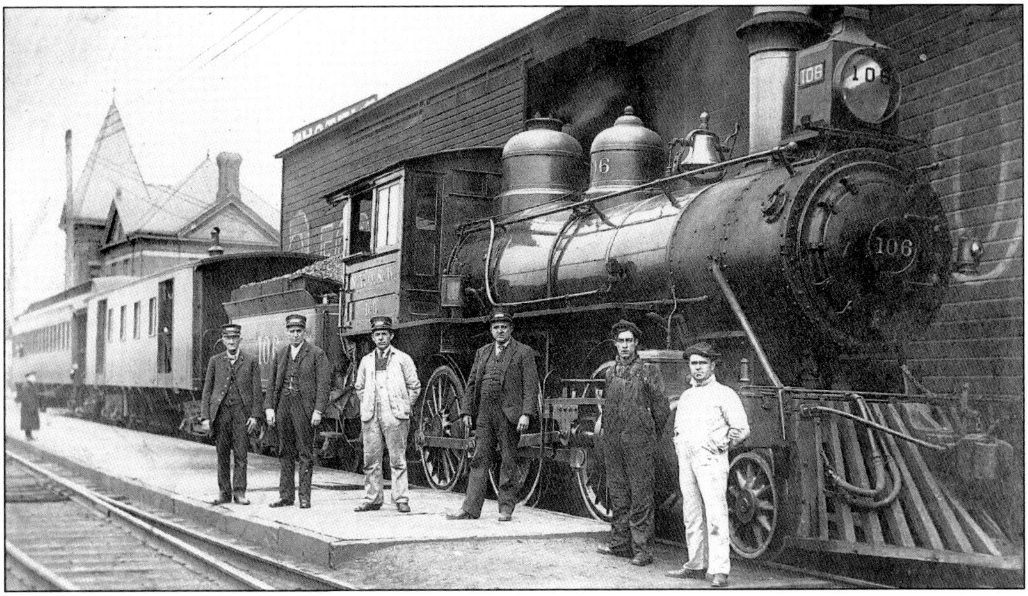

The coal-fired steam engines of the Erie Railroad were magnificent as they chugged into the Port Jervis station. They were in use for a little over 100 years when, in 1949 amid great fanfare, they were replaced with a fleet of diesel engines, resulting in the closing of repair shops and the loss of jobs over the next two decades. The railroad was beginning to go the way of the canal. This early-1900s photograph is a classic picture; everyone seems to be so proud to be working on the railroad. (Courtesy of Robbie Smith.)

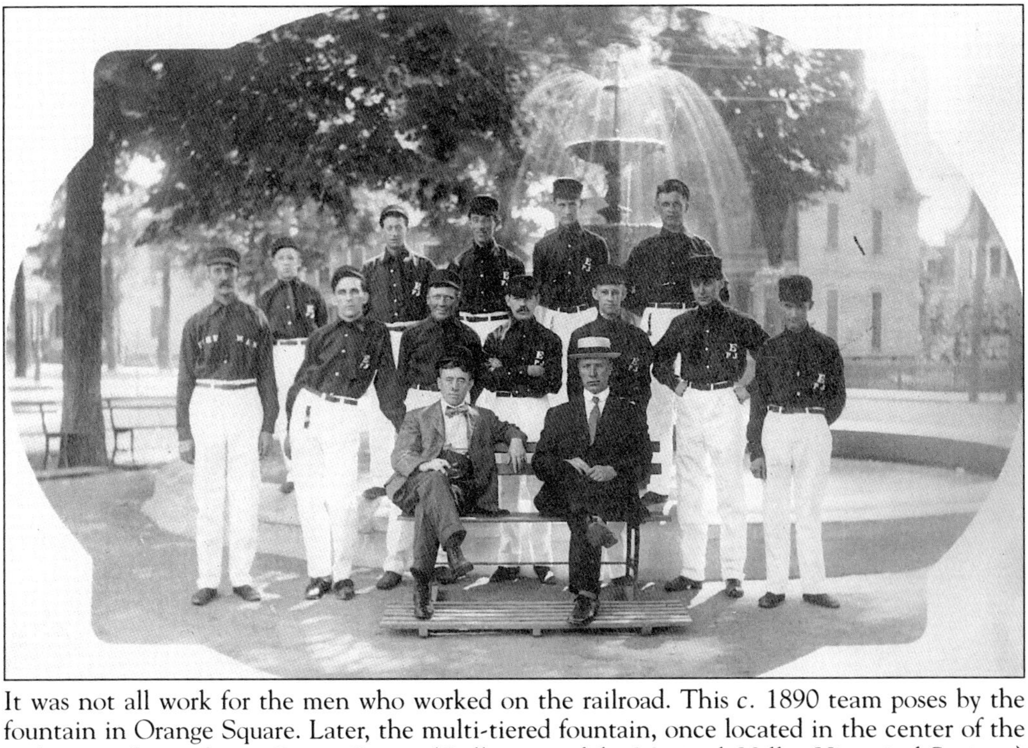
It was not all work for the men who worked on the railroad. This *c.* 1890 team poses by the fountain in Orange Square. Later, the multi-tiered fountain, once located in the center of the park, was relocated near Sussex Street. (Collection of the Minisink Valley Historical Society.)

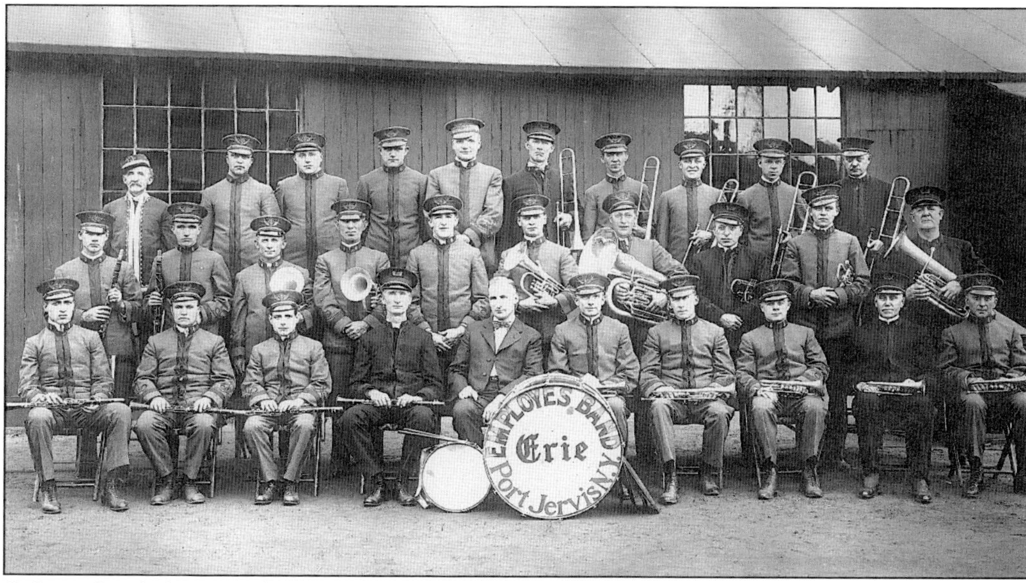

Others decided to try their hand at playing musical instruments. This is the Erie Employees Band, a popular band that performed often at the Orange Square Park. Shown in Port Jervis c. 1918 are, from left to right, the following: (front row) N. Nicolette, R. Adams, unidentified, C. McCoy, F. Wallace, James Latham, W. Mulvaney, W. Wagner, J. Stoll, and J. Bridge; (middle row) G. Strong, H. Lyons, L. Rutan, B. Duane, H. Lehn, B. Stoll, T. Mayfield, J. Bauer, F. Stoll, and G. Boten; (back row) Doc Payne, J. Lyons, E. Murphy, F. Lyons, B. Hamilton, L. Rocklein, M. Stoll, B. Cidel, E. Fuller, and D. Buell. (Collection of the Minisink Valley Historical Society.)

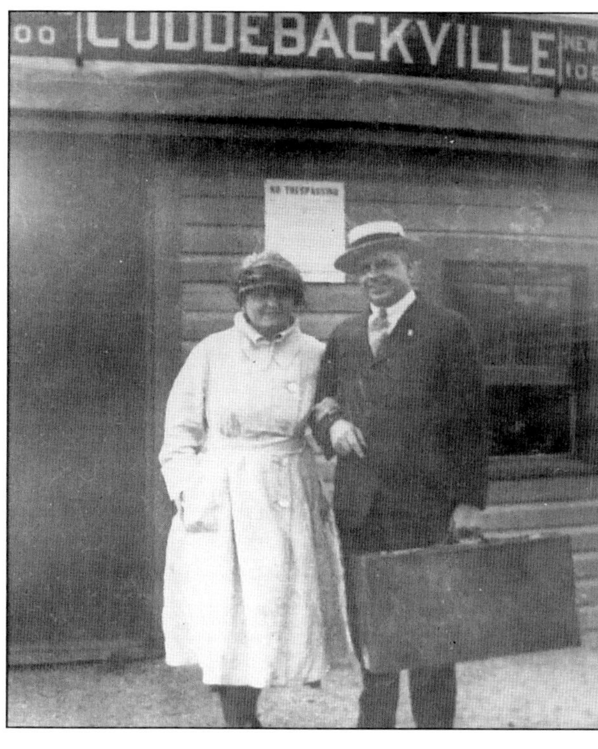

A couple of eager travelers get ready to board the Erie at the Cuddebackville Station. It was nine miles to Port Jervis and 106 to New York City. This pair could have been headed in either direction. (Collection of the Minisink Valley Historical Society.)

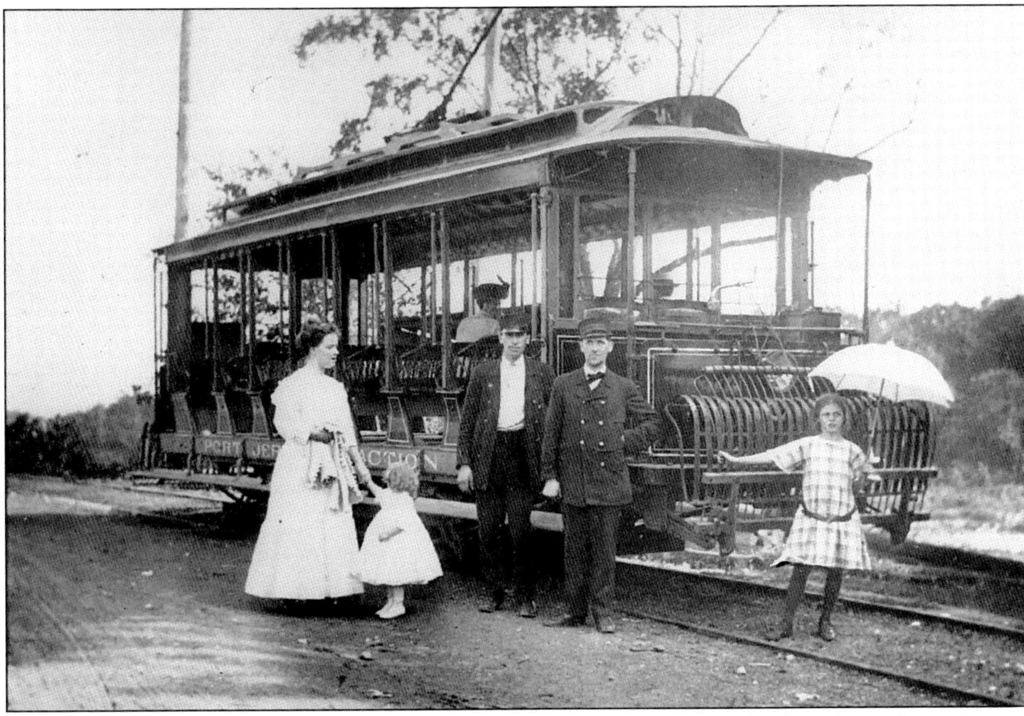

Trolley service began on January 15, 1898. Three trolleys transported riders throughout the city over approximately four miles. (Collection of the Minisink Valley Historical Society.)

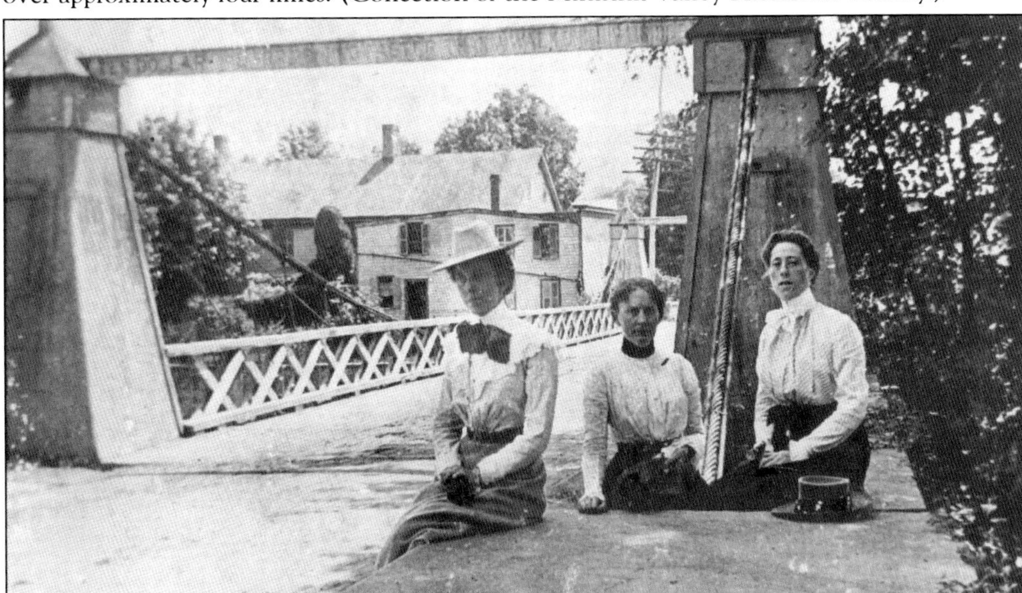

The trolley tracks began at the Tri-States Bridge, known then as Carpenter's Point. In this c. 1900 photograph, three women wait for the trolley to take them into town. In the early years of trolley service, travelers could take the electric trolley to Bamberger's in West End. From there, they transferred to the horse-drawn Sparrowbush Trolley. Eventually, the tracks ran from West End to Sparrowbush. (Collection of the Minisink Valley Historical Society.)

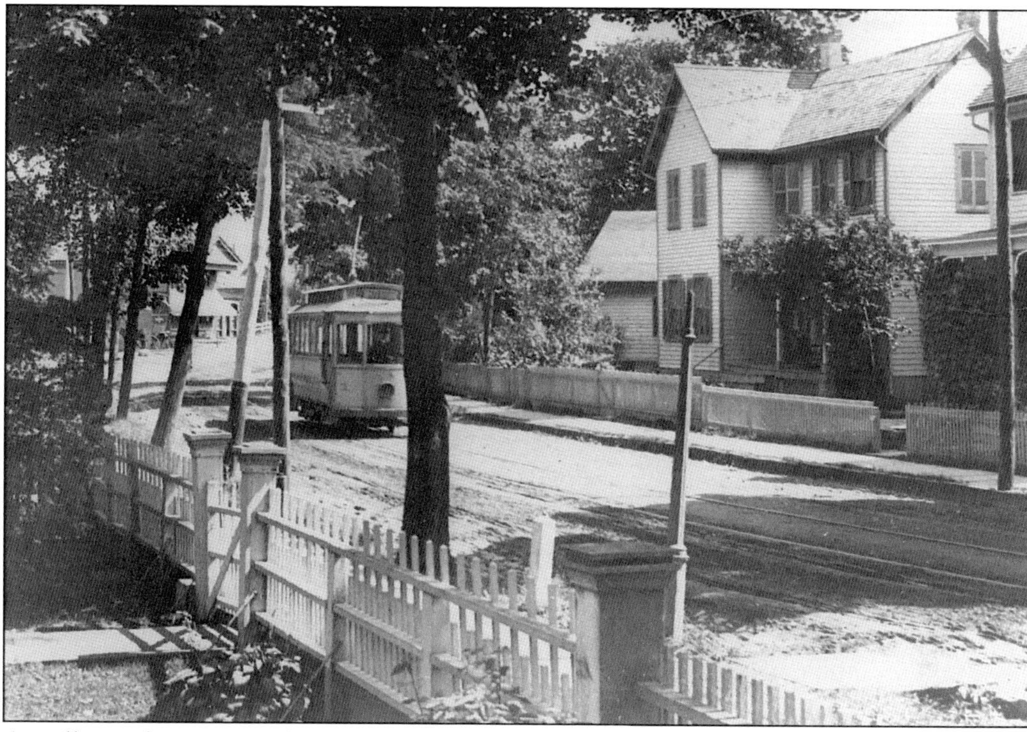

A trolley makes its way along West Main Street to pick up riders at the end of the four-mile trek in West End around the beginning of the 20th century. (Collection of the Minisink Valley Historical Society.)

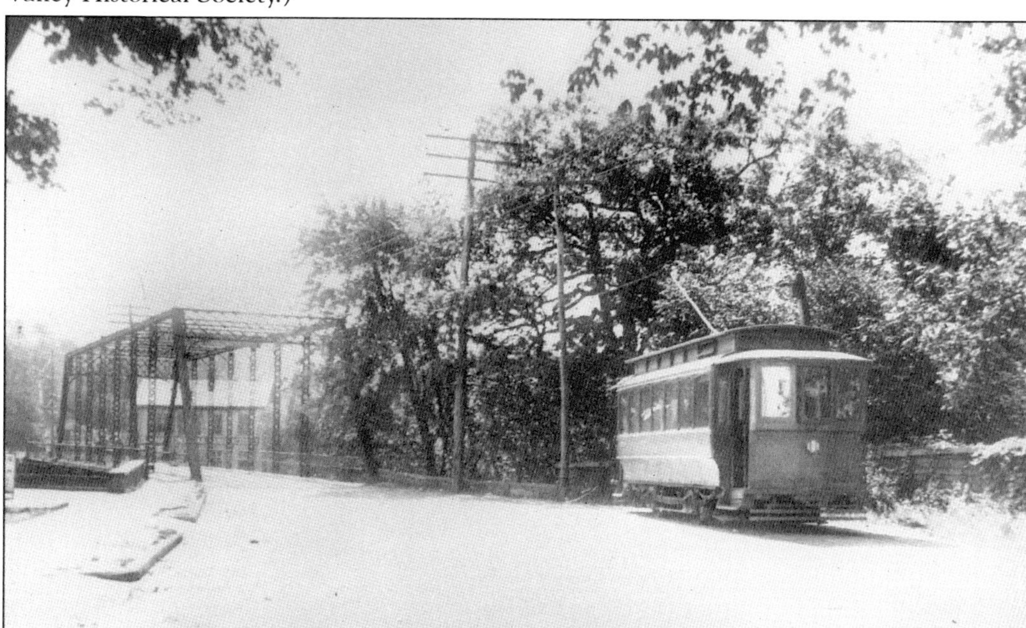

The last eastbound stop on the line was at the Laurel Grove Cemetery. The trolley had to stop short of the Tri-States Bridge due to weight limits. (Collection of the Minisink Valley Historical Society.)

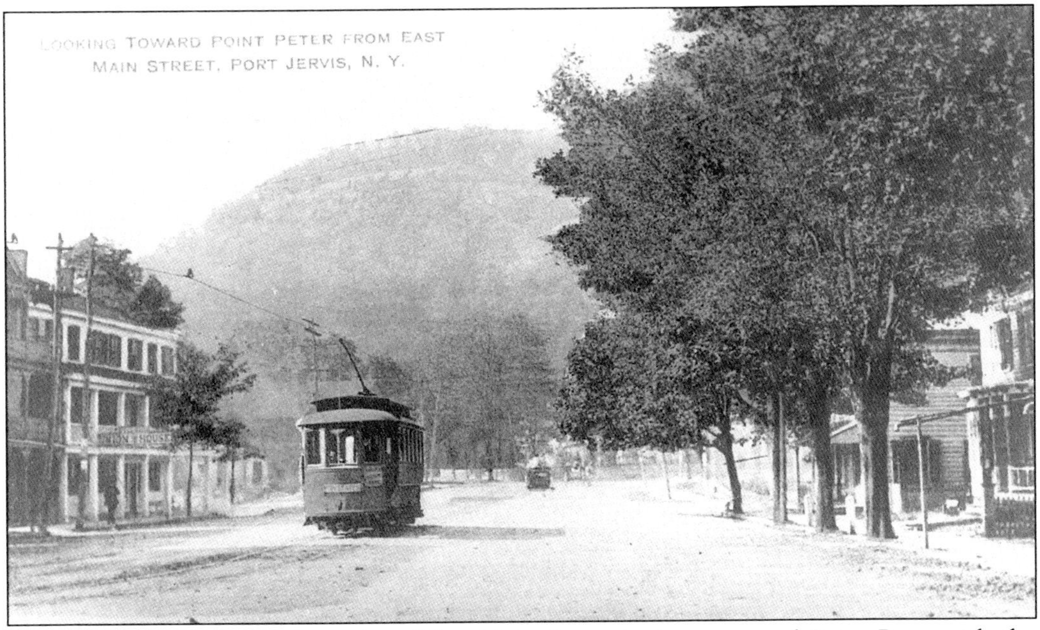

This c. 1916 picturesque scene from West Main Street looks up toward Point Peter with the Union House on the left. (Collection of the Minisink Valley Historical Society.)

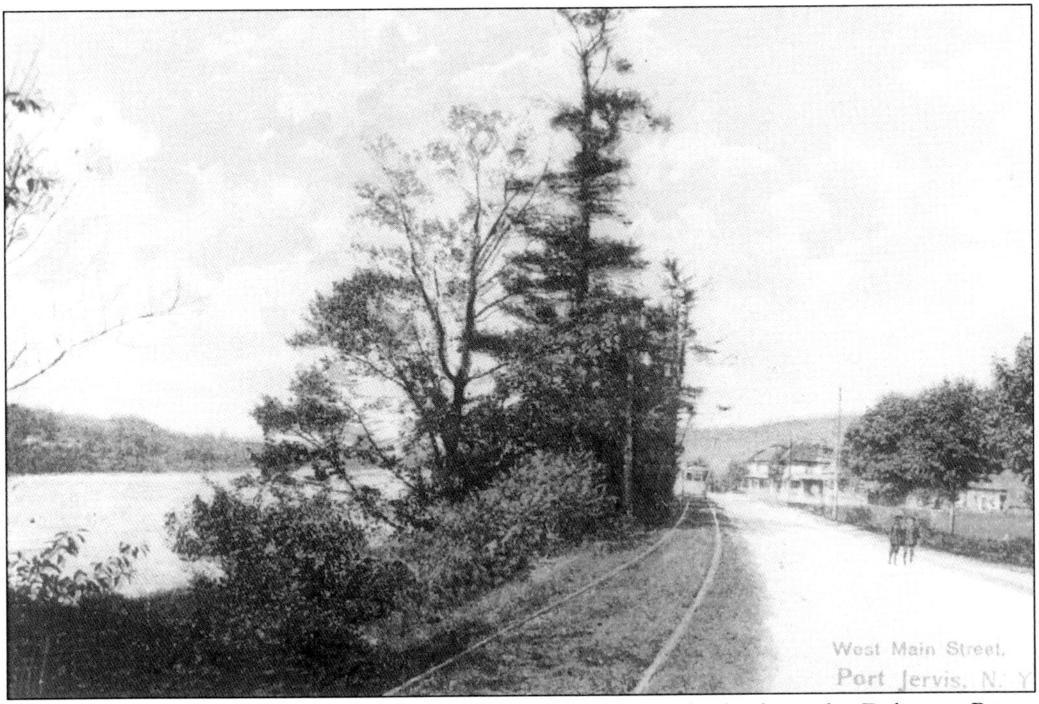

Trolley tracks run along West Main Street up toward Sparrowbush along the Delaware River. The photograph dates from c. 1915. (Collection of the Minisink Valley Historical Society.)

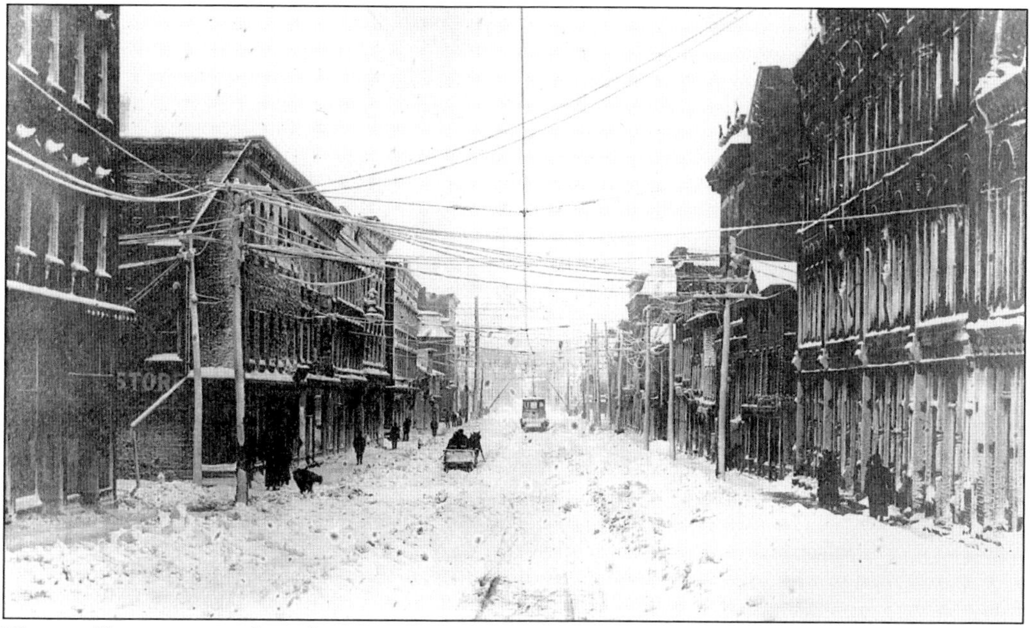

The trolleys equipped with snow sweepers were used to help clear the tracks. This trolley plows its way up Pike Street Hill in the early 1920s. (Collection of the Minisink Valley Historical Society.)

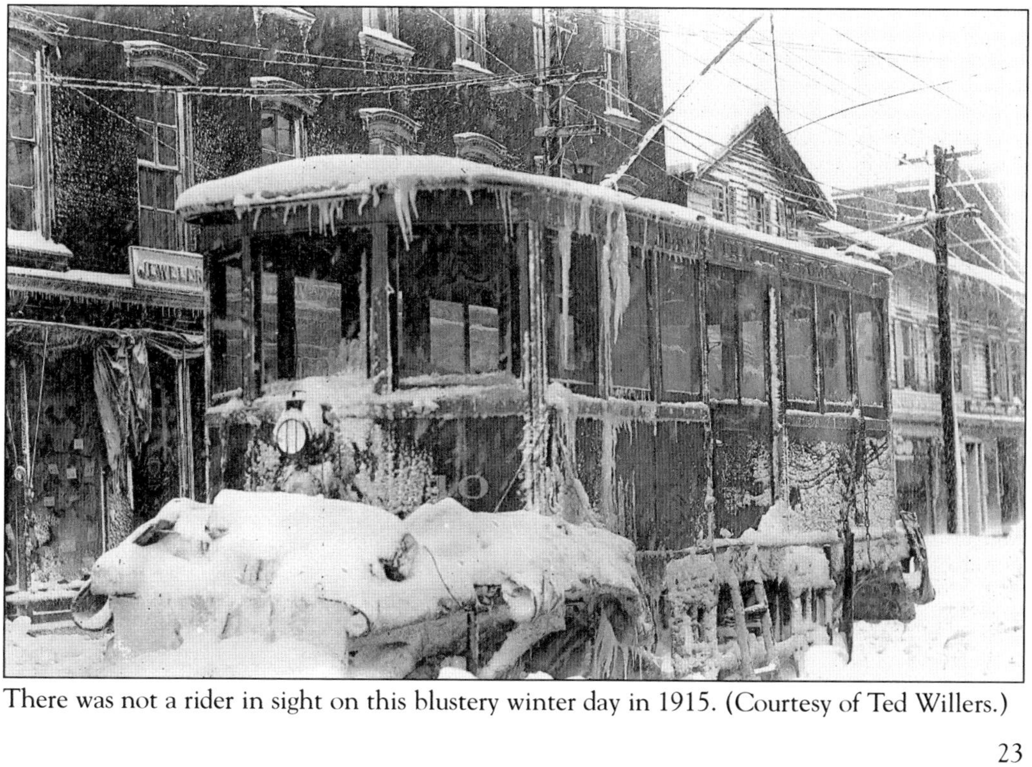

There was not a rider in sight on this blustery winter day in 1915. (Courtesy of Ted Willers.)

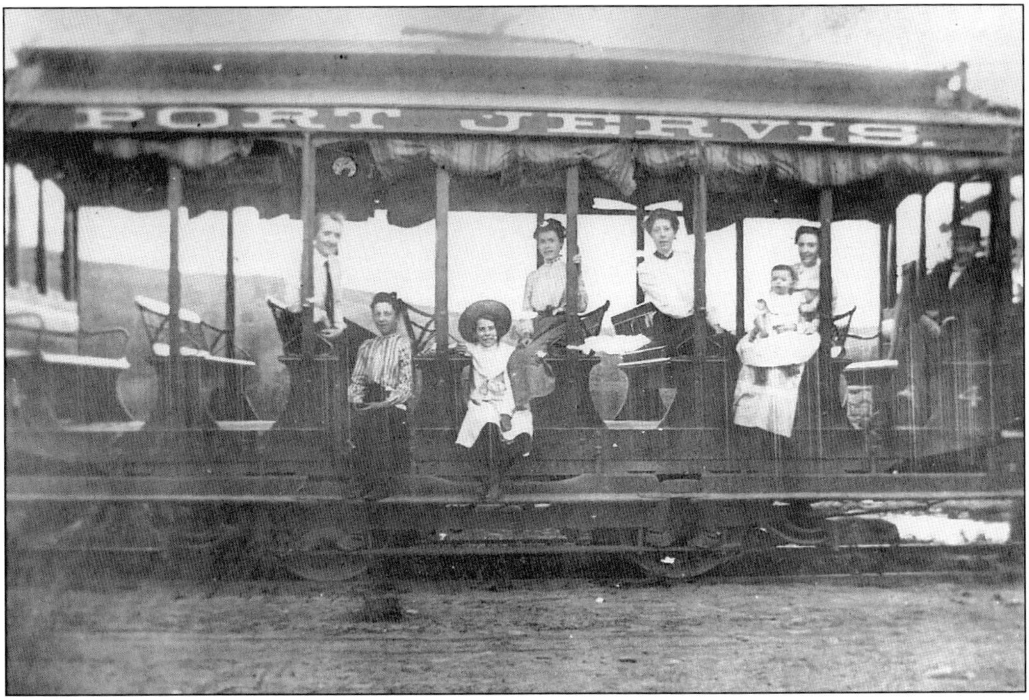

Everyone loved the trolley as a quick and easy way to get around the city. (Collection of the Minisink Valley Historical Society.)

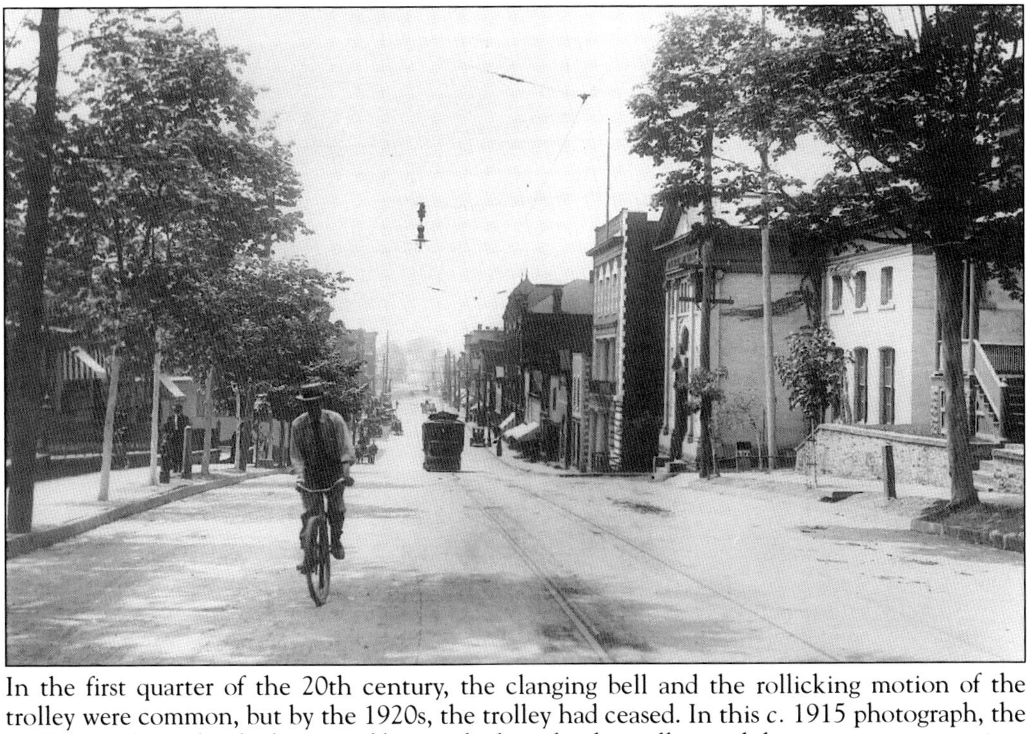

In the first quarter of the 20th century, the clanging bell and the rollicking motion of the trolley were common, but by the 1920s, the trolley had ceased. In this *c.* 1915 photograph, the evolution of travel—the horse and buggy, the bicycle, the trolley, and that new-age innovation, the automobile—is evident. (Collection of the Minisink Valley Historical Society.)

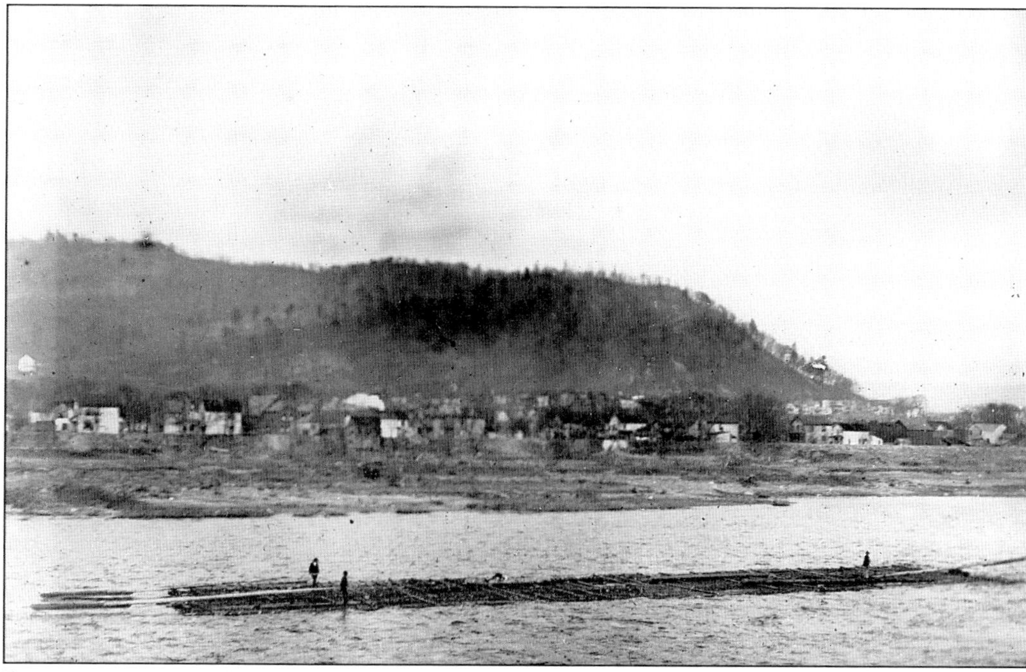

For many years, rafting was a thriving industry on the Delaware River. This method of transporting lumber to Philadelphia, shown *c.* 1890, began as early as 1764; the last raft of its kind carried goods in 1924. (Collection of the Minisink Valley Historical Society.)

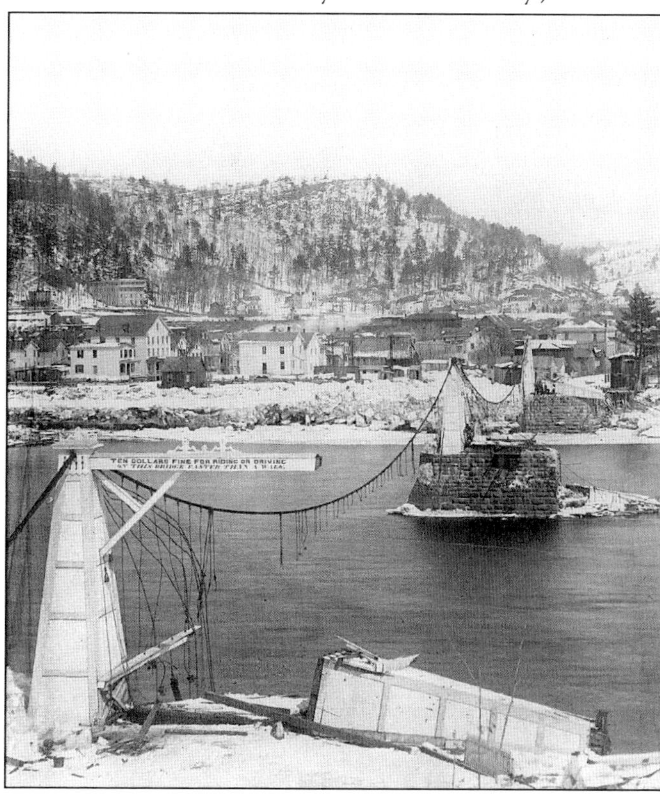

The Erie Railroad was primarily responsible for the establishment of the first bridge that crossed the Delaware between Matamoras and Port Jervis. This photograph, taken on the Pennsylvania side of the Delaware looking toward Point Peter, shows that the ice jam of March 1875 demolished this bridge. After the tragedy, the *Port Jervis Evening Gazette* stated, "What might have been an appalling catastrophe has resulted only in temporary inconvenience." What an understatement. The river had destroyed sections of West End, Riverside, and had washed away the firehouse. (Collection of the Minisink Valley Historical Society.)

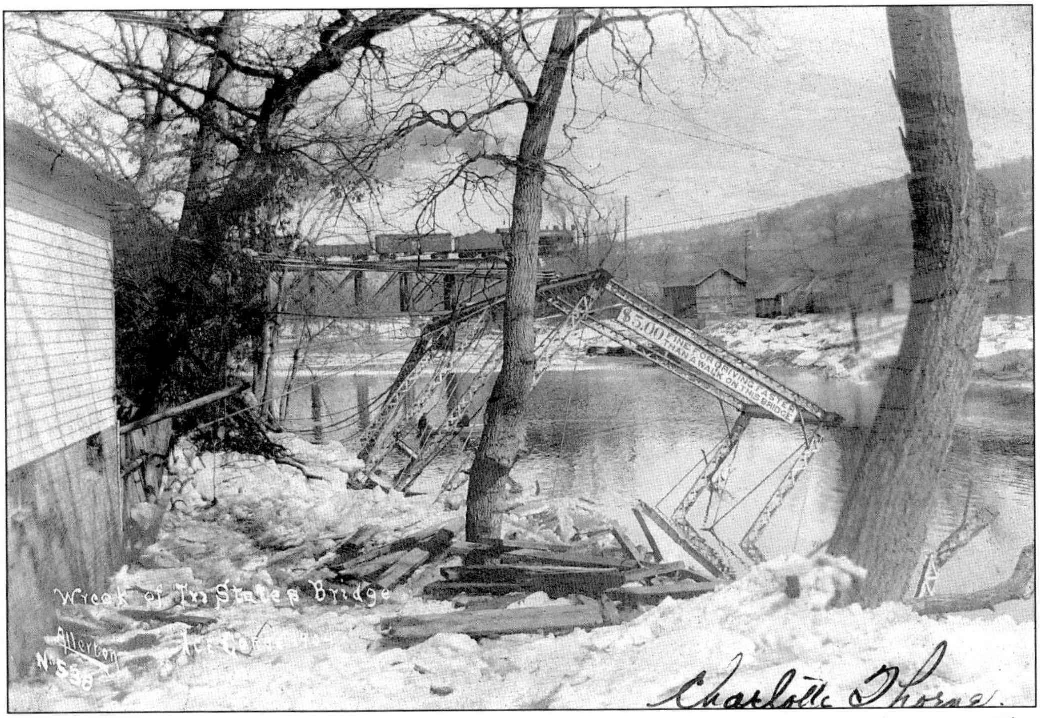

The ice gorge of 1904 wrecked the Tri-States Bridge over the Neversink River. The wood-and-iron suspension bridge had been constructed in 1868. (Collection of the Minisink Valley Historical Society.)

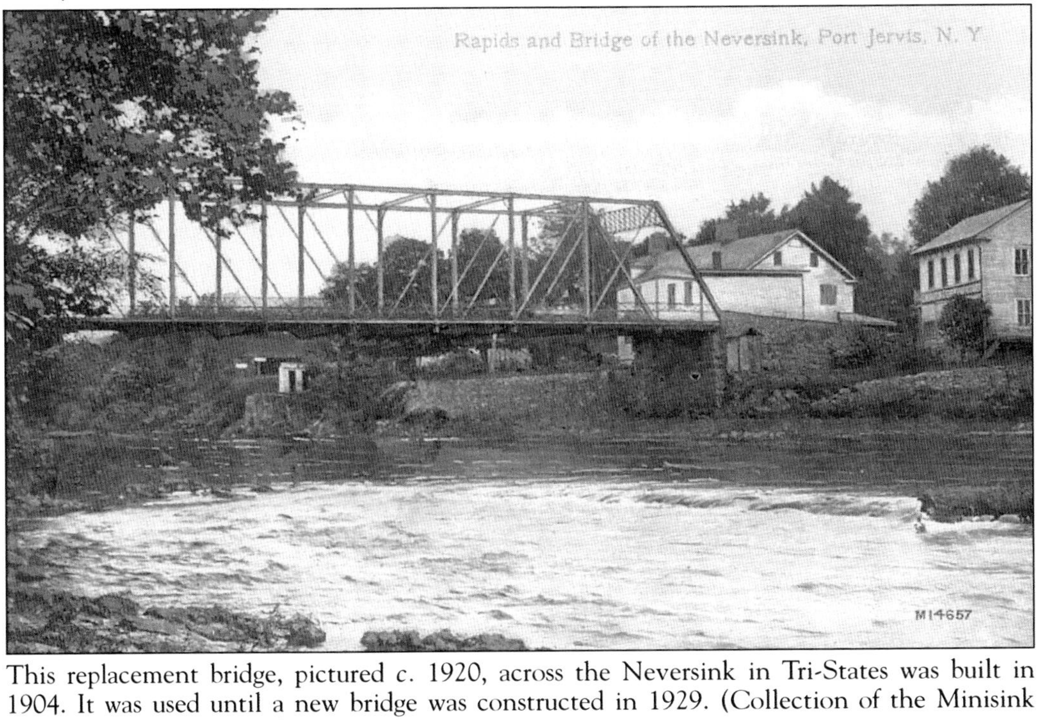

This replacement bridge, pictured *c.* 1920, across the Neversink in Tri-States was built in 1904. It was used until a new bridge was constructed in 1929. (Collection of the Minisink Valley Historical Society.)

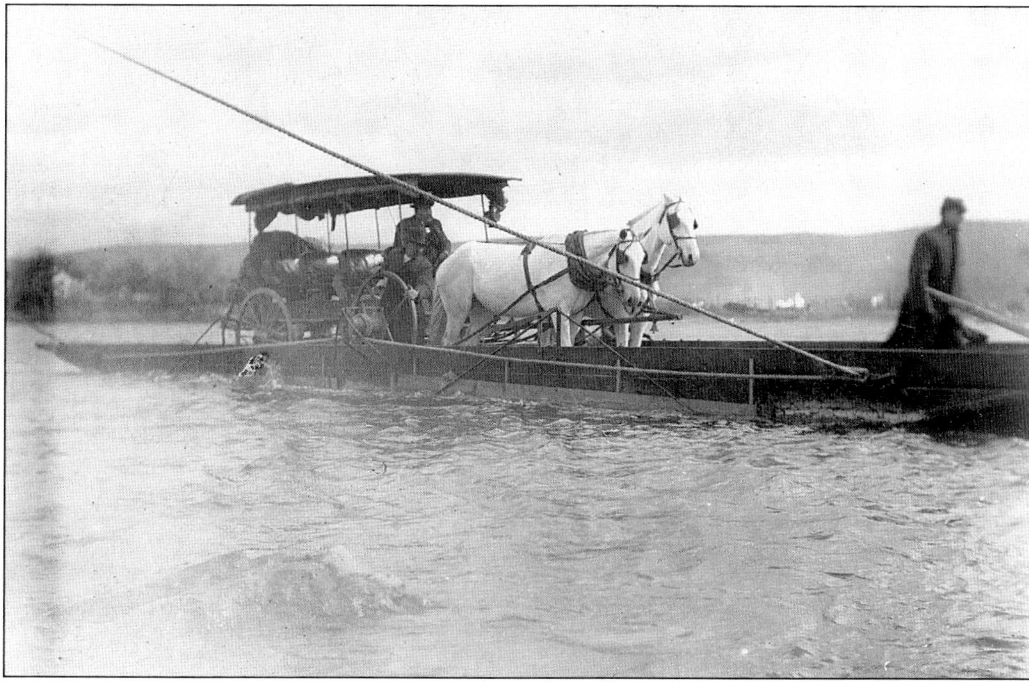

Before the bridges were built secure enough to withstand flooding, travelers relied on ferry service along the Delaware River. Ferry service was put back into use after the 1903 "Pumpkin Flood," which destroyed bridges between Matamoras and Port Jervis. (Collection of the Minisink Valley Historical Society.)

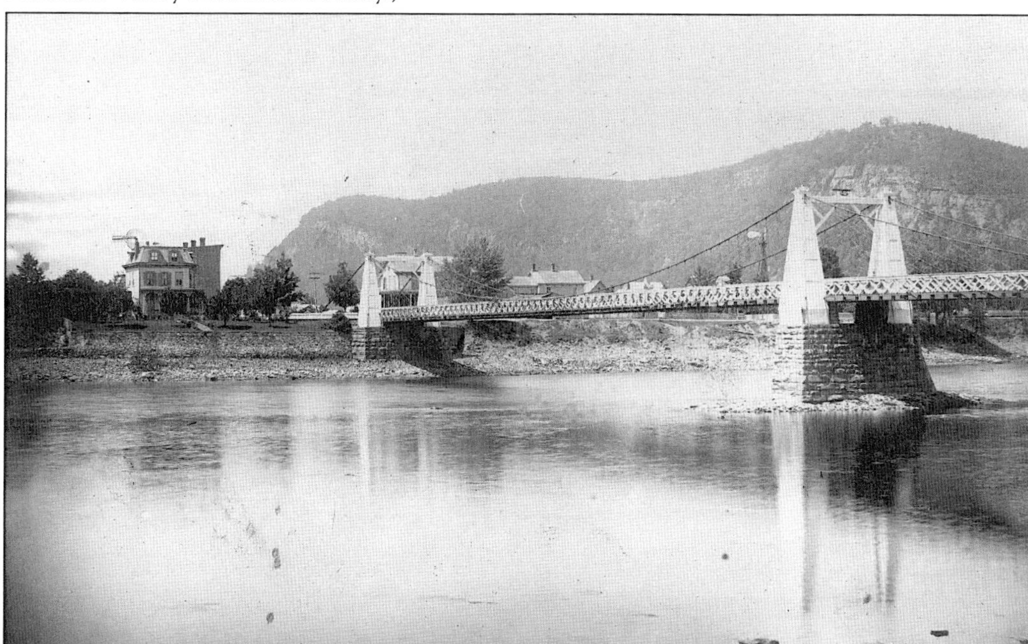

The second Barrett Bridge across the Delaware River, seen from Port Jervis, was used as a toll bridge beginning in 1901. The cost for pedestrians was 2¢. It was 40¢ for each wagon. In 1922, all tolls were discontinued. (Collection of the Minisink Valley Historical Society.)

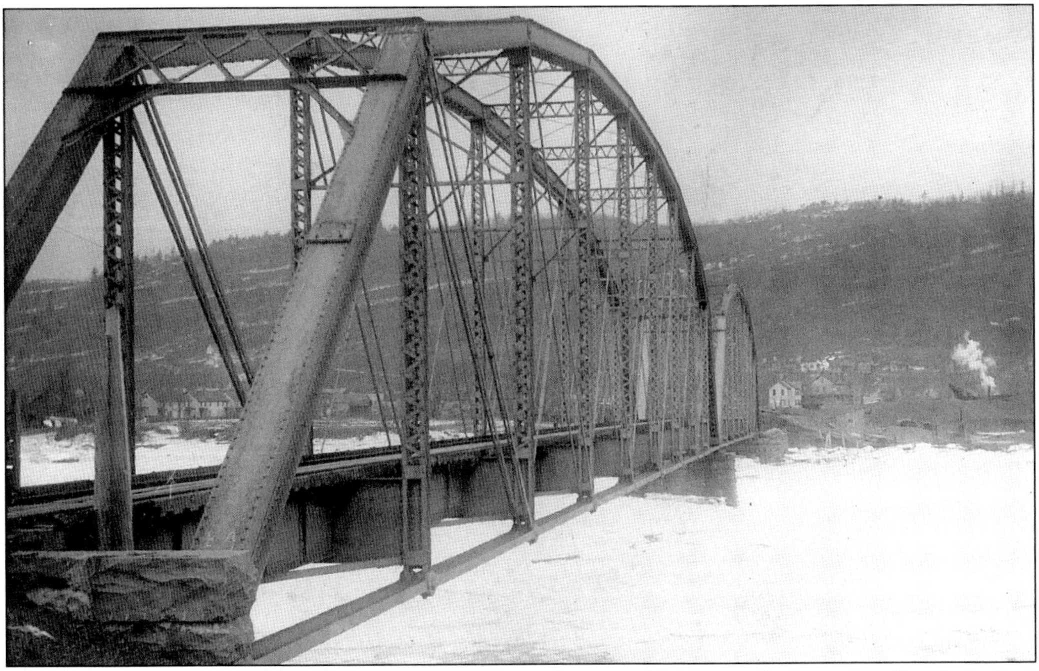

This picture, looking toward Matamoras, was taken in 1903 just before the flood. It had been hoped that the railroad bridge, built in 1898, would bring rail travel from Port Jervis to Stroudsburg, Pennsylvania. The 1903 flood washed away these dreams. (Collection of the Minisink Valley Historical Society.)

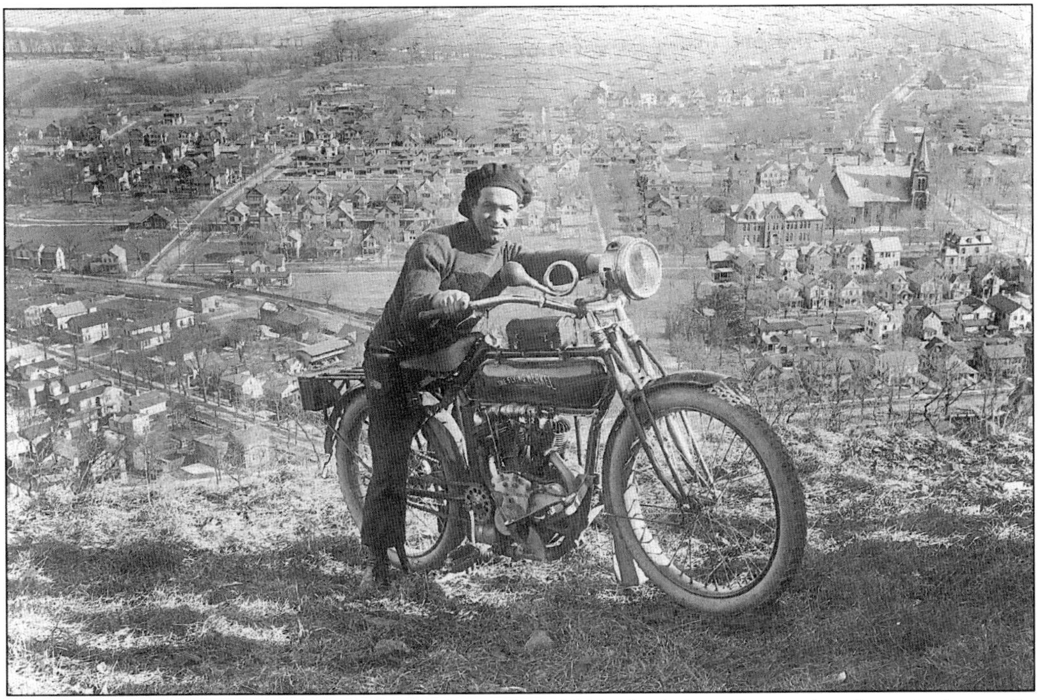

Here comes the Flying Merkel. Before it burned in 1918, the Main Street Academy is shown in this view taken from Point Peter. (Collection of the Minisink Valley Historical Society.)

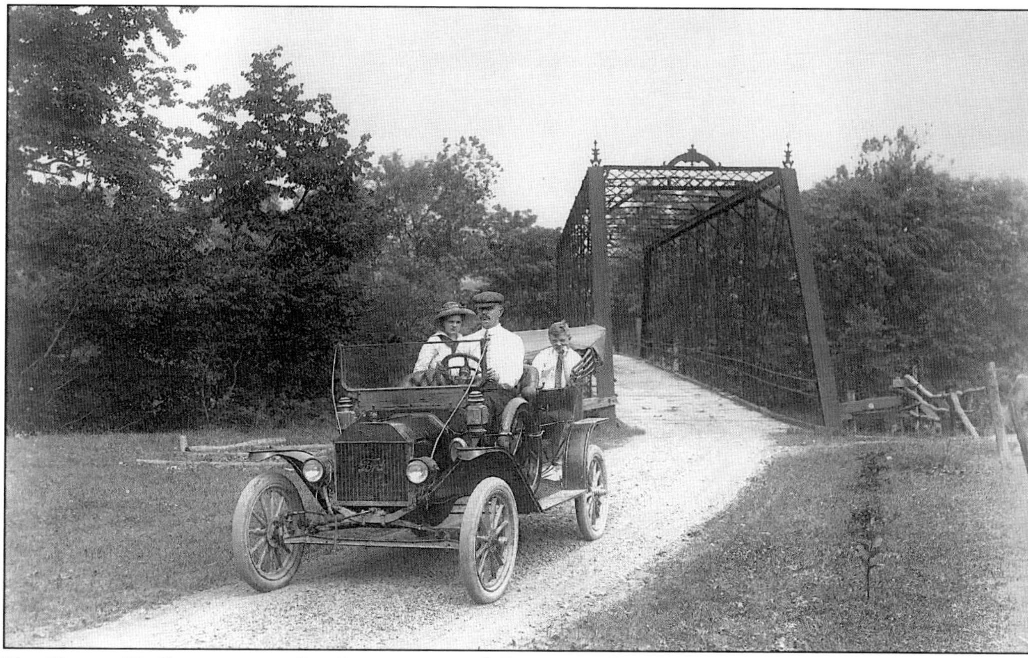

Dr. Henry B. Swartwout, the first mayor of the city of Port Jervis, crosses one of the several bridges over the Neversink River. He was also one of the few people in Port Jervis who owned an automobile when this picture was snapped c. 1909. (Collection of the Minisink Valley Historical Society.)

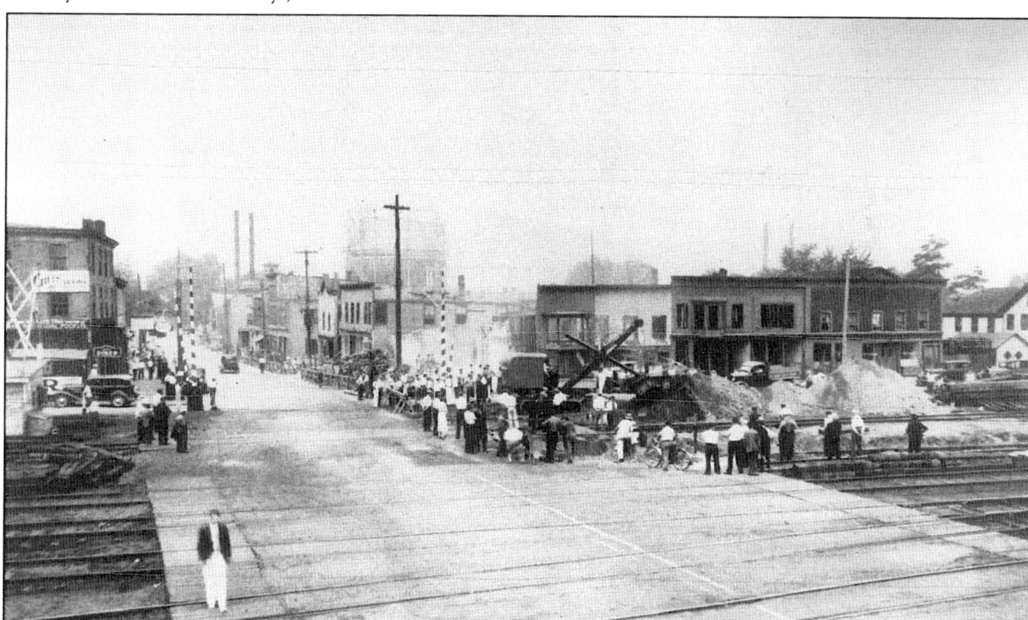

The construction of the underpass on Pike Street was considered by some to be one of the most significant improvements in the history of Port Jervis. Construction began in 1936 and completed in June 1937. Never again would people have to be fearful of being caught on the railroad tracks with the gates down. (Collection of the Minisink Valley Historical Society.)

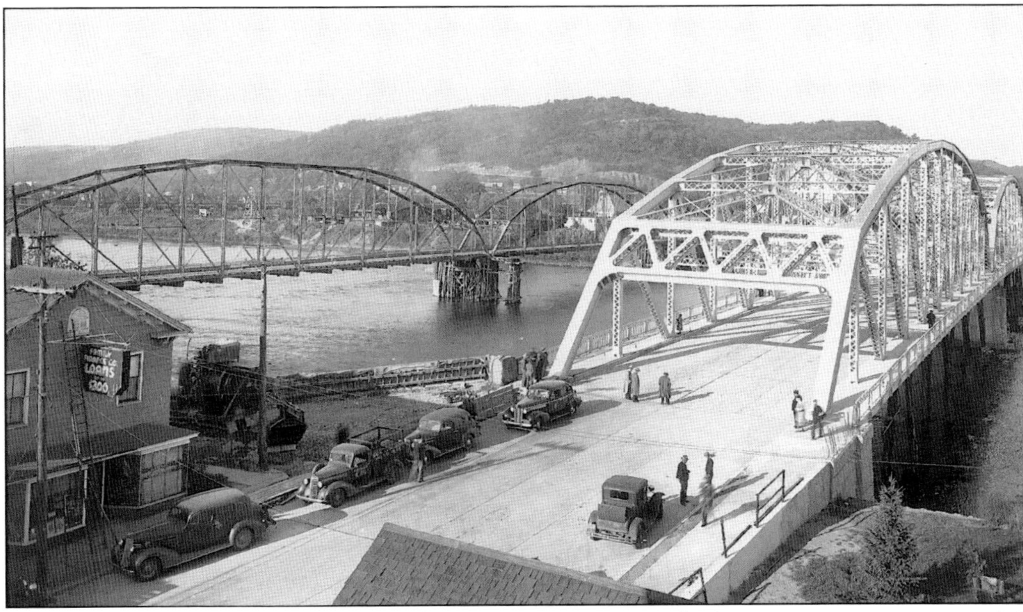

In the mid-1930s, the present bridge between Port Jervis and Matamoras was constructed. It replaced a bridge that had been in use for about 30 years. When construction on the new bridge began, the old bridge was moved upstream and used for more than a year while the building was under way and finally completed. This photograph shows both bridges in place. (Collection of the Minisink Valley Historical Society.)

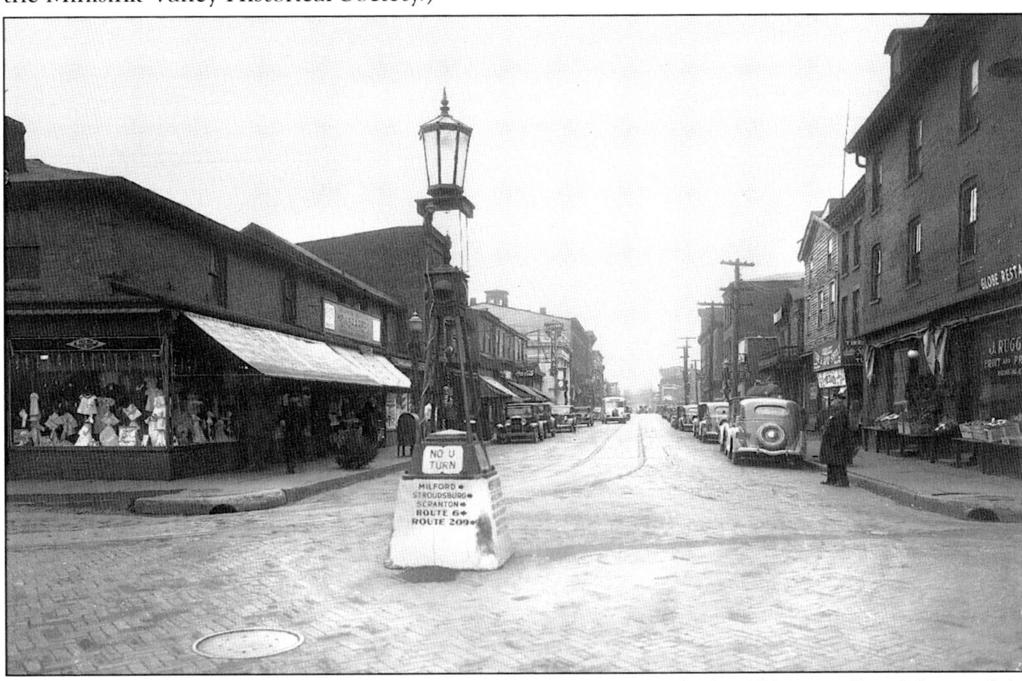

For more than 200 years, Port Jervis has been a transportation hub. Old Mine Road (one of the country's first highways), the D & H Canal, the Erie Railroad, and three major U.S. highways (Routes 6 and 209 and Interstate 84) all converged in Port Jervis. (Collection of the Minisink Valley Historical Society.)

Two

FAITH

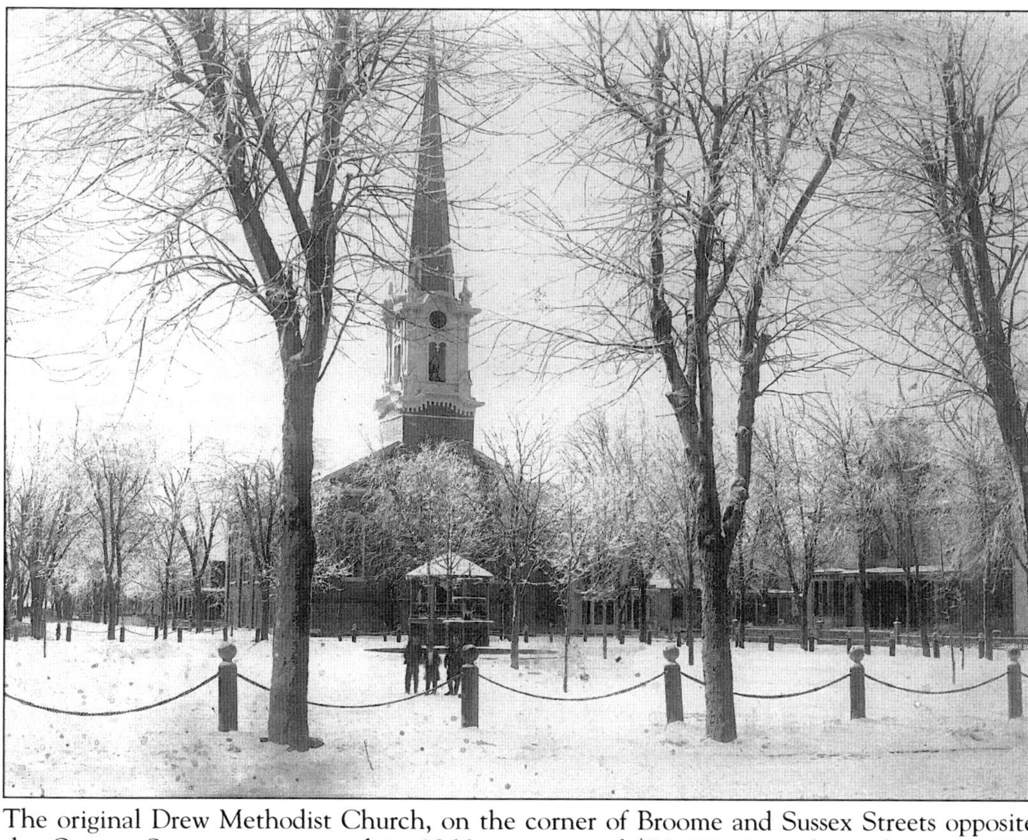

The original Drew Methodist Church, on the corner of Broome and Sussex Streets opposite the Orange Square, was erected in 1866 at a cost of $28,000. It is shown here *c.* 1886. Jonathan Townley Crane, the father of writer Stephen Crane, was the minister from 1878 until 1880. On April 13, 1893, the steeple was destroyed by a cyclone, effectively destroying the entire church as well. A new church was built in 1894. That church stood until the late 20th century. (Collection of the Minisink Valley Historical Society.)

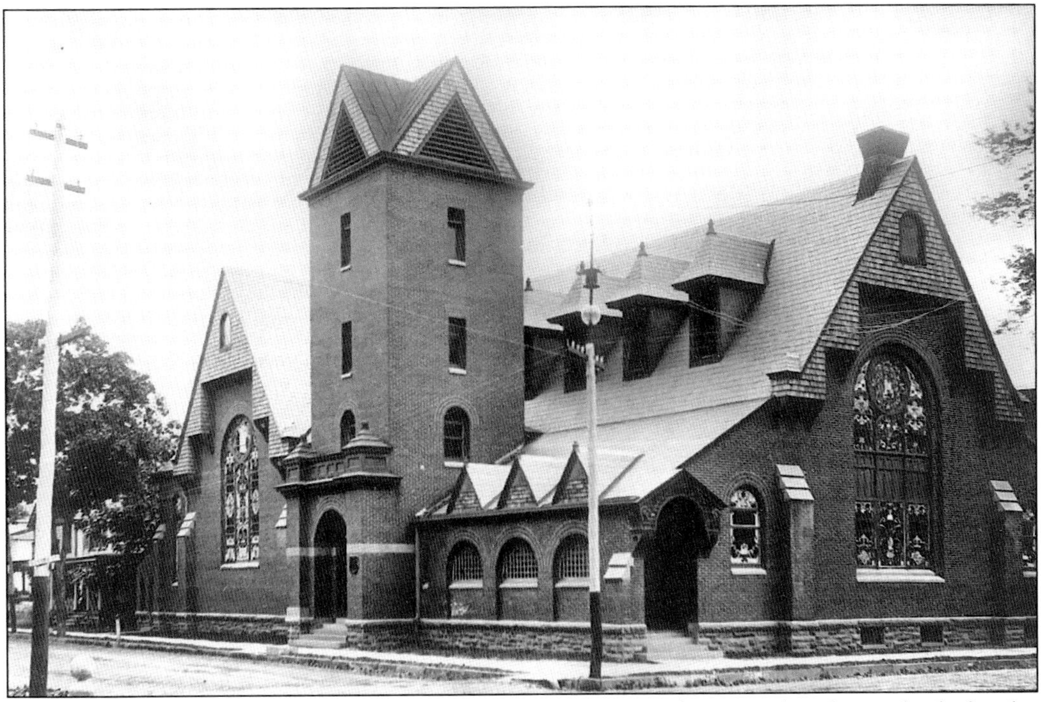

The 1894 Drew Methodist Church burned in the 1990s, and a new church was built for the congregation in the late 1990s. (Collection of the Minisink Valley Historical Society.)

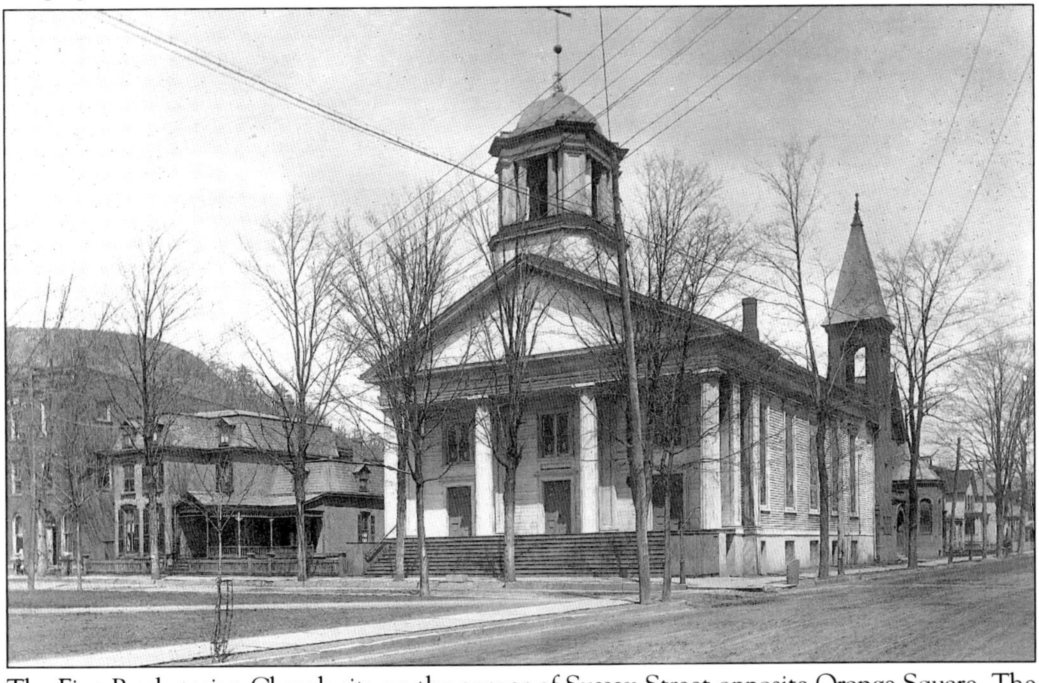

The First Presbyterian Church sits on the corner of Sussex Street opposite Orange Square. The congregation was organized on June 3, 1851. Services were first held at the Baptist church, until this building could be erected in 1852. A brick chapel was added in 1889. This picture shows the church and parsonage c. 1909. (Collection of the Minisink Valley Historical Society.)

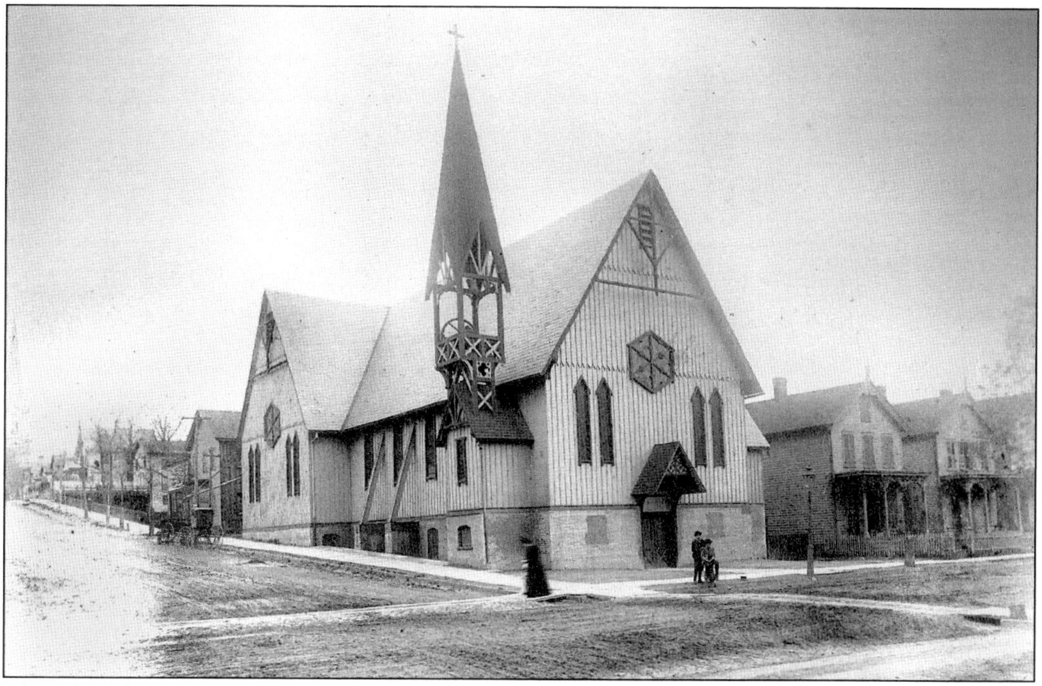

This church stood on the corner of Sussex and Hammond Streets and was first used by the Episcopalians and later the Lutherans. In the background, up the hill, is the Drew Methodist Church. (Collection of the Minisink Valley Historical Society.)

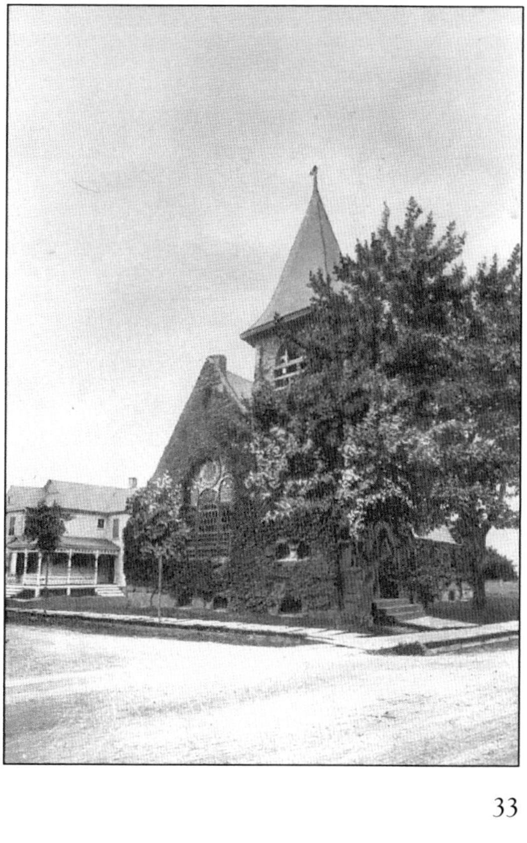

The Grace Episcopal Church was first organized in 1853. In 1868, a church was built on East Main Street. This building was later sold and the congregation met at Brown's Hall. A second church was erected at Sussex and Hammond Streets (above) and was sold to the Lutherans. The current Episcopal church, pictured here, was built in 1891 and is located on the corner of East Main Street and Seward Avenue. (Courtesy of Matt and Carol Osterberg.)

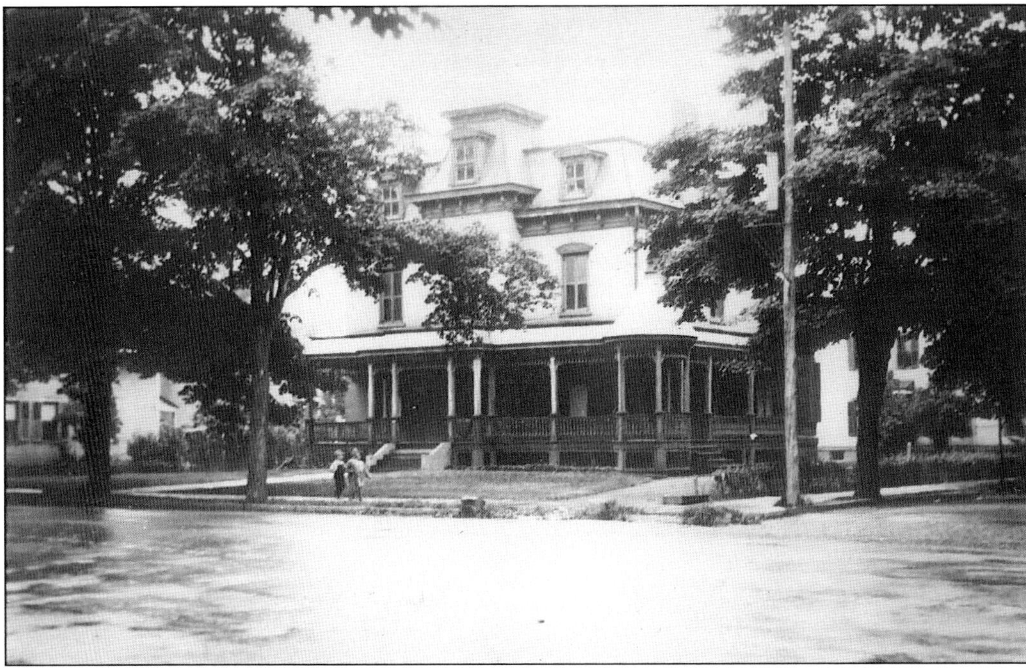

This photograph shows the original architecture of the building at the corner of East Main Street and Sullivan Avenue with a full wraparound porch. (Courtesy of Brian Lewis.)

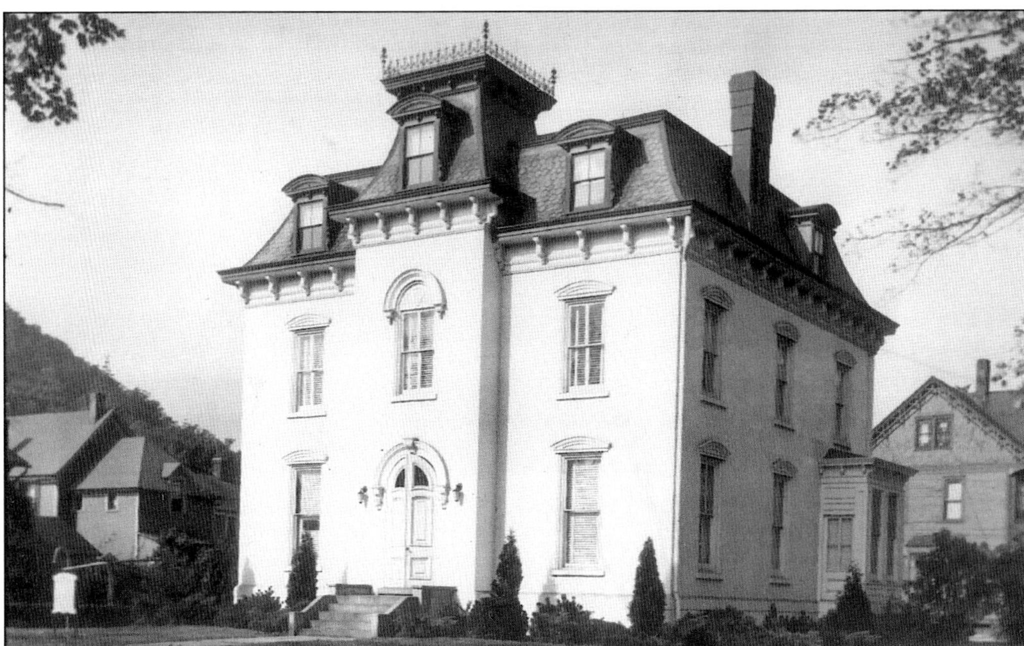

The same building at a later date is shown with the porch removed and ornate ironwork added to the cupola. (Courtesy of Brian Lewis.)

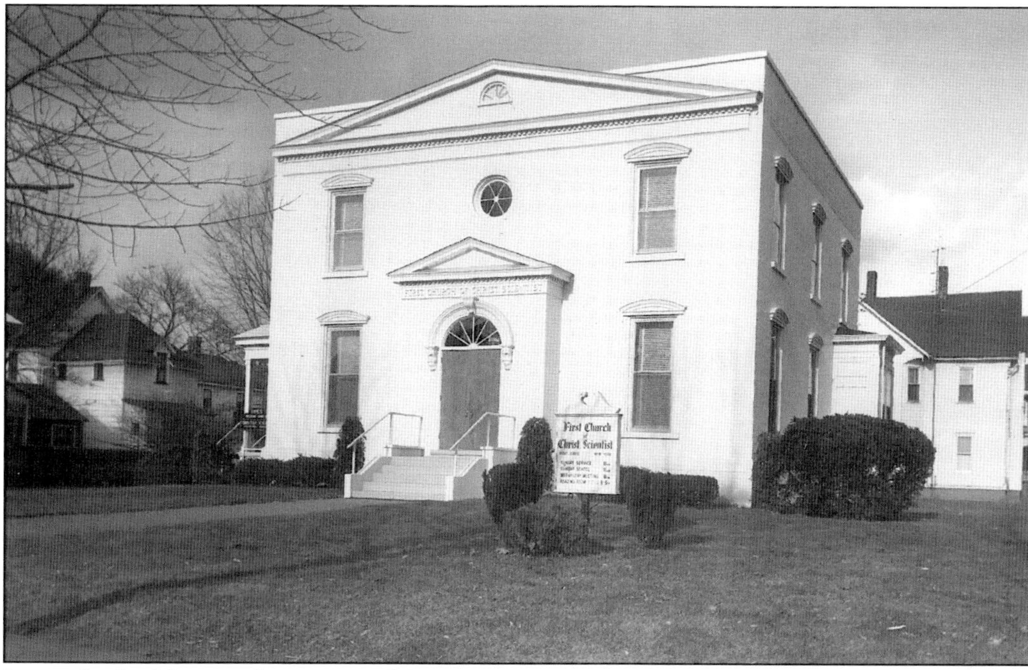

Later, the building at the corner of East Main Street and Sullivan Avenue became the home of the First Church of Christ, Scientist. All the original architectural features, except for the windows, have been removed. (Courtesy of Brian Lewis.)

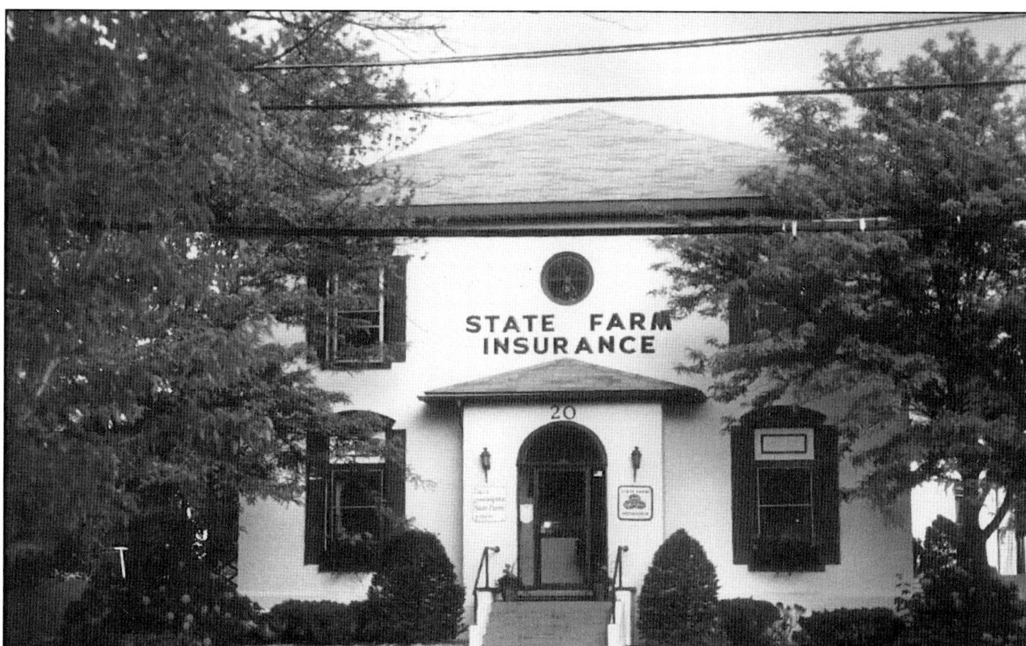

Today, the building is occupied by the James W. Reyle State Farm Insurance Company at 20 East Main Street. (Courtesy of Matt and Carol Osterberg.)

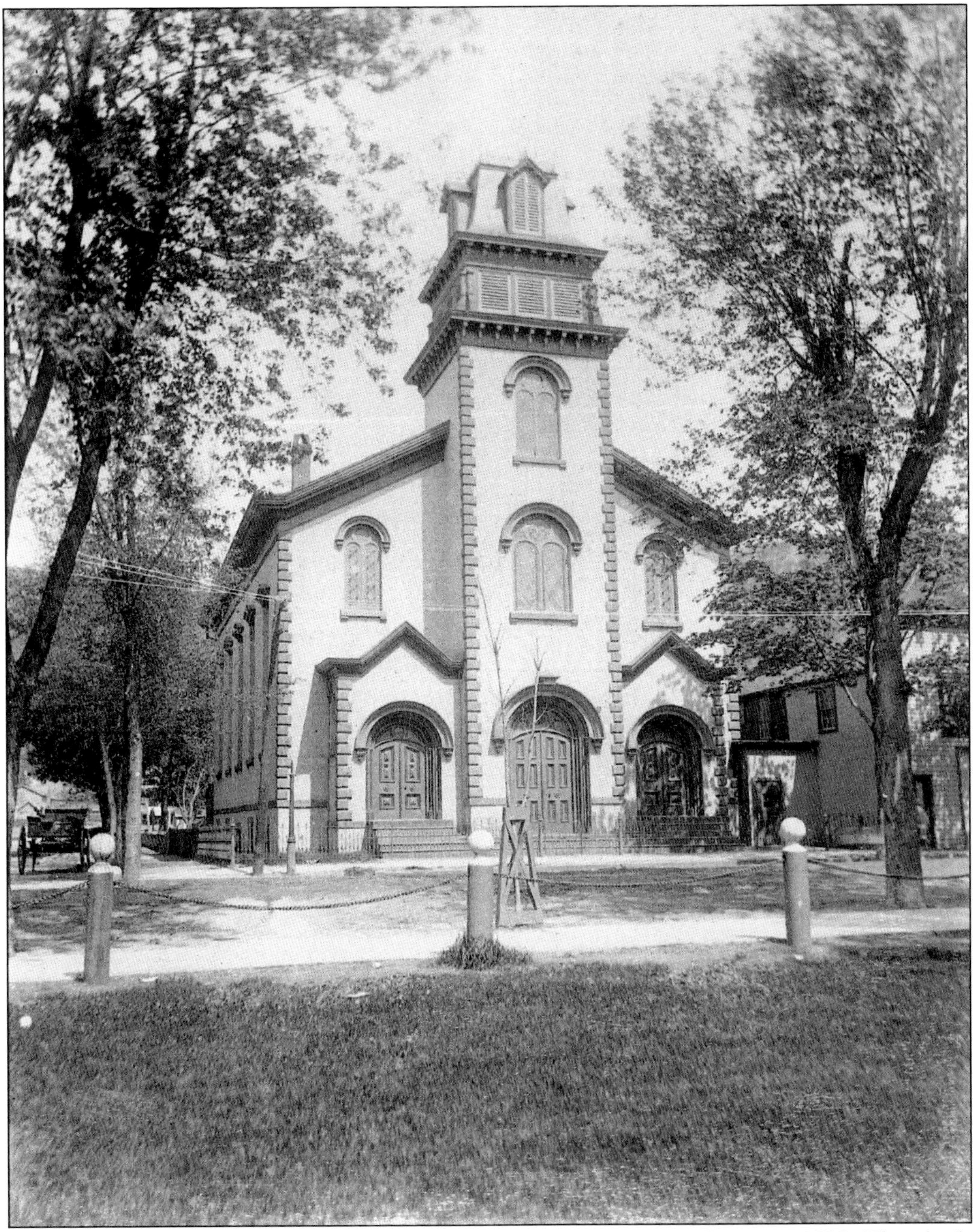

Five men and five women organized a Baptist congregation in Port Jervis in 1838. They built their first church on Hudson Street in 1848. A second church, seen here, was erected on Pike Street in 1865. In September 1894, this building partially burned. The congregation then built a new house of worship on East Main Street. This structure became the Deerpark Club. (Collection of the Minisink Valley Historical Society.)

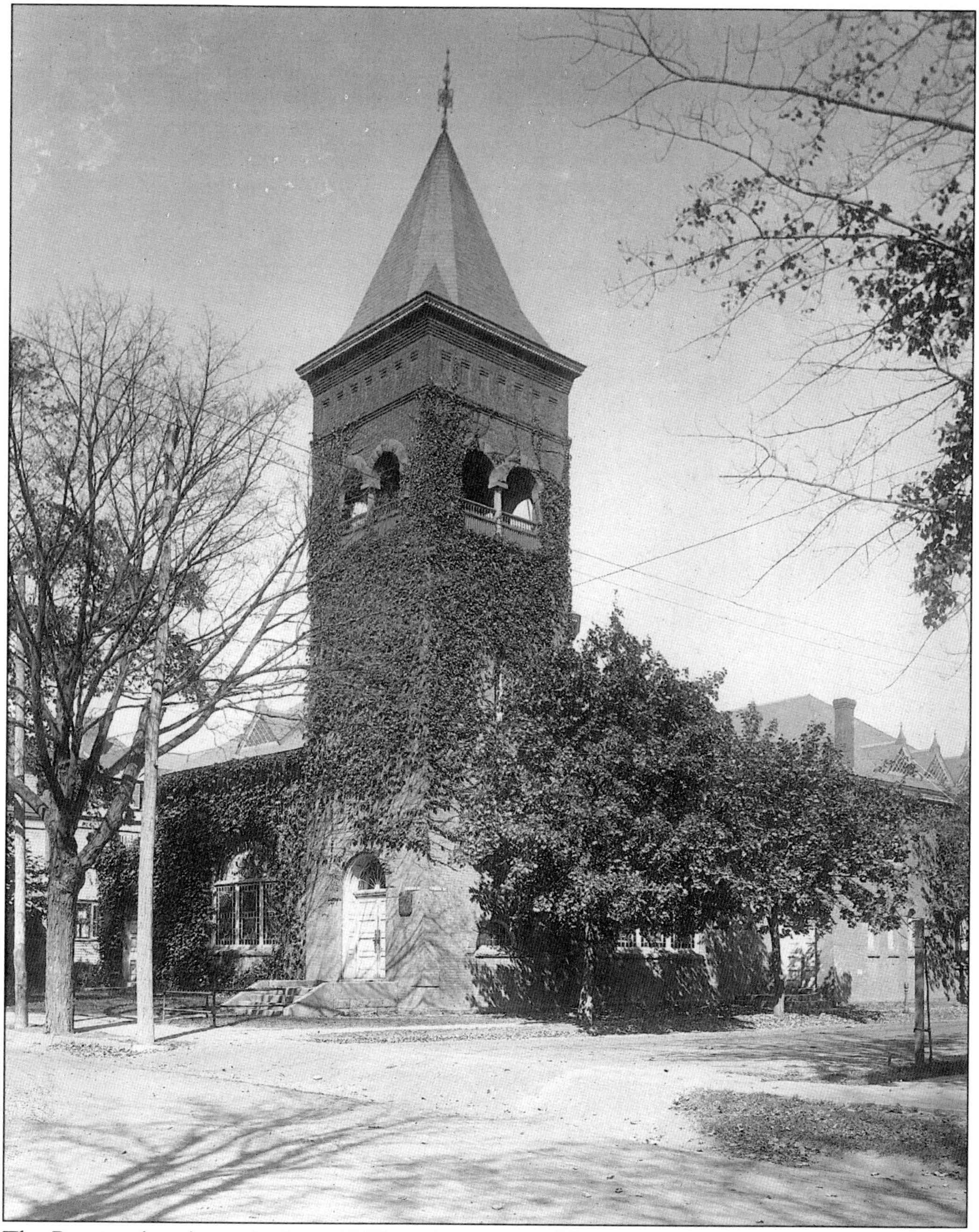

The Baptist church was built in 1895 on the corner of Ferguson Avenue and East Main Street after the church on Pike Street had been damaged by fire a year earlier. (Collection of the Minisink Valley Historical Society.)

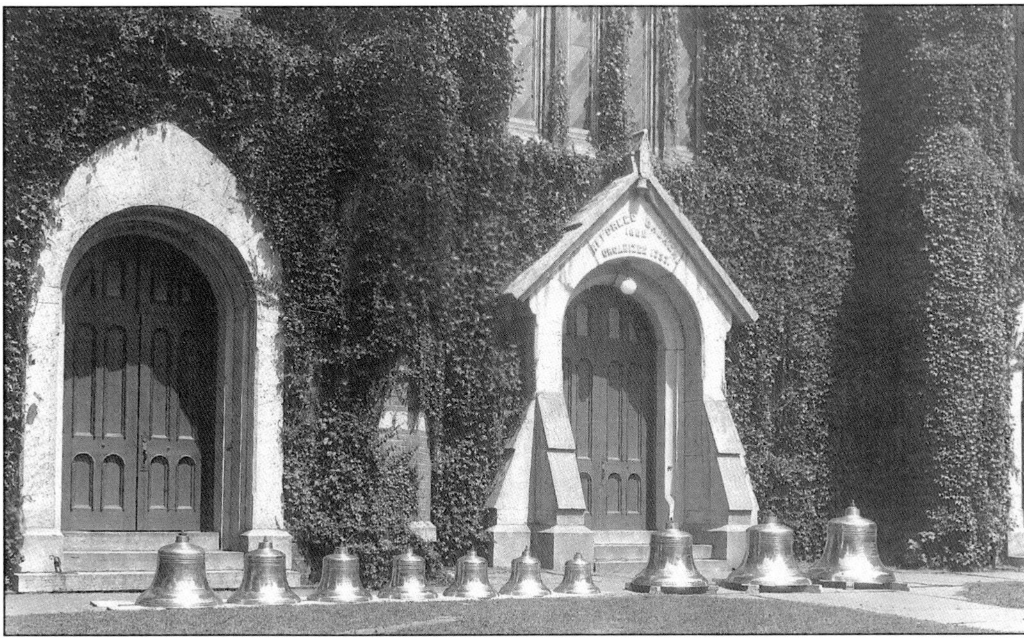

In 1928, Alfred Clark Carpenter donated a set of carillon bells to the Deerpark Dutch Reformed Church. These were in memory of his parents, Ora Grinell Carpenter and Phoebe Wickham Carpenter. The bells were hoisted by rope into the steeple. The nearest known carillon bells are in Syracuse, New York, and Hartford, Connecticut. (Courtesy of Robbie Smith.)

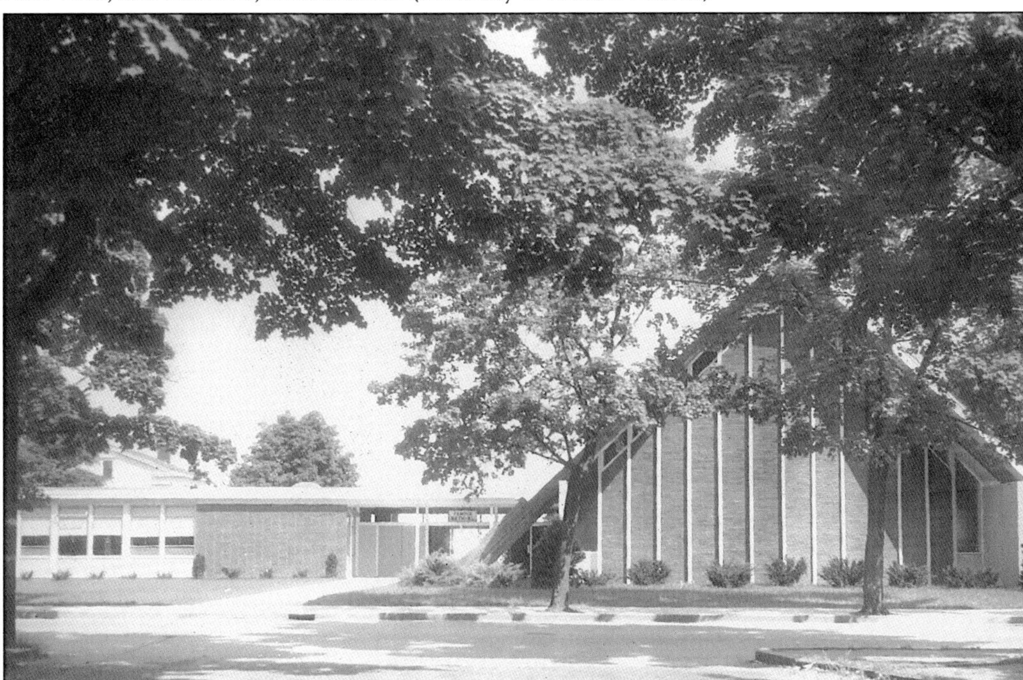

The Jewish Temple and community center at 88 East Main Street was dedicated on September 20, 1959. Previously, services had been held at the synagogue at Seward Avenue and Hammond Street. (Collection of the Minisink Valley Historical Society.)

St. Mary's Church, built in 1879 on Ball Street, is also known as the Church of the Immaculate Conception. The congregation was established in 1852. In 1915, a parochial school was established for area students and lasted for many years. The building on the right was a convent and at one time was used as an orphanage. Today, the Tri-States Day Care Center occupies this building. (Courtesy Ed Nikles Jr.)

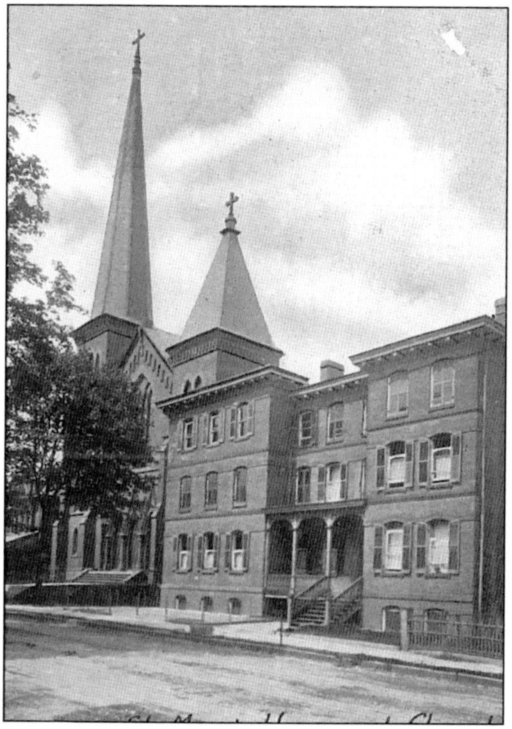

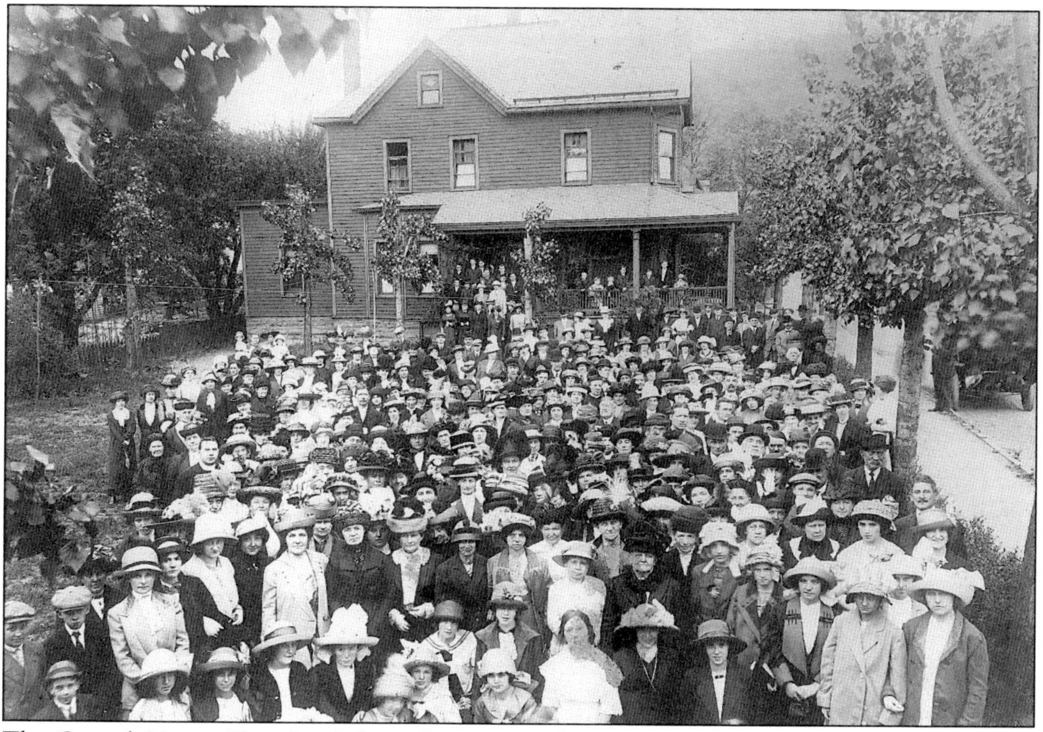

The Sacred Heart Church, dedicated in November 1898, is on West Main Street in the West End area of Port Jervis. Pictured here is the congregation in the 1920s. (Collection of the Minisink Valley Historical Society.)

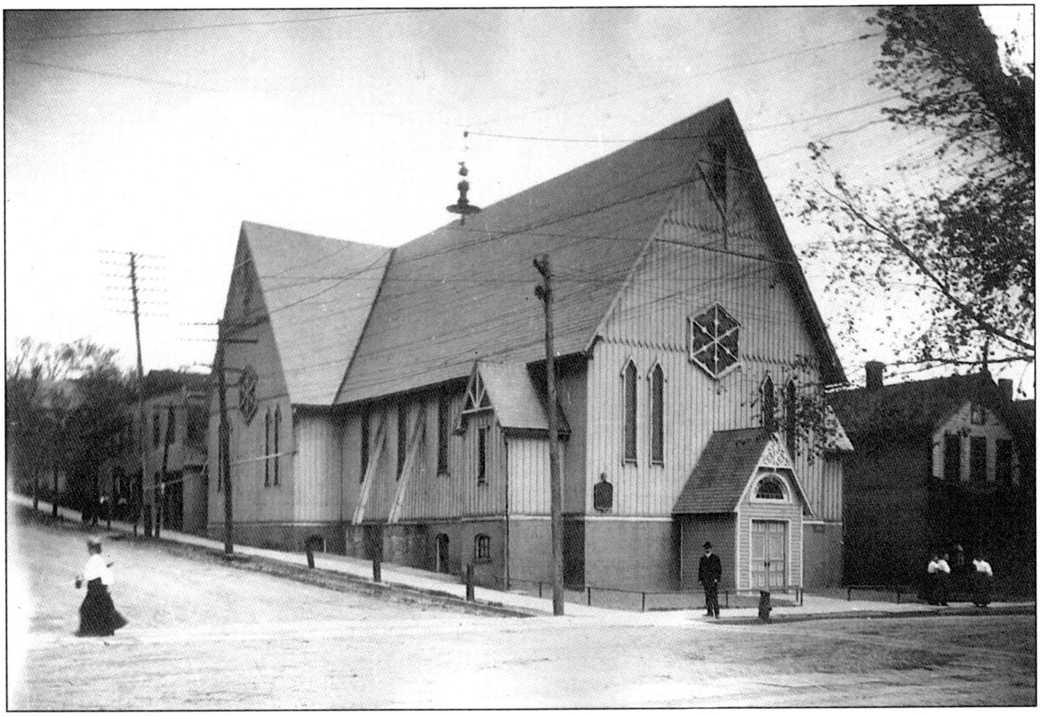

The Lutheran church, on the corner of Sussex and Hammond Streets, sat upon the present location of the Port Jervis City Hall. (Collection of the Minisink Valley Historical Society.)

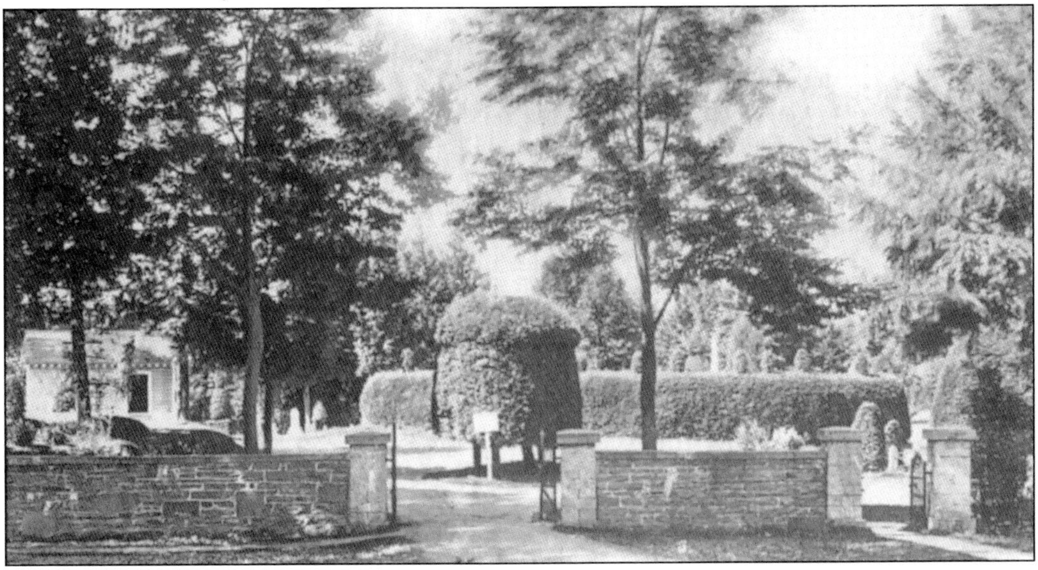

Laurel Grove Cemetery, designed by New York architect Howard Daniels, opened on July 15, 1856. Daniels had been one of the finalists in the competition to design Central Park in New York City. The cemetery is laid out in a parklike design with winding roads, hemlocks, pines, and mountain laurels. At the tip of the cemetery is Carpenter's Point, where Carpenter's Ferry once crossed. Located on the banks of the Neversink and Delaware Rivers, the cemetery is the final resting place for the Carpenter family. The Tri-States monument can also be found in this cemetery. (Courtesy of Matt and Carol Osterberg.)

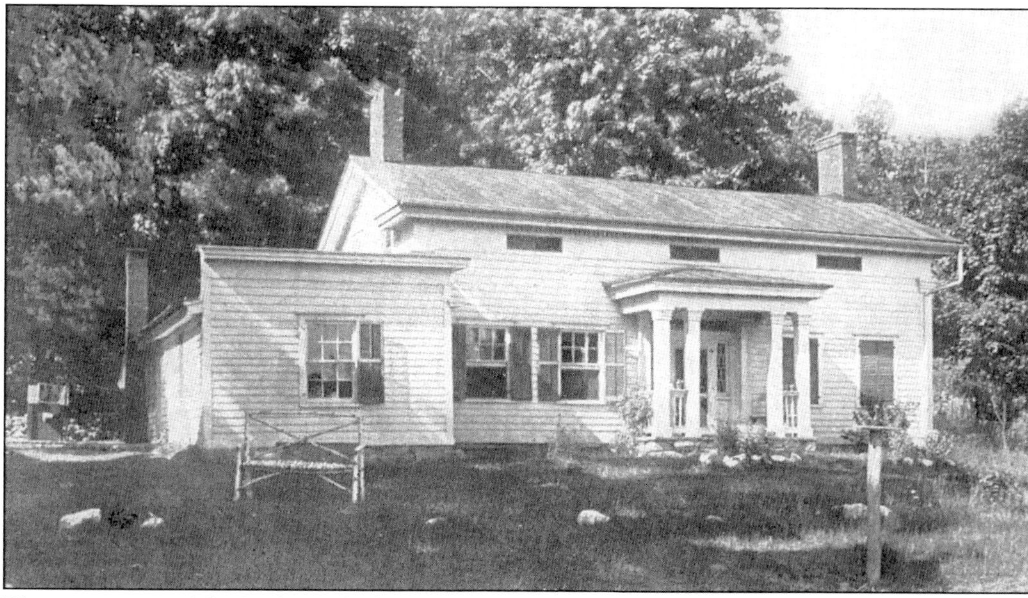

The parsonage of the Reformed Church in Cuddebackville was on Oakland Valley Road. Now a private residence, the building was still being used as a parsonage when this postcard was produced in the early 1900s. (Collection of the Minisink Valley Historical Society.)

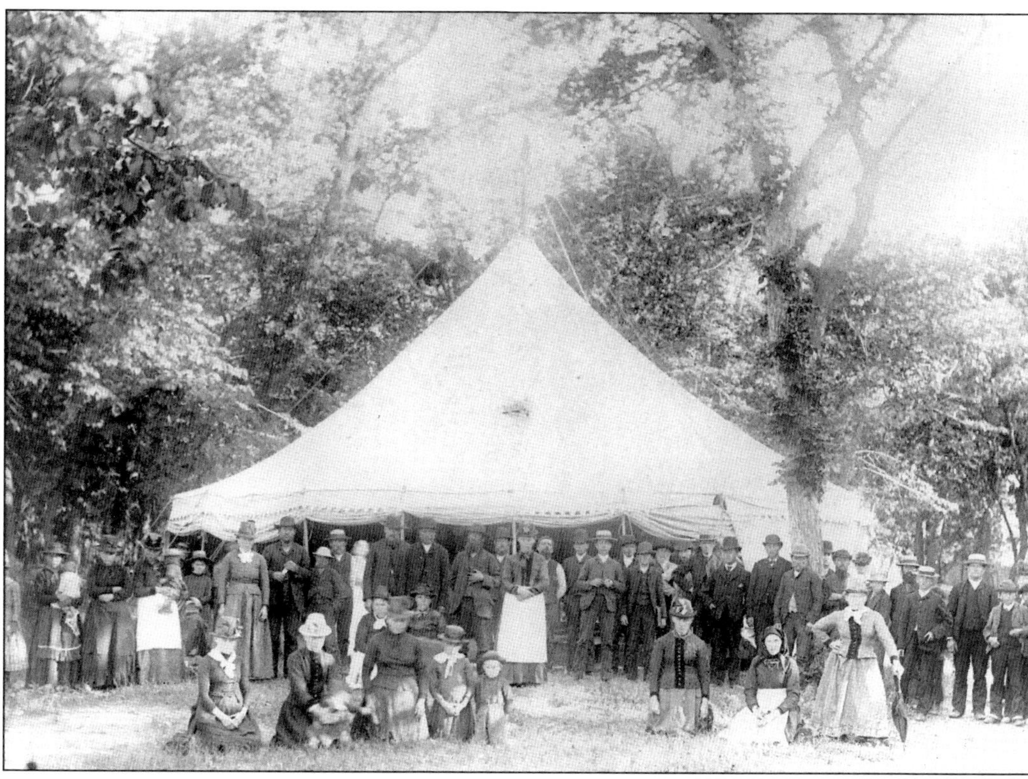

A group of parishioners from the Sparrowbush Church attends a spiritual revival meeting in the 1890s. (Collection of the Minisink Valley Historical Society.)

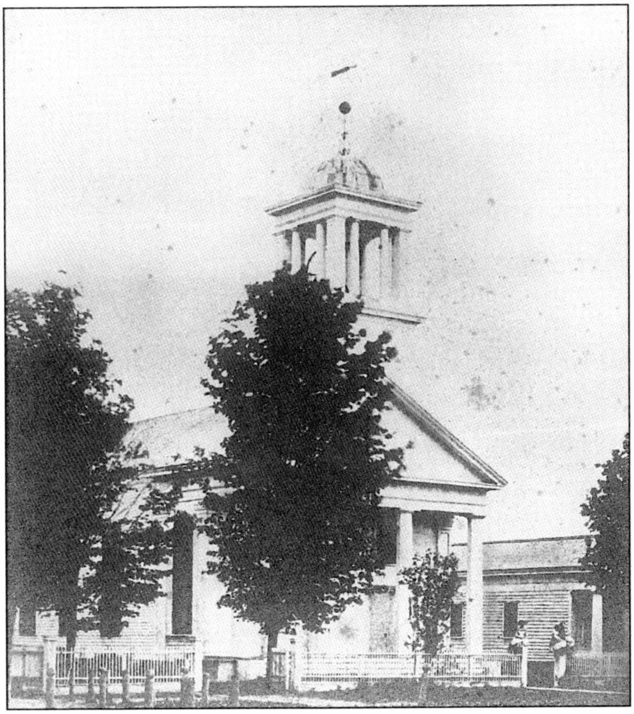

The third Deerpark Reformed Church served the congregation from 1836 to 1868. Built on East Main Street, it replaced the two previous churches on the site of the Moghogomock Cemetery. The Deerpark Reformed Church has been in existence since 1737. Many faithful ministers have served this church, including Rev. Elias VanBunschoten, who was instrumental in helping to establish Queens College, which became Rutgers University. (Collection of the Minisink Valley Historical Society.)

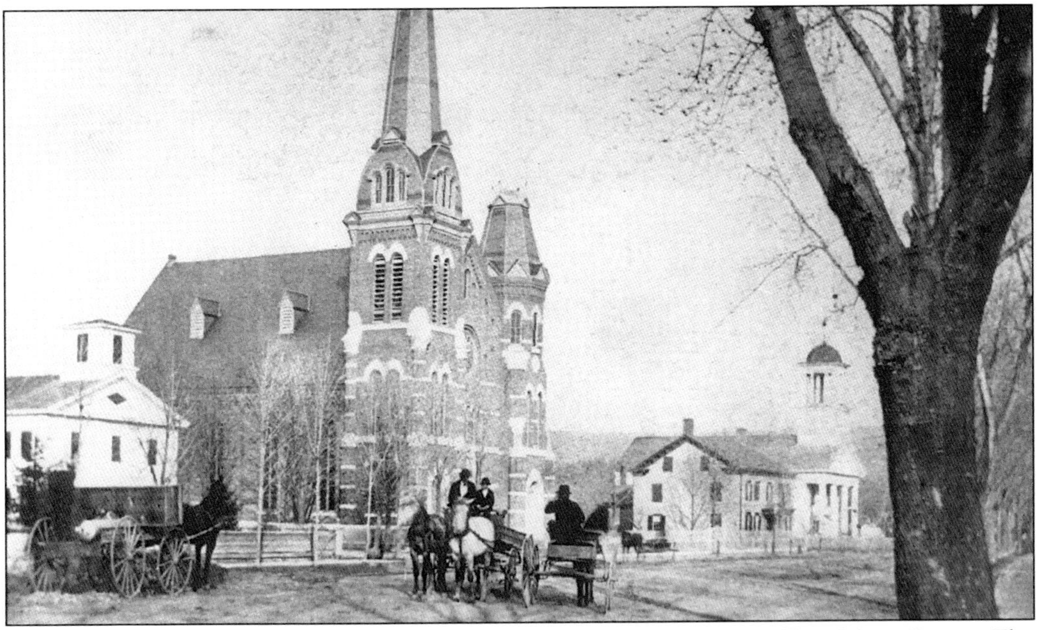

The fourth Deerpark Reformed Church was constructed in 1868 on East Main Street. The white building on the left is the former Sullivan Avenue School. The third building on the right was the home of the D & H Canal offices. The fourth building on the right is the third Deerpark Reformed Church. This building was moved to the Laurel Grove Cemetery, where it was used as a chapel until swept away by the flood of 1904. The tall steeple shown was destroyed by a windstorm in 1886. The photograph dates from between 1868 and 1886. (Collection of the Minisink Valley Historical Society.)

Three

THE THREE RS

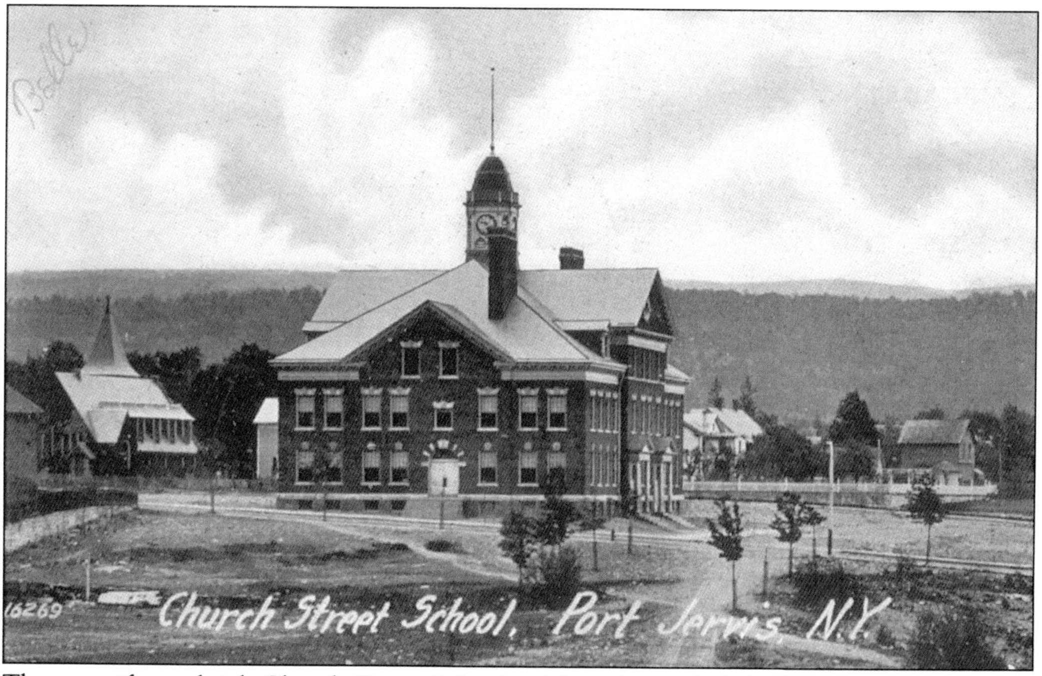

The magnificent brick Church Street School, with its four-sided clock tower, was erected in 1899. In 1987, it was demolished to make way for the Church Street Park and Playground. The building on the left is the Grace Episcopal Church on East Main Street. (Courtesy of Brian Lewis.)

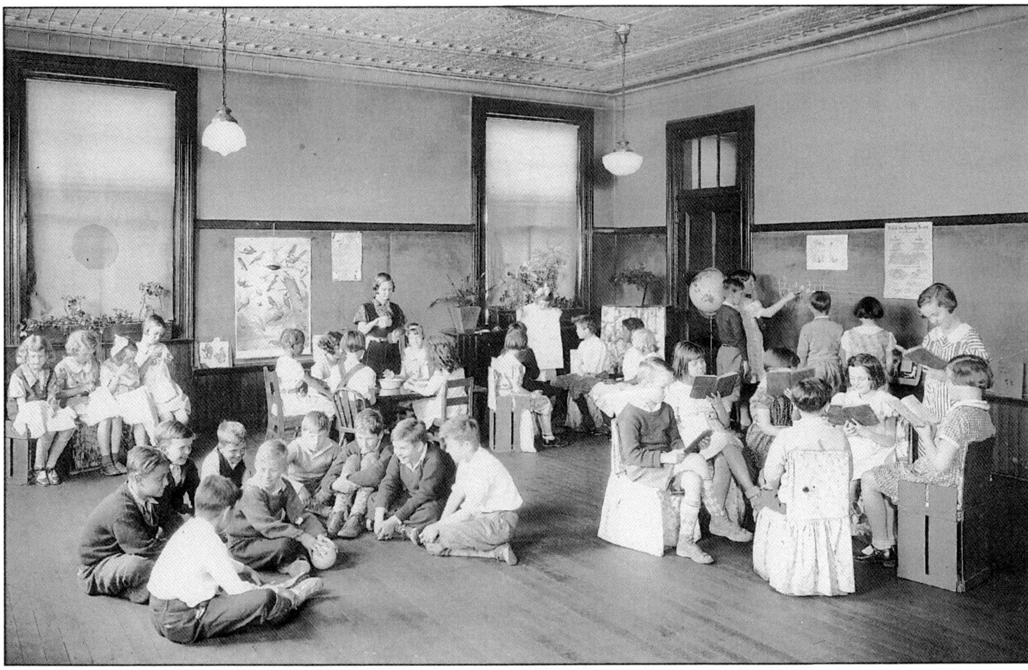

The interior of the second Church Street School was as elaborate as its exterior, with metal embossed ceilings and beautiful woodwork. Miss Write, center, conducts a fourth-grade class in 1933. (Courtesy of Brian Lewis.)

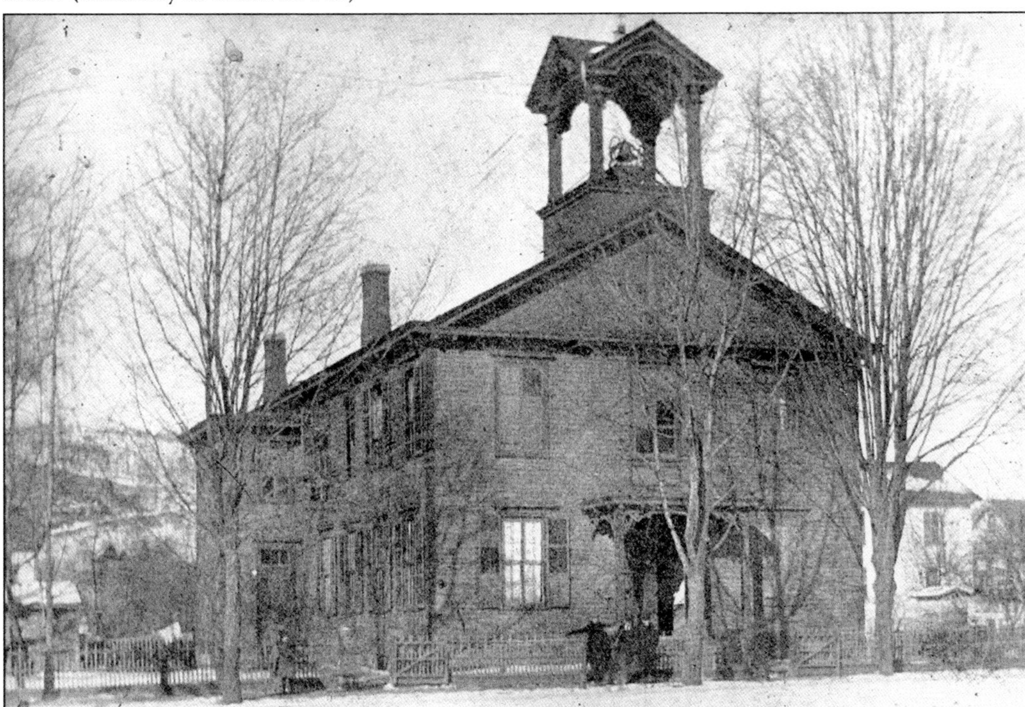

The original Church Street School, built in 1867 at Hammond and Church Streets, was used until the new school was erected in 1899. (Collection of the Minisink Valley Historical Society.)

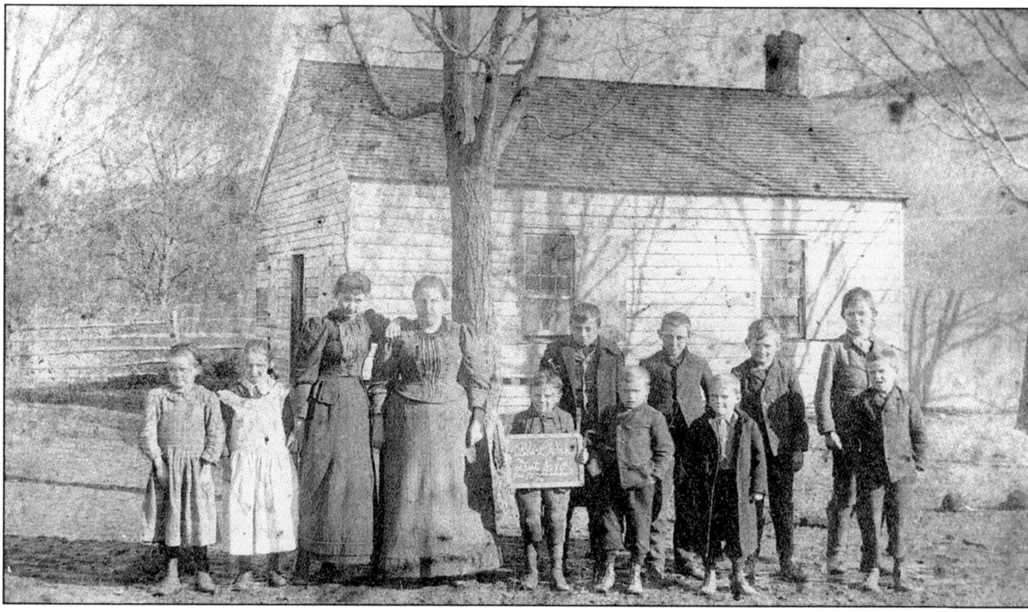

This class photograph was taken *c.* 1900 at the Black Rock School in Huguenot. This is one of the oldest one-room schools in Orange County. (Collection of the Minisink Valley Historical Society.)

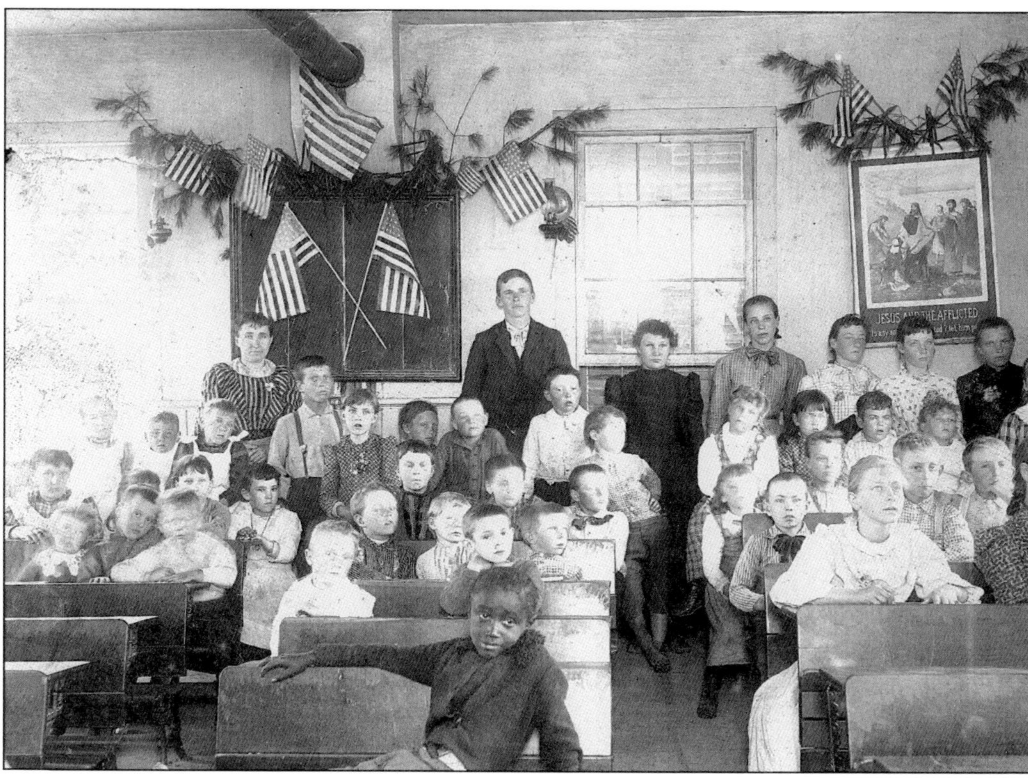

A class poses for a picture at the Myers Grove School in Goddefroy. This building is still standing near Canal Road. (Collection of the Minisink Valley Historical Society.)

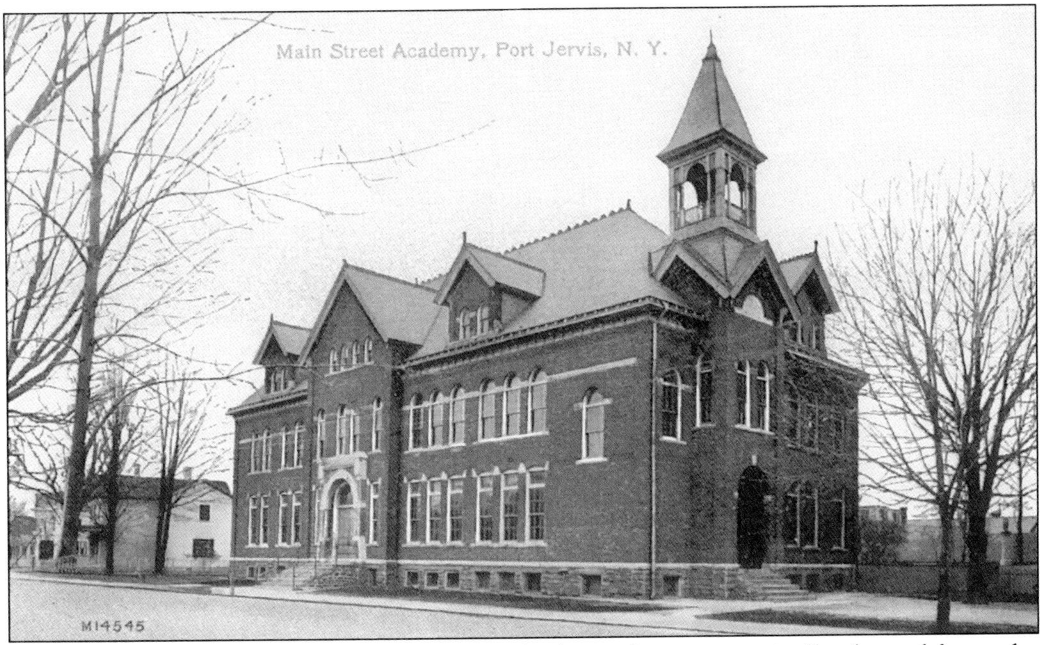

The Main Street Academy was built in 1888. The lower floor was originally planned for grades one through four, but eventually part of the first floor functioned as a high school. The structure was lost to fire in 1918. (Courtesy of Ed Nikles Jr.)

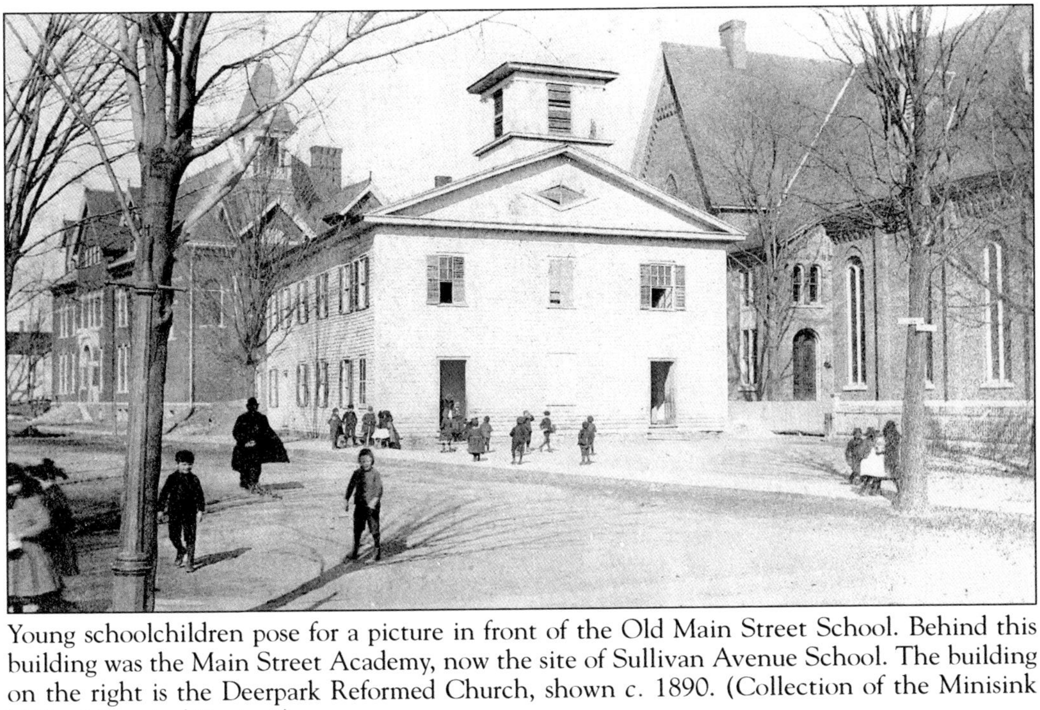

Young schoolchildren pose for a picture in front of the Old Main Street School. Behind this building was the Main Street Academy, now the site of Sullivan Avenue School. The building on the right is the Deerpark Reformed Church, shown *c.* 1890. (Collection of the Minisink Valley Historical Society.)

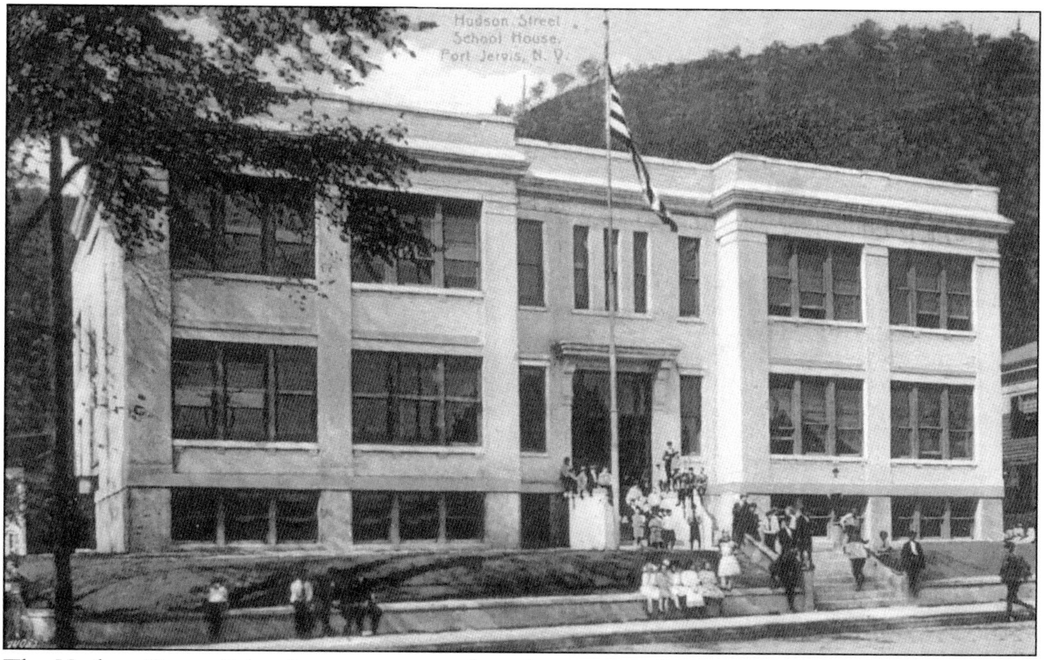

The Hudson Street School was constructed on the corner of West Main and Hudson Streets in 1911. The building was used for a short time but, because of poor workmanship, was demolished in 1919. The site is now the home of St. Peter's Lutheran Church, which was built in the 1950s. (Courtesy of Matt and Carol Osterberg.)

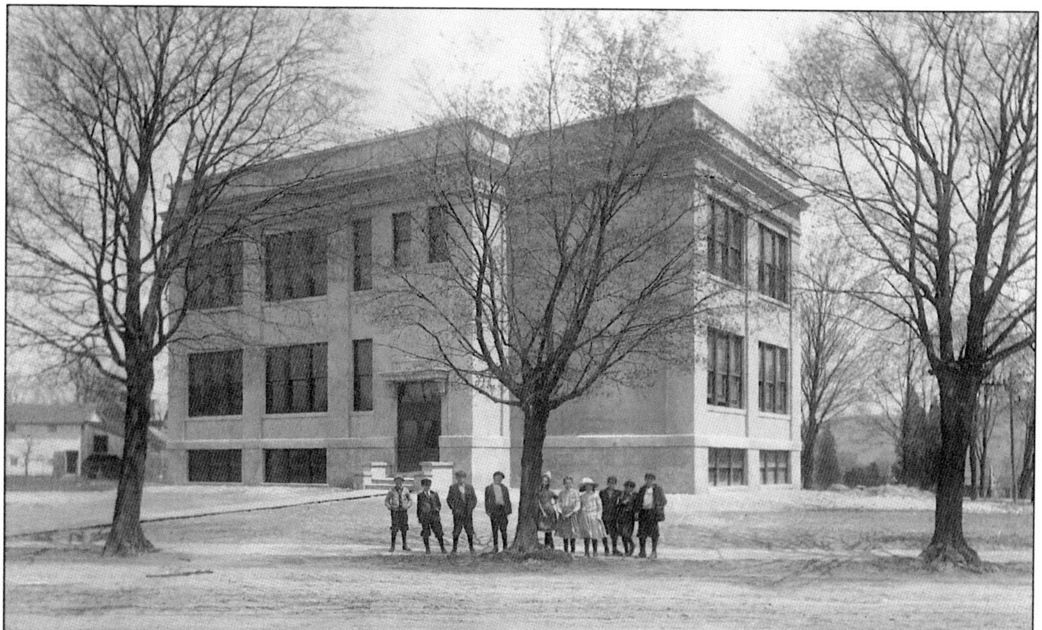
A group of schoolchildren poses in front of a tree at the East Main Street School, built in 1911. Machackemach Village Senior Housing Complex is now situated on this corner of East Main Street and Jersey Avenue. (Collection of the Minisink Valley Historical Society.)

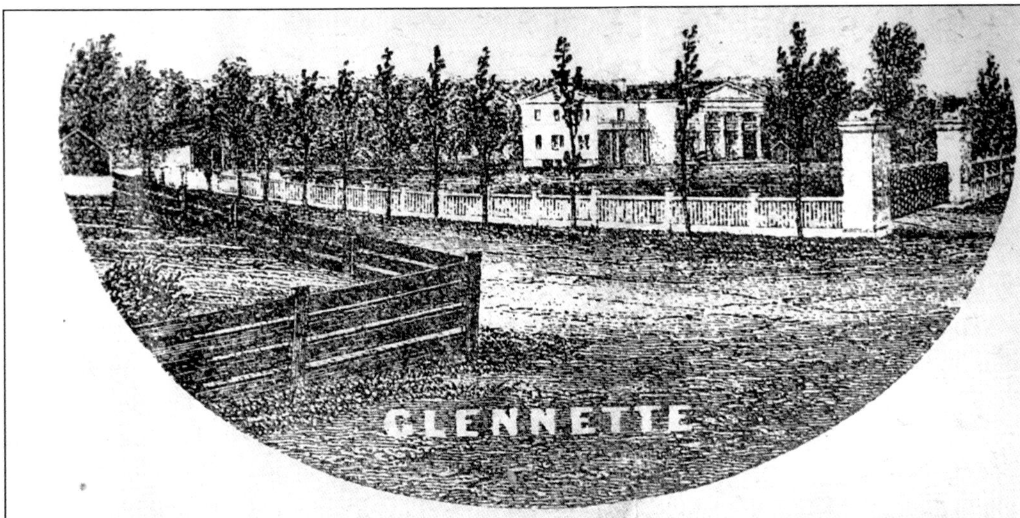

THE PORT JERVIS RESIDENCE OF COL. SAM FOWLER

Glennette Fowler was the wife of Col. Samuel Fowler. The colonel's estate, Glennette Field, is used by the Port Jervis School District for home football games. (Courtesy of Robbie Smith.)

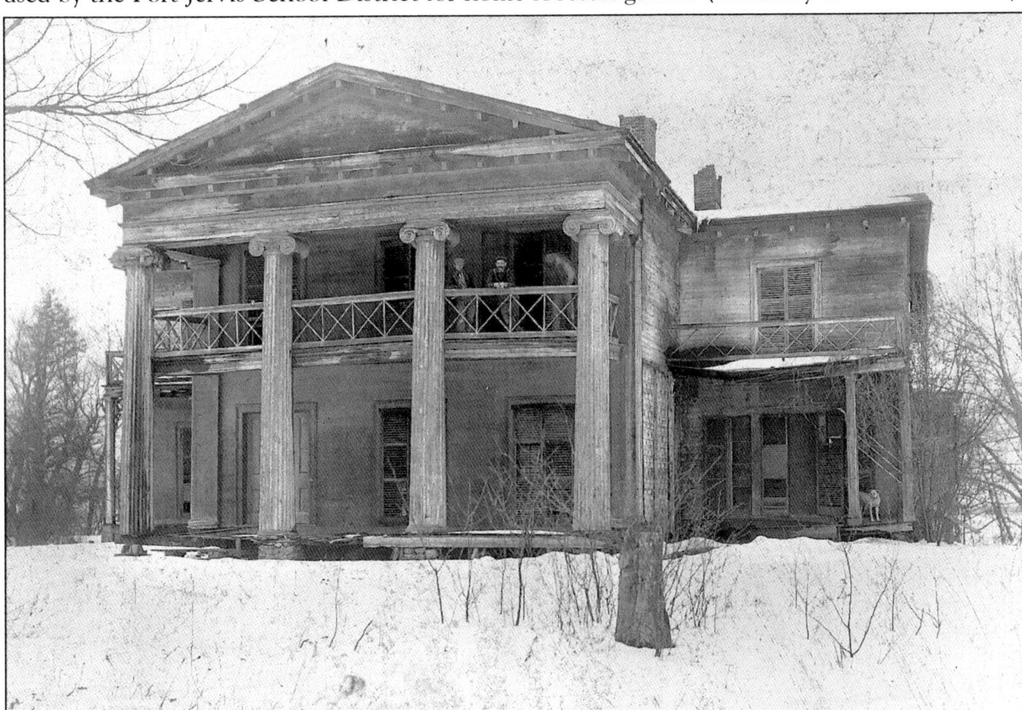

This was the estate of Col. Samuel Fowler, considered by some to be the most influential person to develop the community of Port Jervis. His home, built in the 1850s, resembled an old-time plantation, with a manor house and stables. An underground tunnel connected these two buildings. At the time this photograph was taken in the early 1900s, the building was in disrepair. Soon after, it was demolished and the Port Jervis School District purchased the land for future school buildings. (Collection of the Minisink Valley Historical Society.)

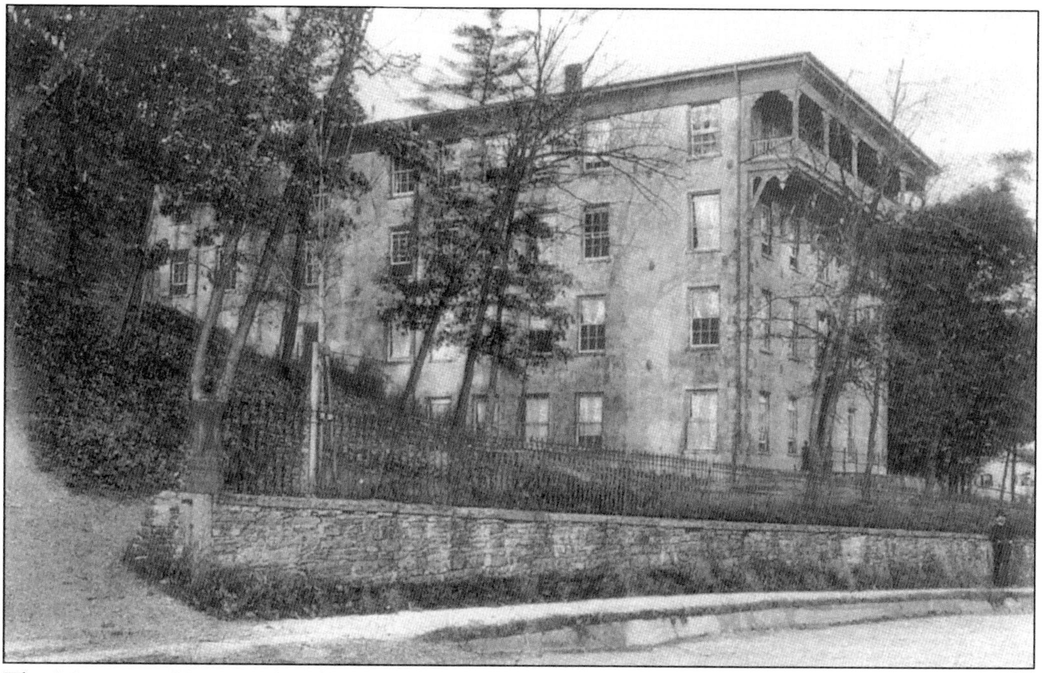

The Mountain House School building was a hotel in the 1870s but in use as a school from the 1880s until 1924. Located on West Main Street, shown *c.* 1907, it could hold 100 students. It was demolished in 1929. (Courtesy of Matt and Carol Osterberg.)

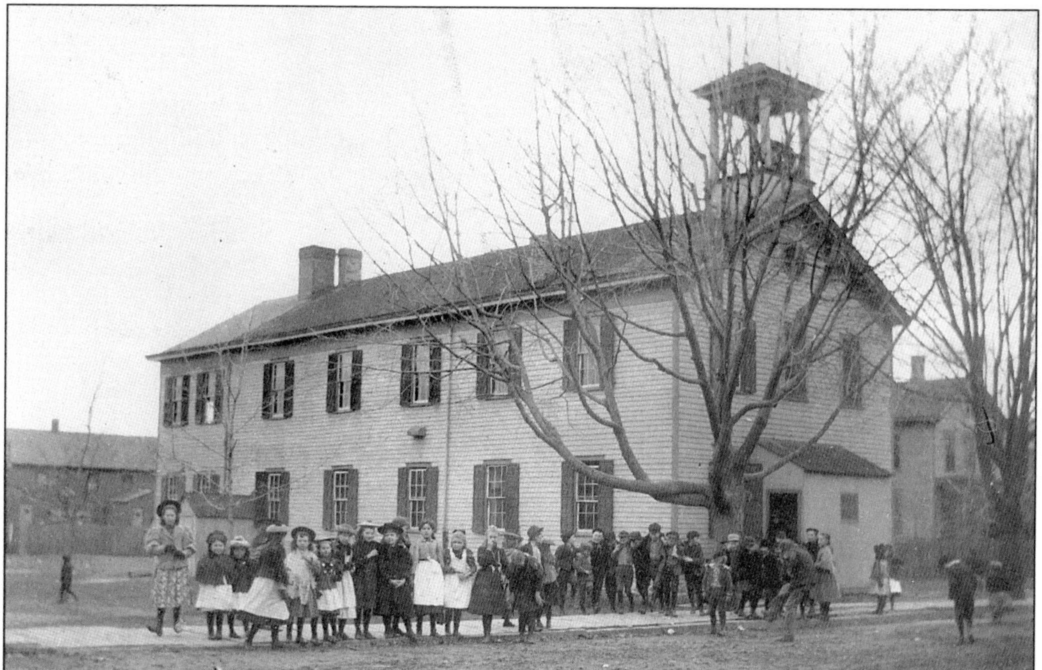

The West End section of Port Jervis was originally called Germantown due to the large population of German immigrants who settled there. This is the Germantown School *c.* 1900. (Collection of the Minisink Valley Historical Society.)

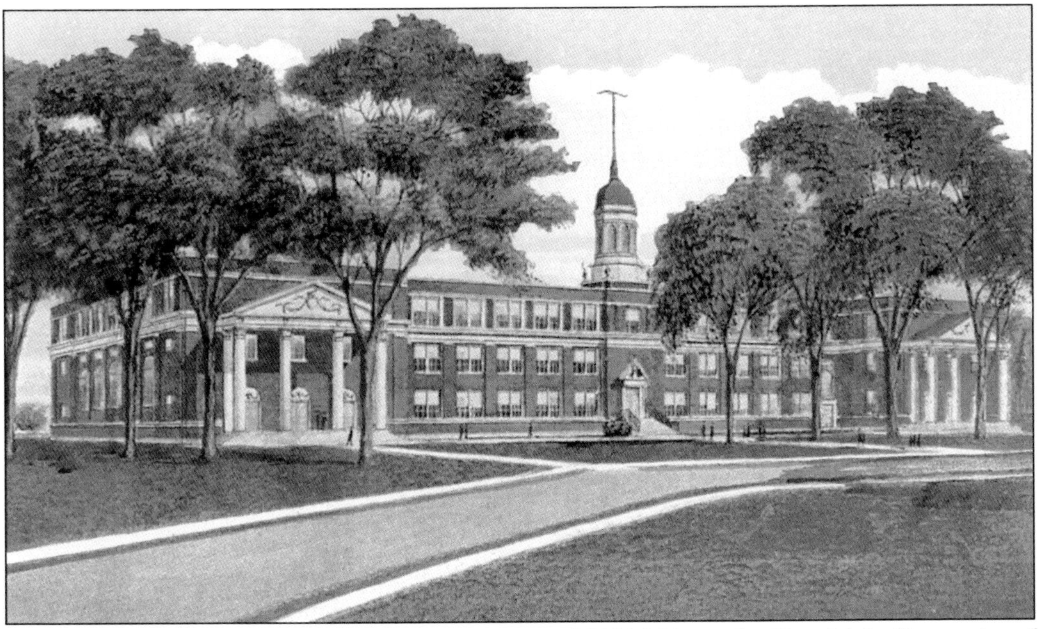

A new high school was erected in 1922 at a cost of $400,000 on the East Main Street site of Glennette, the former homestead of Col. Samuel Fowler. Today, the building is used as the Port Jervis Middle School. The school is shown *c.* the 1920s. (Courtesy of Matt and Carol Osterberg.)

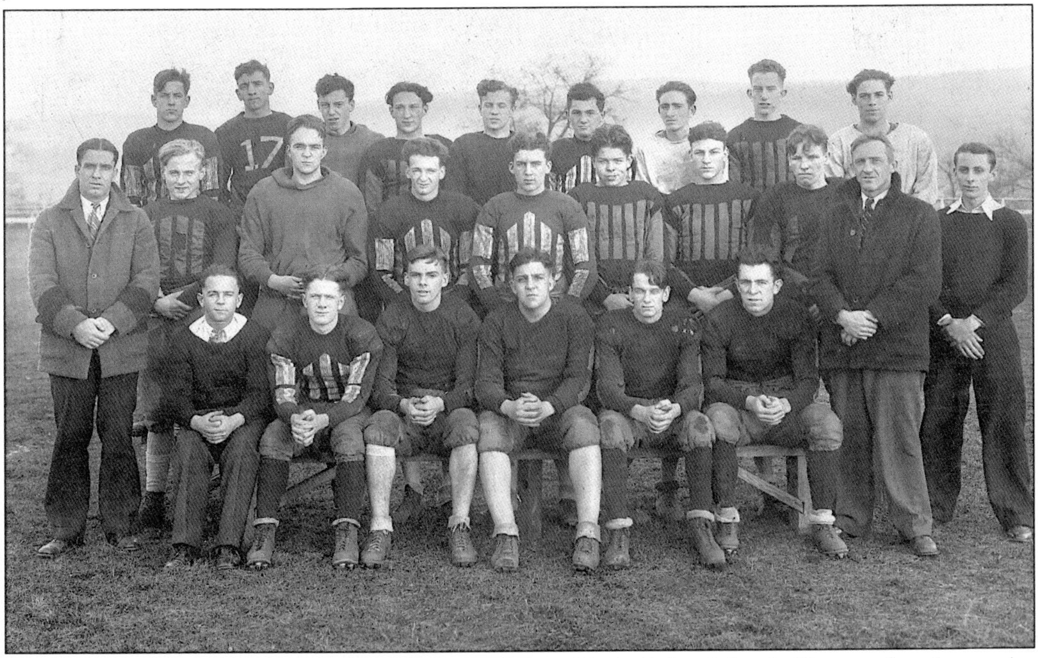

As long as anyone can remember, the Port Jervis High School football team has been the pride of the city. The 1930 Red Raiders pictured are, from left to right, as follows: (front row) Knight (coach), Curtiss, Casterline, T. Balmos, Buchanan, Birmingham, and Chase (coach); (middle row) Klein, Briard, Soudant, Amey, Boyle, Carroll, and Backus; (back row) Schantz, Adell, Nolan, Oliver, L. Balmos, Perl, Cohen, Leavy, and Schofield. (Collection of the Minisink Valley Historical Society.)

Four

Volunteering and Relaxing

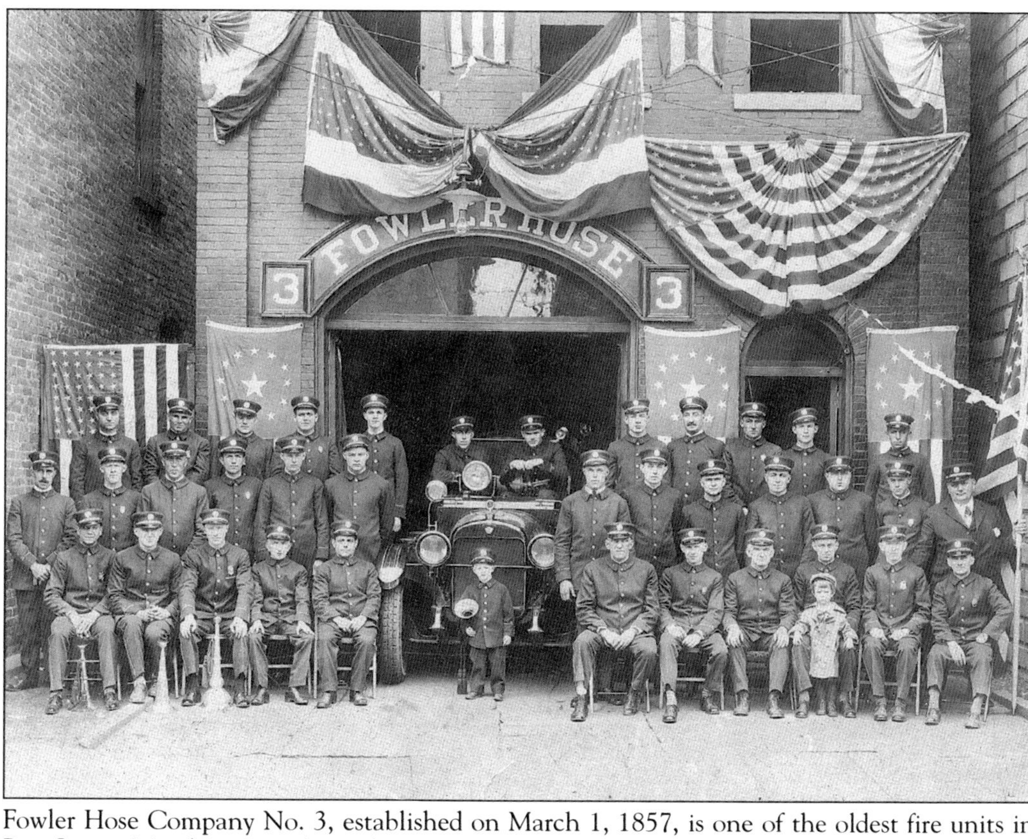

Fowler Hose Company No. 3, established on March 1, 1857, is one of the oldest fire units in Port Jervis. Members pose for a photograph in July 1925 prior to the annual Fire Department Inspection Parade. The boy in the center is Dan Dwyer Jr.; his father, Dan Dwyer Sr., is on the right. This building is now the home of Woogie's Deli on Pike Street near King Street. This fire company was named after Col. Samuel Fowler. (Courtesy of Dan Dwyer.)

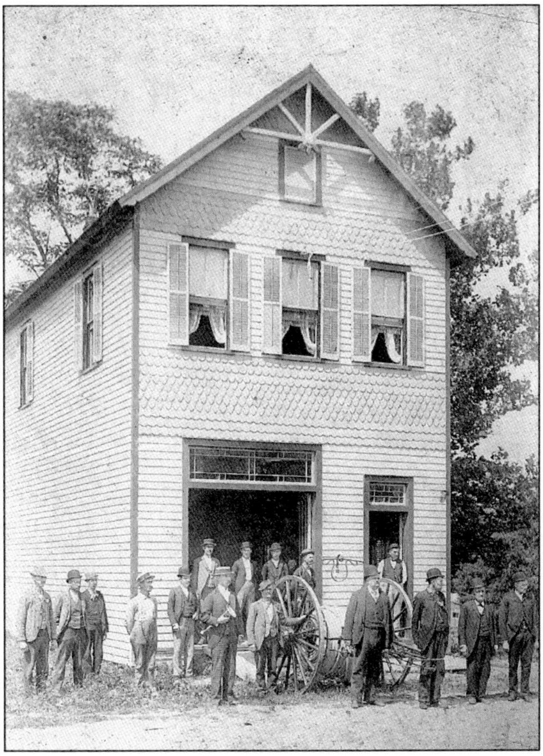

Tri-States Hose Company No. 6 is the youngest fire company in Port Jervis. It was formed to protect the community in Tri-States, which is just over the Neversink Bridge. The firehouse is shown c. 1890. (Collection of the Minisink Valley Historical Society.)

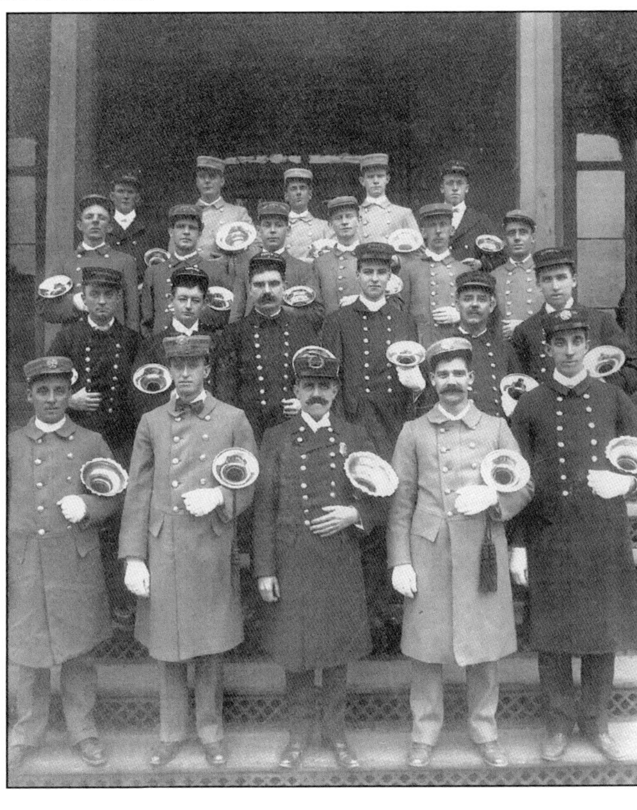

Volunteer fire companies have protected Port Jervis and the surrounding communities since 1857. Today, there are six fire units protecting the city. This c. 1890 photograph shows a local company standing proud after marching in the annual firemen's parade. (Collection of the Minisink Valley Historical Society.)

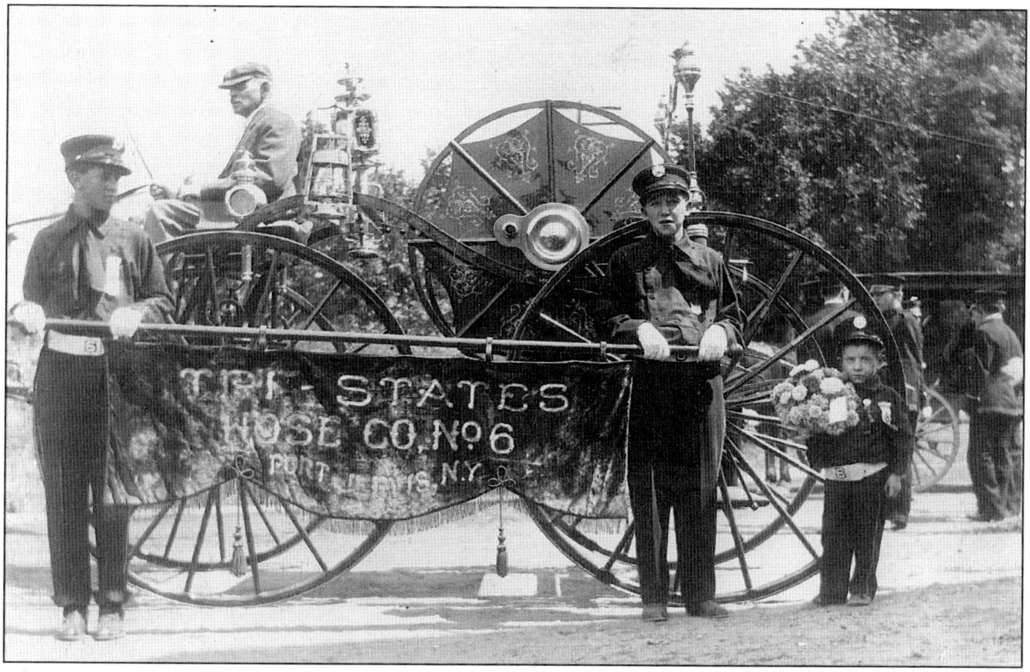

This was the winning apparatus in the 1910 parade. Members of Tri-States Hose Company No. 6 proudly display their banner. (Collection of the Minisink Valley Historical Society.)

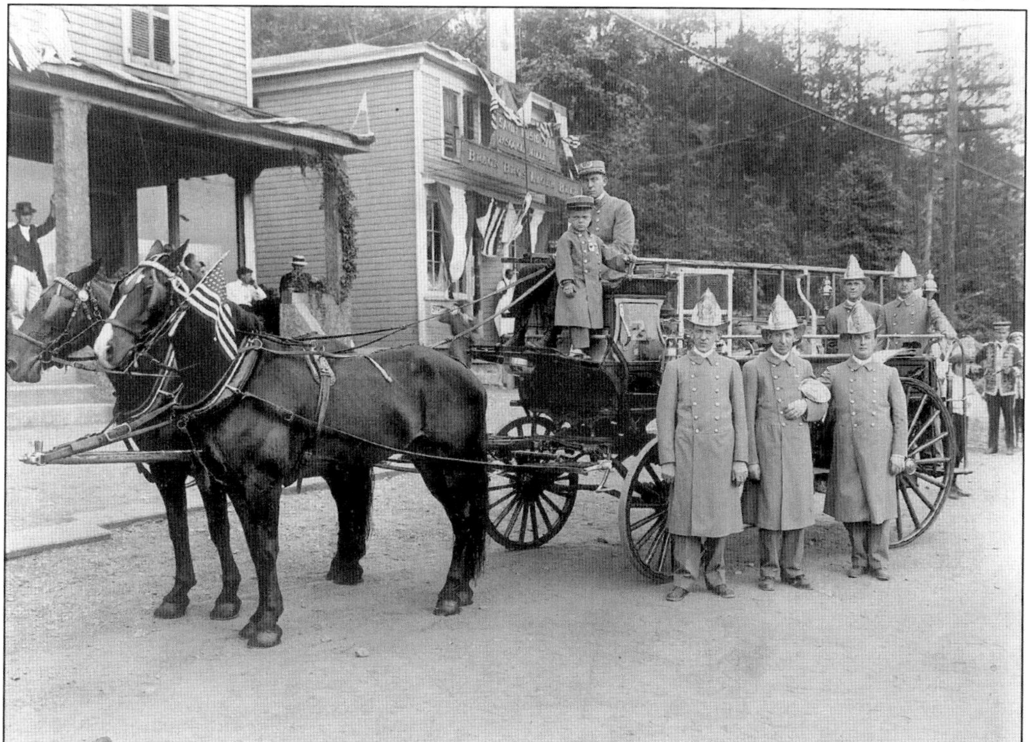

The Delaware Hose Company No. 2 was proud to be invited to the firemen's parade held in Suffern, New York, on August 5, 1914. (Collection of the Minisink Valley Historical Society.)

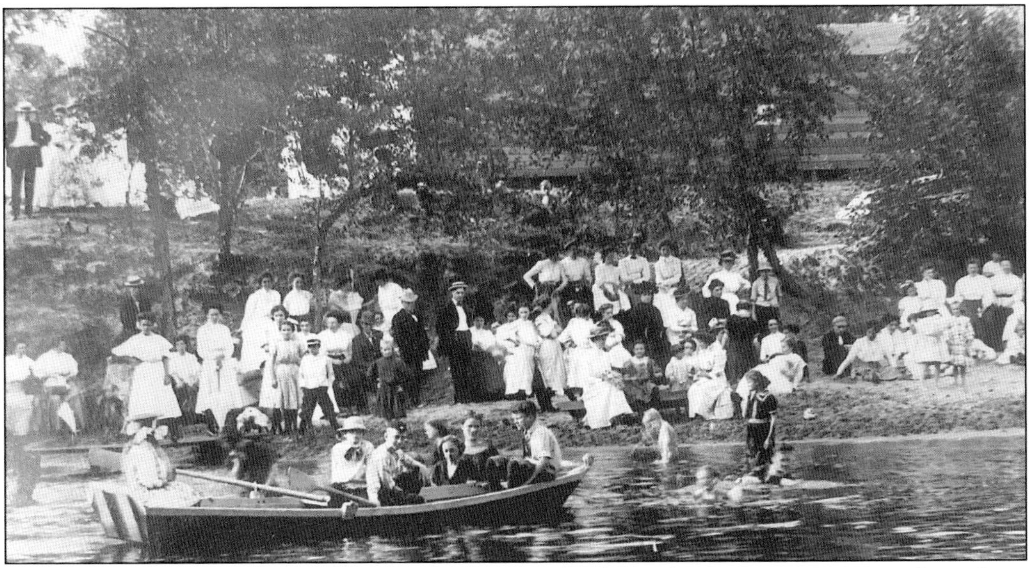

These people enjoy a beautiful summer day at Joyland Beach c. 1910. Many people seeking summer fun discovered boating on the Neversink River. (Collection of the Minisink Valley Historical Society.)

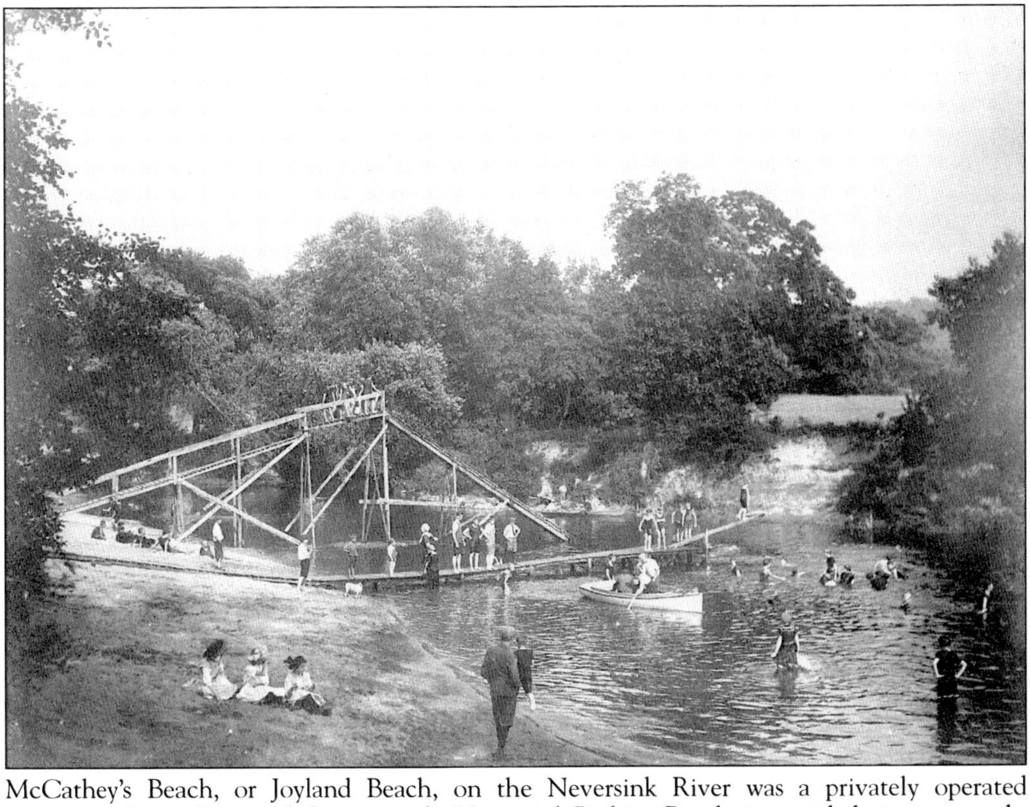

McCathey's Beach, or Joyland Beach, on the Neversink River was a privately operated recreational area. Previously known as the Neversink Bathing Beach, it provided picnic grounds, auto camping, a dancing facility, 200 bathhouses, and a large pavilion. It became the most popular recreational facility in the area. (Collection of the Minisink Valley Historical Society.)

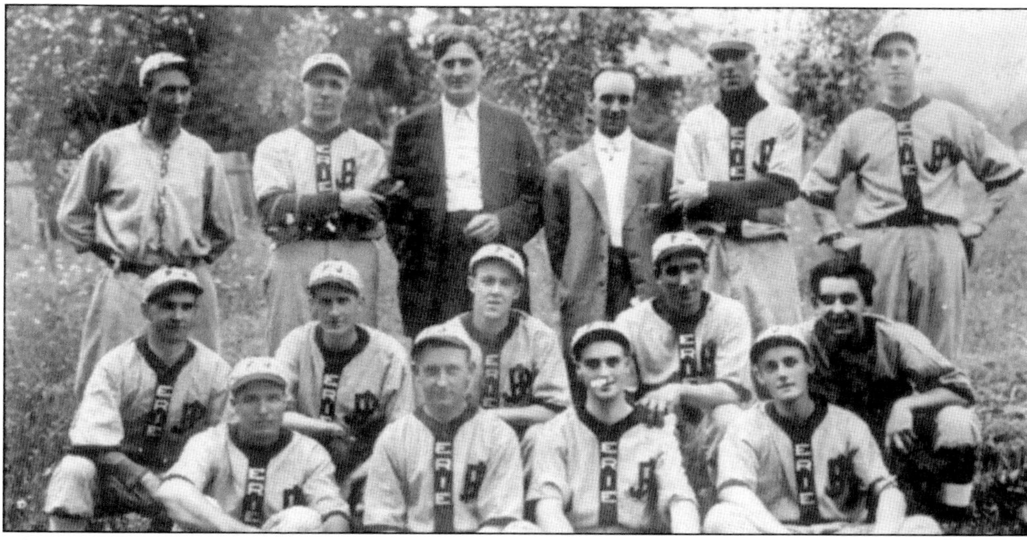

The Erie baseball team was one of the finest in the area in 1915. Team members pictured are, from left to right, as follows: (front row) Peewee Carey, Bill Adams, Odgen Clark, and Tom Hoppey; (middle row) Frank Eagen, Ed Conroy, George Patterson, unidentified, and John Powrie; (back row) Hortense Luckey, Paul Regen, George Tiebolt, Eddie Flanagan, William Monahan, and Sidney Winan. (Courtesy of Robbie Smith.)

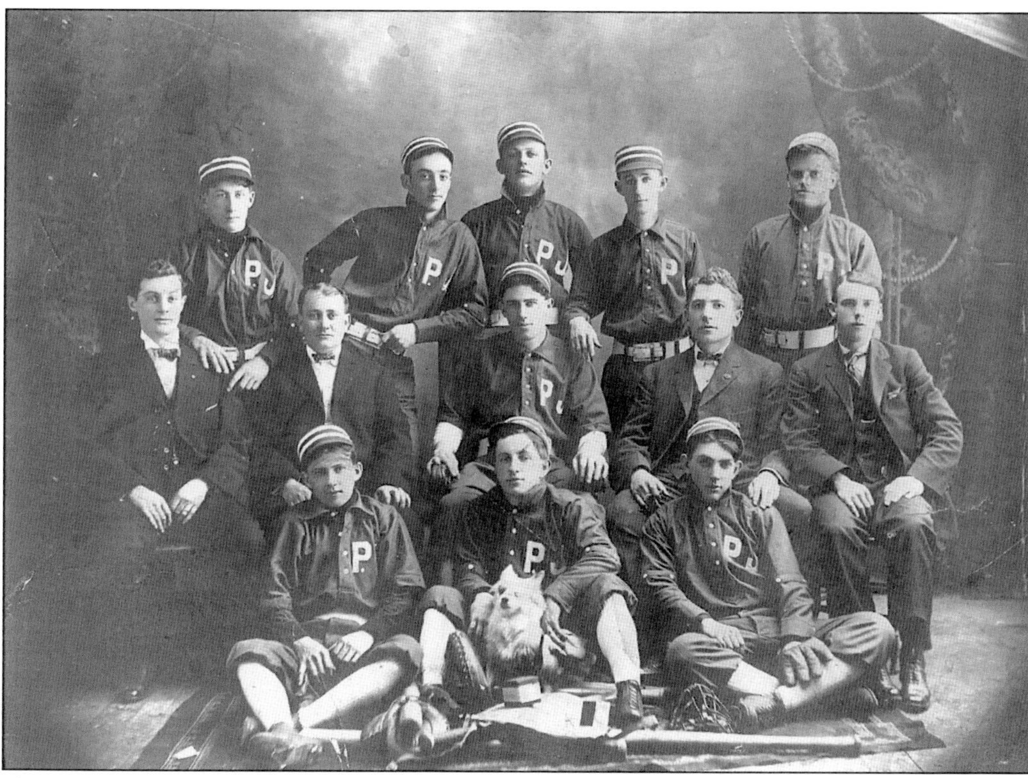

If you played for the Port Jervis baseball club in 1906, you played in every game. There were no bench warmers in this group. (Collection of the Minisink Valley Historical Society.)

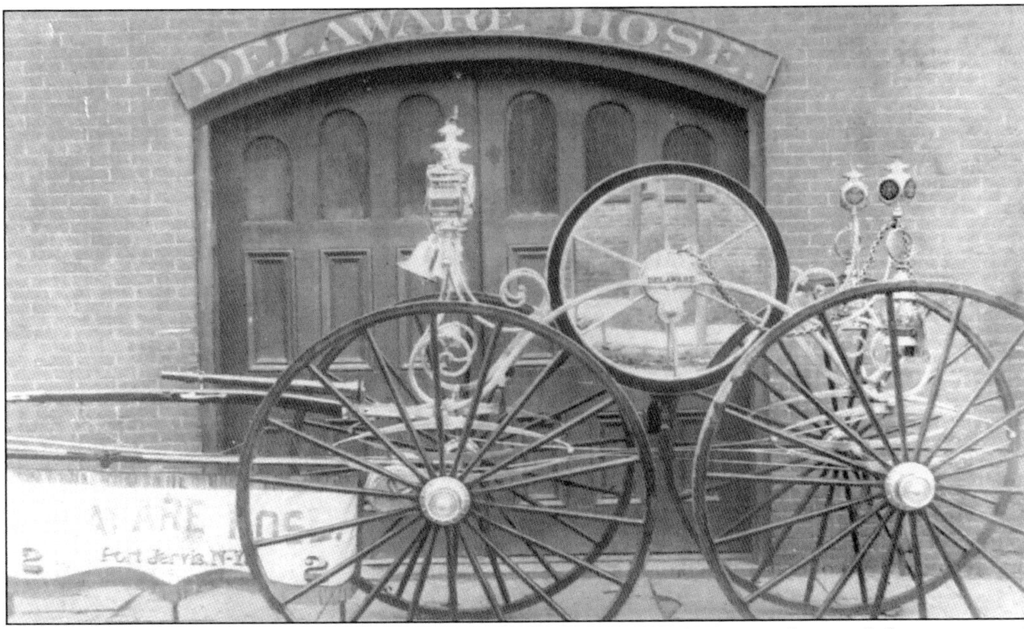

The Delaware Hose Company No. 2 and its equipment are shown in front of the company's original firehouse on Sussex Street near Ball Street *c.* 1910. (Collection of the Minisink Valley Historical Society.)

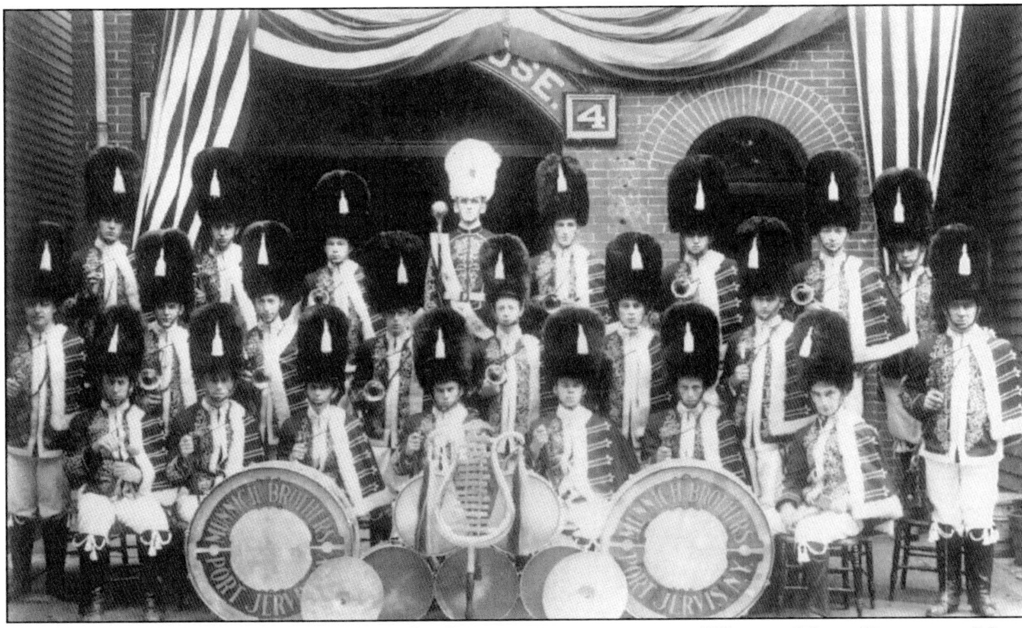

In 1876, a new fire company organized. This company was named Everitt Hose Company No. 4 after one of its founding members, John E. Everitt. In 1883, the company was renamed the Port Jervis Hose Company No. 4, a name that remained until 1936. It was once again renamed in honor of Howard Wheat, fire chief from 1910 until 1936. The Munnich Brothers Band of Port Jervis stands in front of Hose Company No. 4 before the annual Firemen's Inspection Day Parade. This building is on Seward Avenue. (Collection of the Minisink Valley Historical Society.)

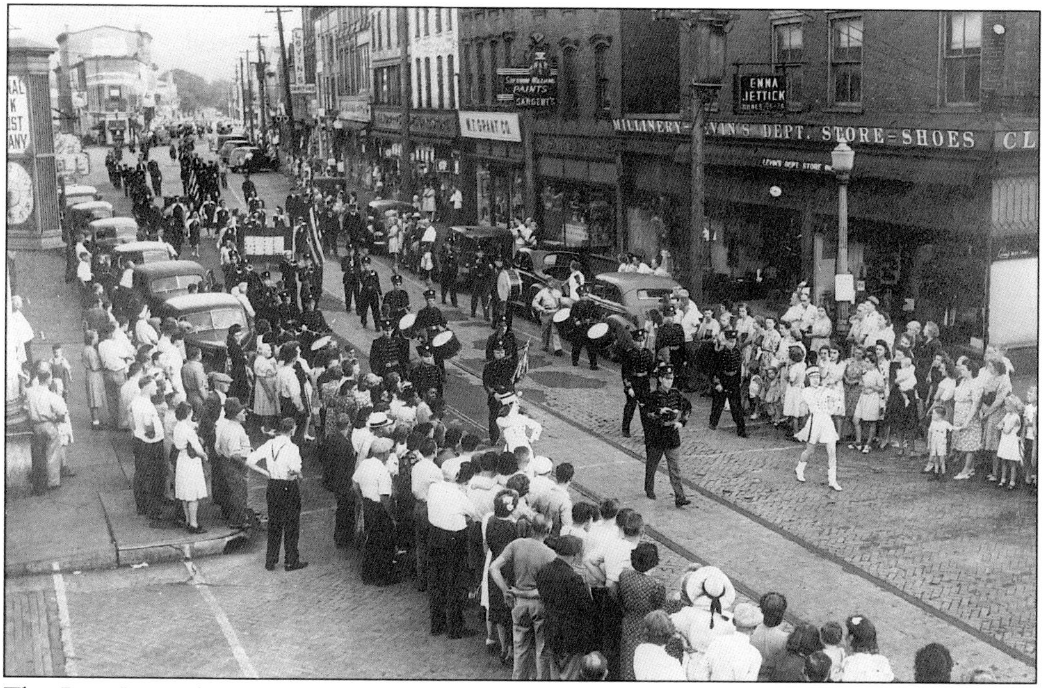

The Port Jervis firemen's parade, held every July, has been a city tradition for more than 100 years. The parade proceeds down Front Street in the 1940s. (Collection of the Minisink Valley Historical Society.)

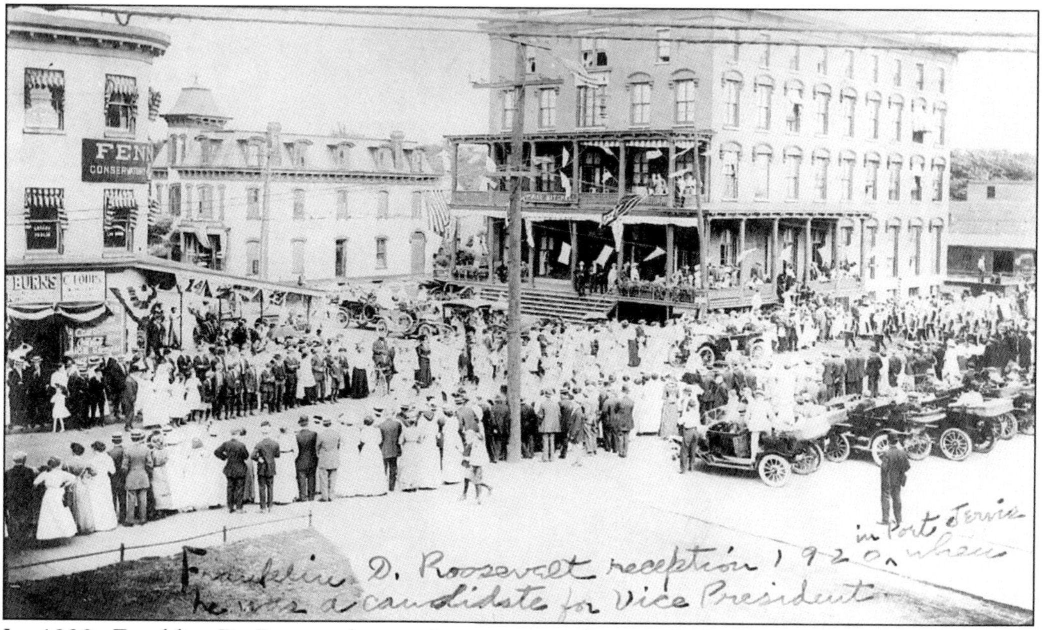

In 1920, Franklin D. Roosevelt ran for vice president with James M. Cox, a Democratic nominee for president. His visit to Port Jervis brought out thousands of people, seen in this picture in front of the Erie Depot. The building in the center is the Hotel Mitchell, formerly known as the Fowler House, on the corner of Fowler Street and Jersey Avenue. (Collection of the Minisink Valley Historical Society.)

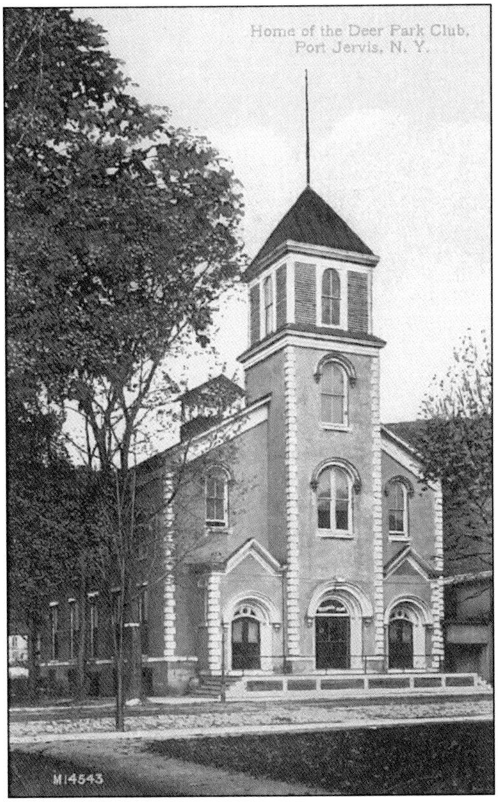

When this photograph was taken in the early 1900s, the Deerpark Club was still open. The social club was on the corner of Pike and West Broome Streets, where the telephone company is today. The club operated in what had been the Baptist church. (Courtesy of Matt and Carol Osterberg.)

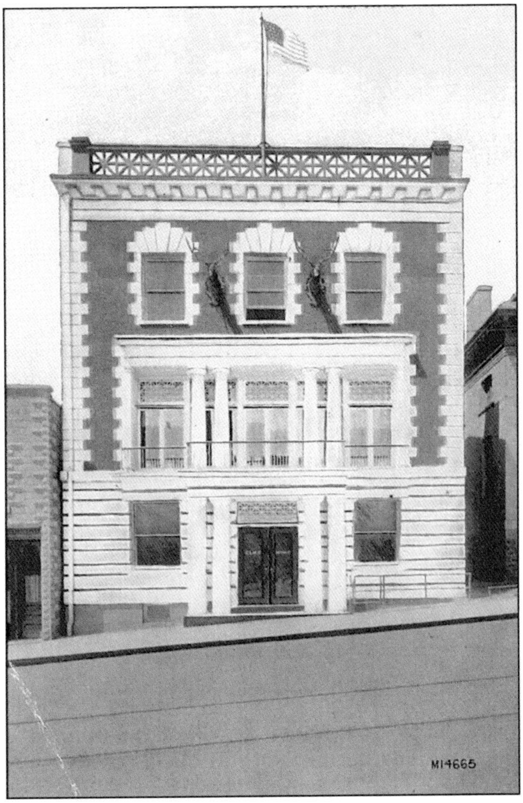

The Port Jervis Elks was officially instituted on January 3, 1901. In 1907, they purchased land on Pike Street from P.E. Farnum for $1,500. A building was erected, and dedicated on September 2, 1909. The organization began the 20th century with a chartered membership of 65. Today there are more than 800 members in the Elks Club. (Courtesy of Ed Nikles Jr.)

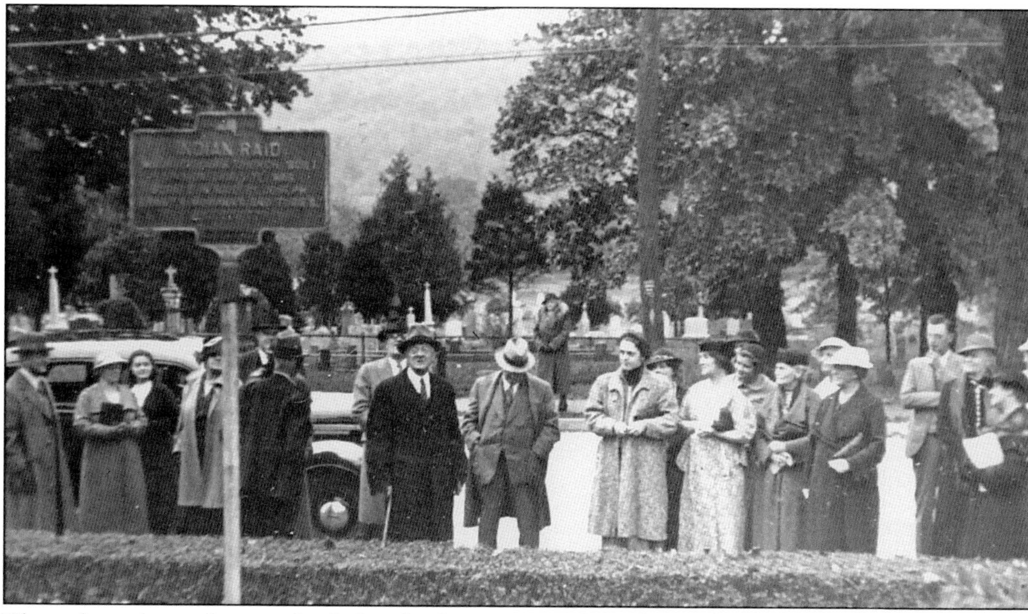

There has always been a high level of interest in Port Jervis history. The Minisink Valley Historical Society began in 1889 and is the second oldest historical society in Orange County. Over the years, they have gathered a vast collection of photographs and information. Their archives are housed in the Port Jervis Free Library. In 1970, the society purchased the Fort Decker in West End and totally refurbished the building. There are many historical plaques in the city and in the Town of Deerpark, the establishment of which is credited to the society. This one was dedicated on East Main Street on October 2, 1937. (Courtesy of Robbie Smith.)

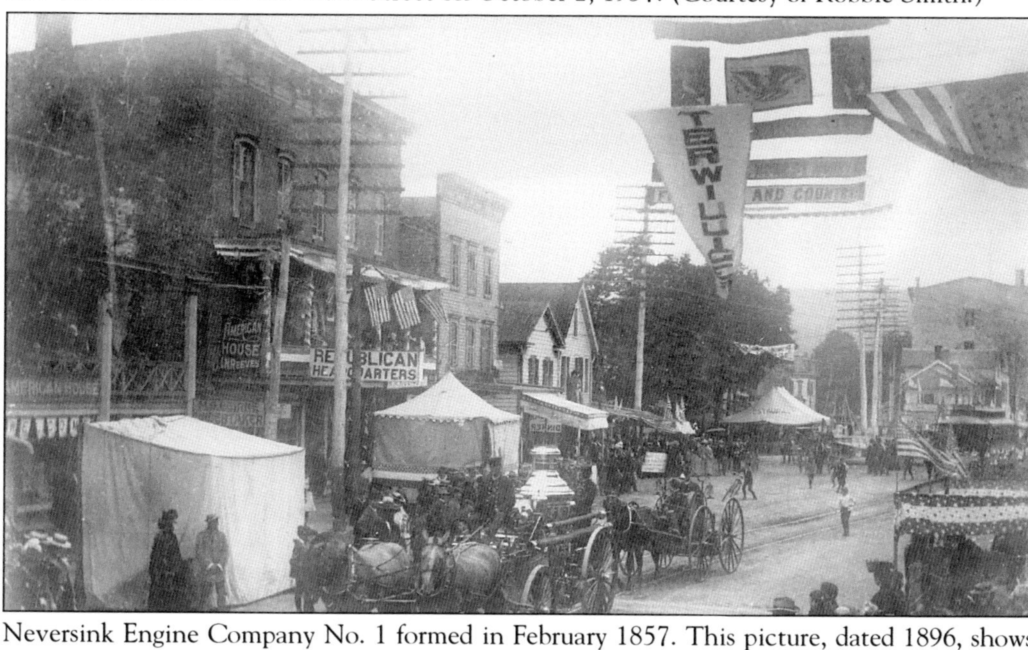

Neversink Engine Company No. 1 formed in February 1857. This picture, dated 1896, shows the company in a parade on Front Street. Terwilligers Store can be seen on the right. Other establishments include American House and A.G. Beirne, undertaker, on the left. (Collection of the Minisink Valley Historical Society.)

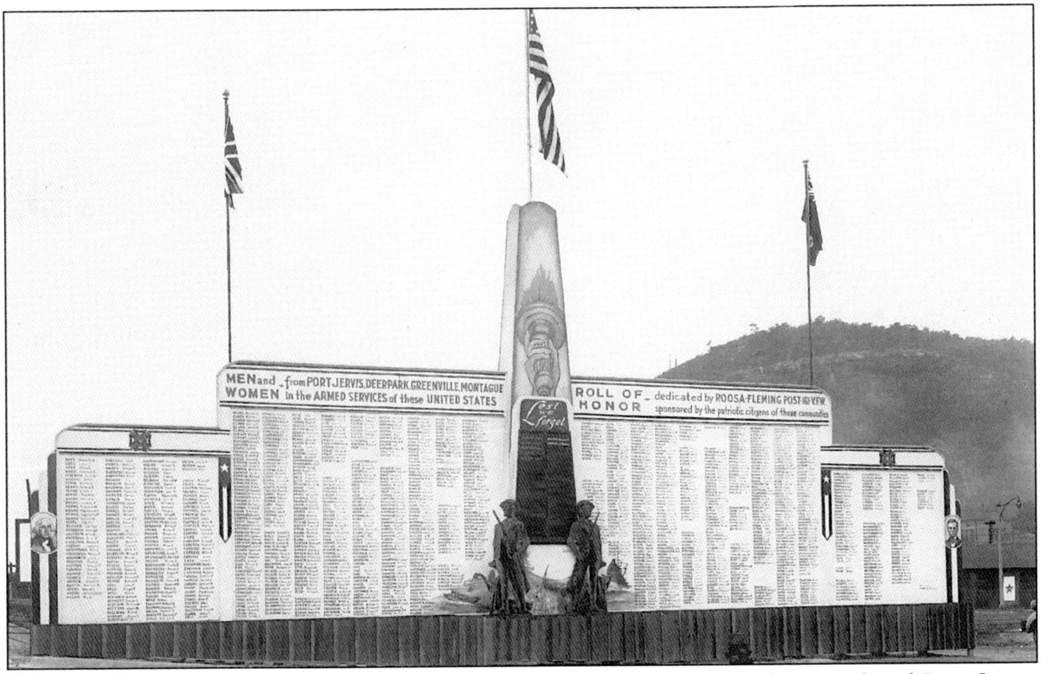

By 1943, many young Americans were fighting in World War II. The people of Port Jervis showed their respect for the young men and women with a Roll of Honor, dedicated by the Roosa-Fleming Post 161 of the Veterans of Foreign Wars and sponsored by the patriotic citizens of the community. This was located near the present-day Burger King. (Collection of the Minisink Valley Historical Society.)

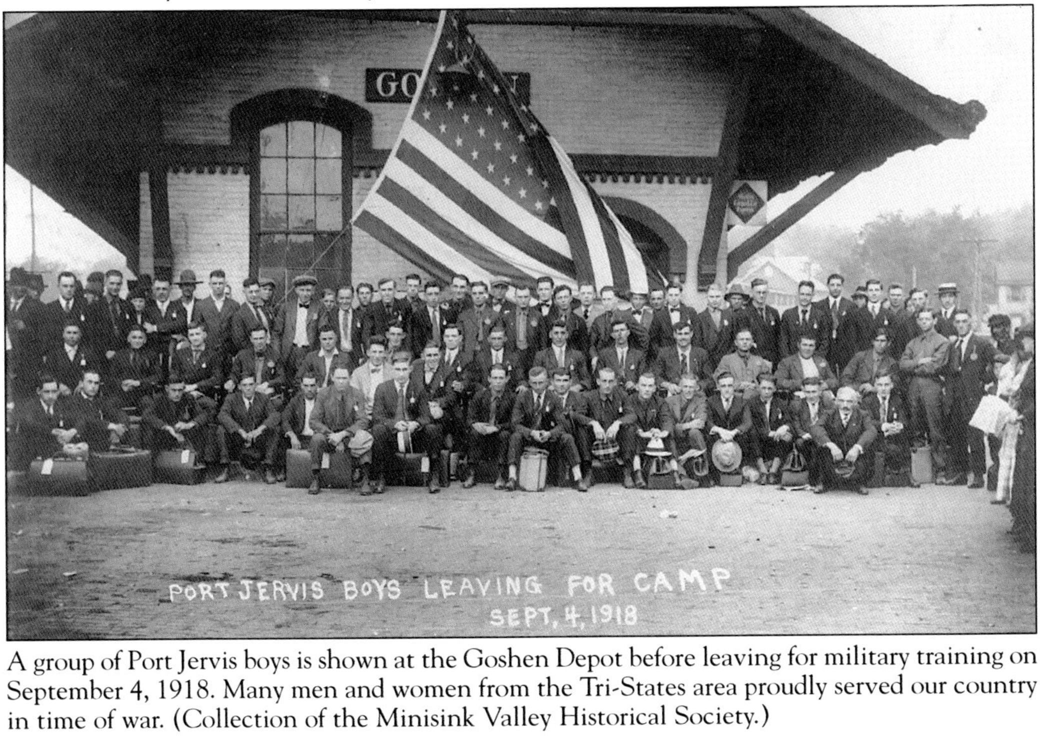

A group of Port Jervis boys is shown at the Goshen Depot before leaving for military training on September 4, 1918. Many men and women from the Tri-States area proudly served our country in time of war. (Collection of the Minisink Valley Historical Society.)

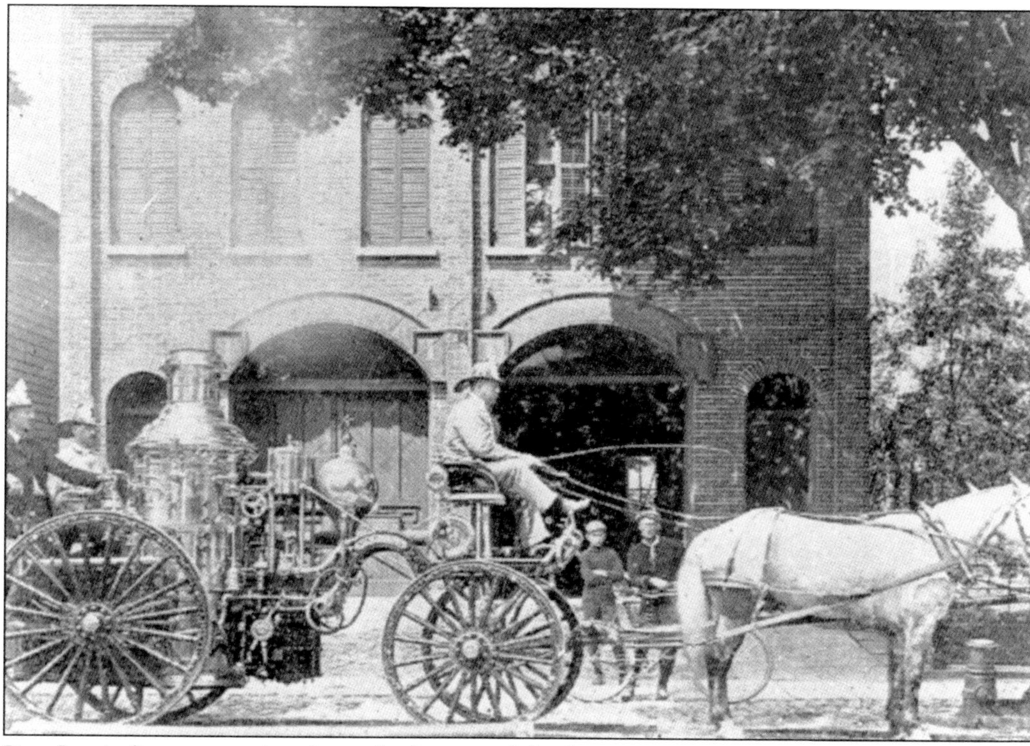

Port Jervis fire companies always had some of the best equipment in the area. Here in 1896, the Neversink Engine Company No. 1 shows off its latest fire apparatus. (Collection of the Minisink Valley Historical Society.)

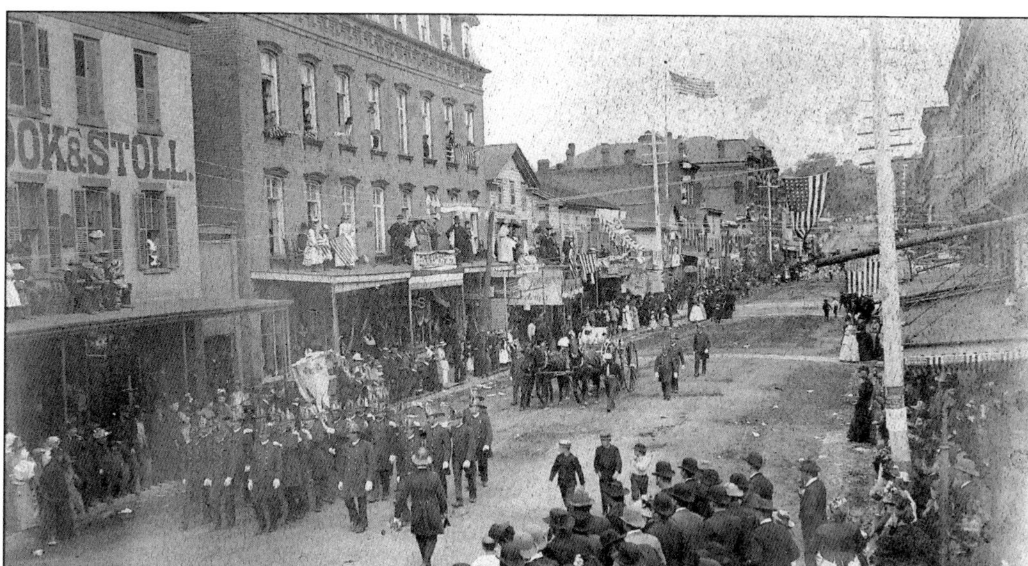

The Delaware Hose Company No. 2 marches up Pike Street near the corner of Front Street in 1885. The company has served the city since 1857. (Collection of the Minisink Valley Historical Society.)

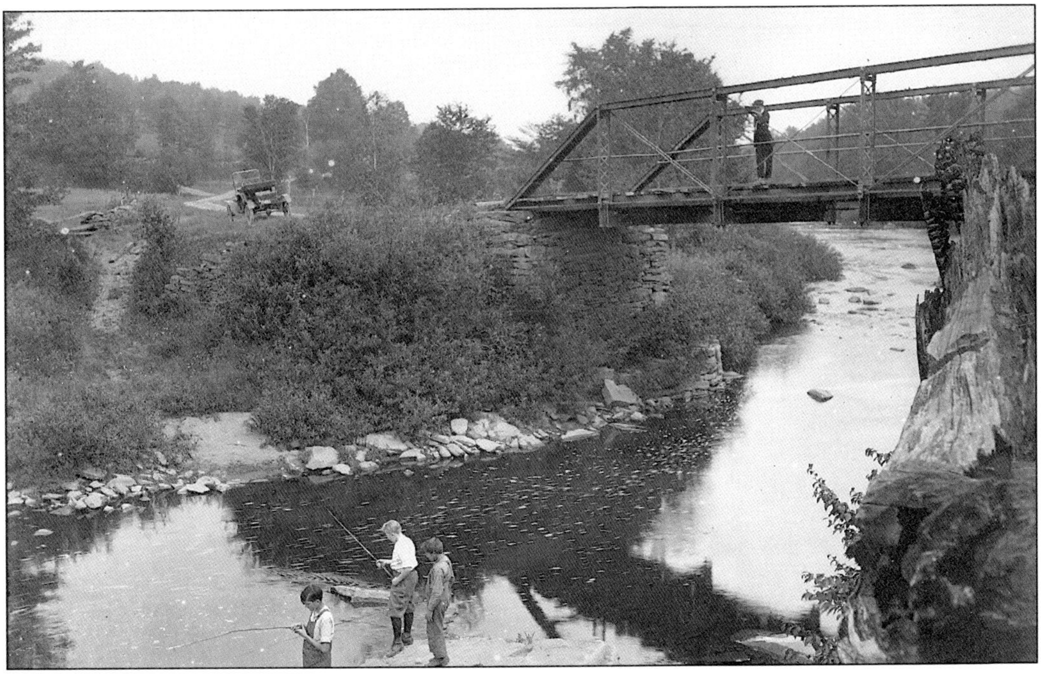

Fishing on a summer day along the Neversink River remains a favorite pastime for many young boys. Three boys try to catch the "big one" while an older boy tries his luck on the Neversink Bridge *c.* 1920. (Collection of the Minisink Valley Historical Society.)

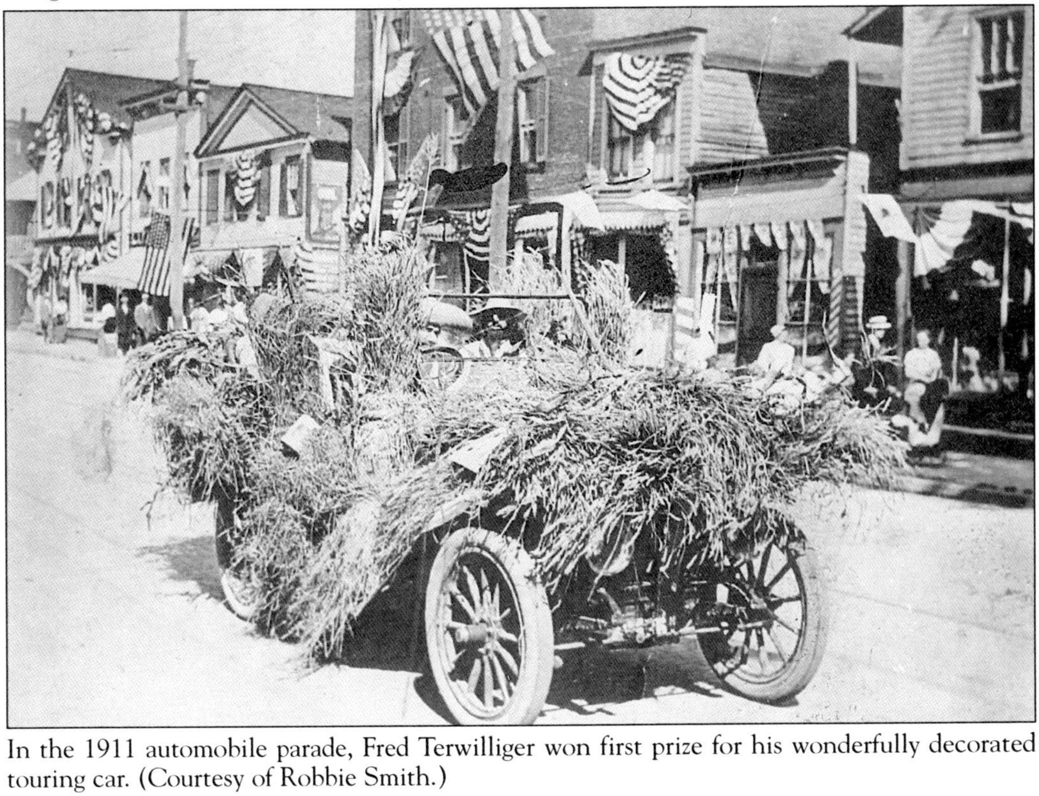

In the 1911 automobile parade, Fred Terwilliger won first prize for his wonderfully decorated touring car. (Courtesy of Robbie Smith.)

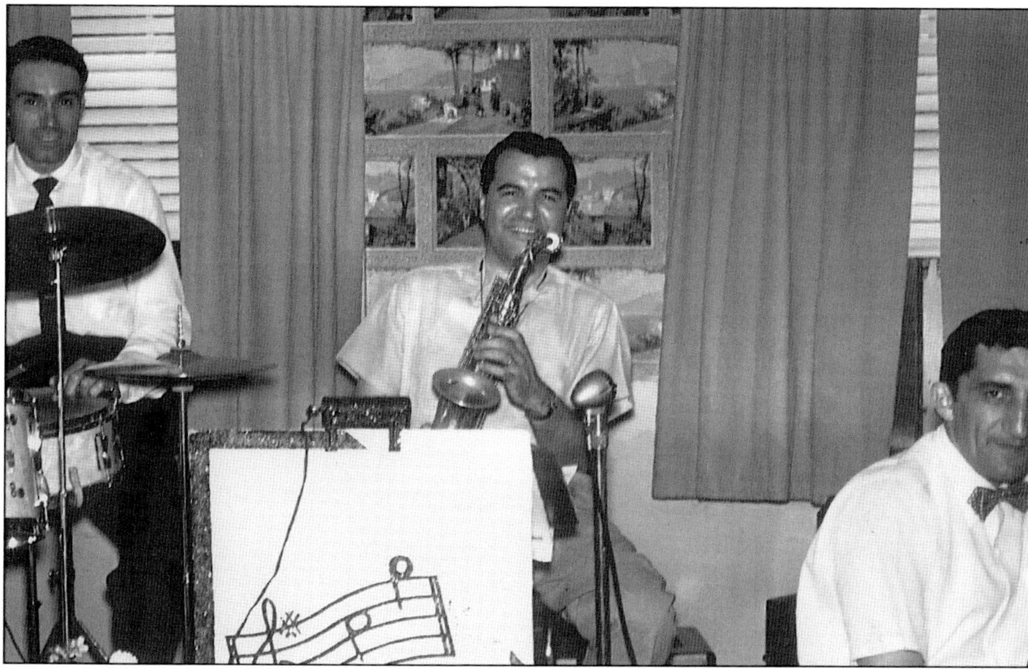

Music was a popular pastime for many local men and women. This band performed at area restaurants for nightclub entertainment. Pictured in 1955 are, from left to right, Pete Gurino, Jim Colaiaco Sr., and Carmen Caputo. (Courtesy of Fannie Colaiaco.)

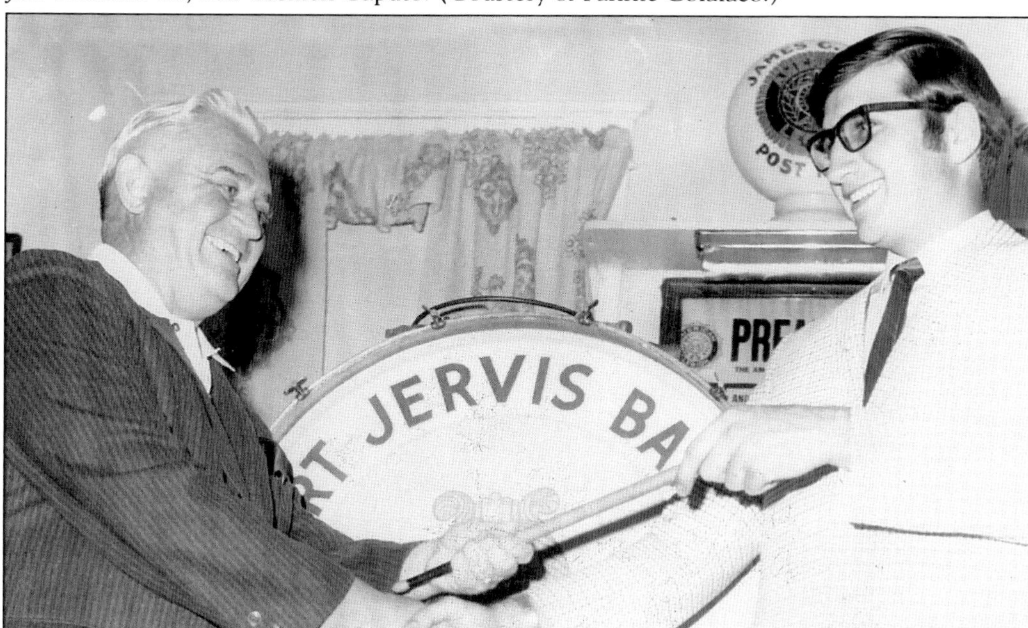

Strike up the band! Musicians Union Local 667 was formed in May 1903. Many members of the local performed in the Port Jervis City Band. In the summer of 1969, the conducting baton was passed from Earl Cummings to West Chester University student and future Port Jervis Middle School Band teacher Jim Colaiaco Jr. They played summer concerts for many years at the Rose Garden on Orange Street. (Courtesy of Fannie Colaiaco.)

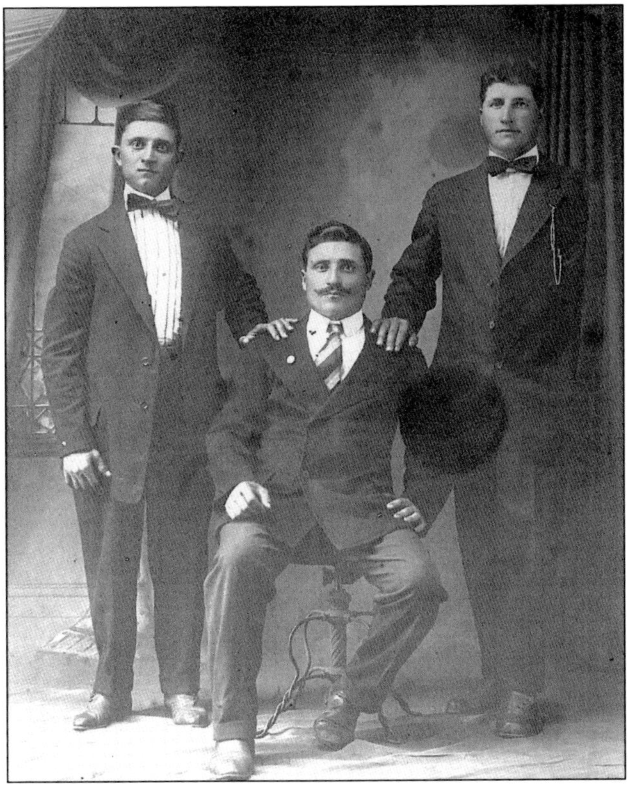

Shown from left to right are Donato Callichio, Frank Caputo, and Jacob Caputo, in 1921. The men were Italian immigrants living in Port Jervis. Jacob Caputo and Tony English founded the Mount Carmel Society in 1923, because they were tired of attending meetings of the society in Middletown, New York. Fifteen charter members gave $20 each to buy a statue of Our Lady of Mount Carmel. This feast day is celebrated on July 16. (Courtesy of Fannie Colaiaco.)

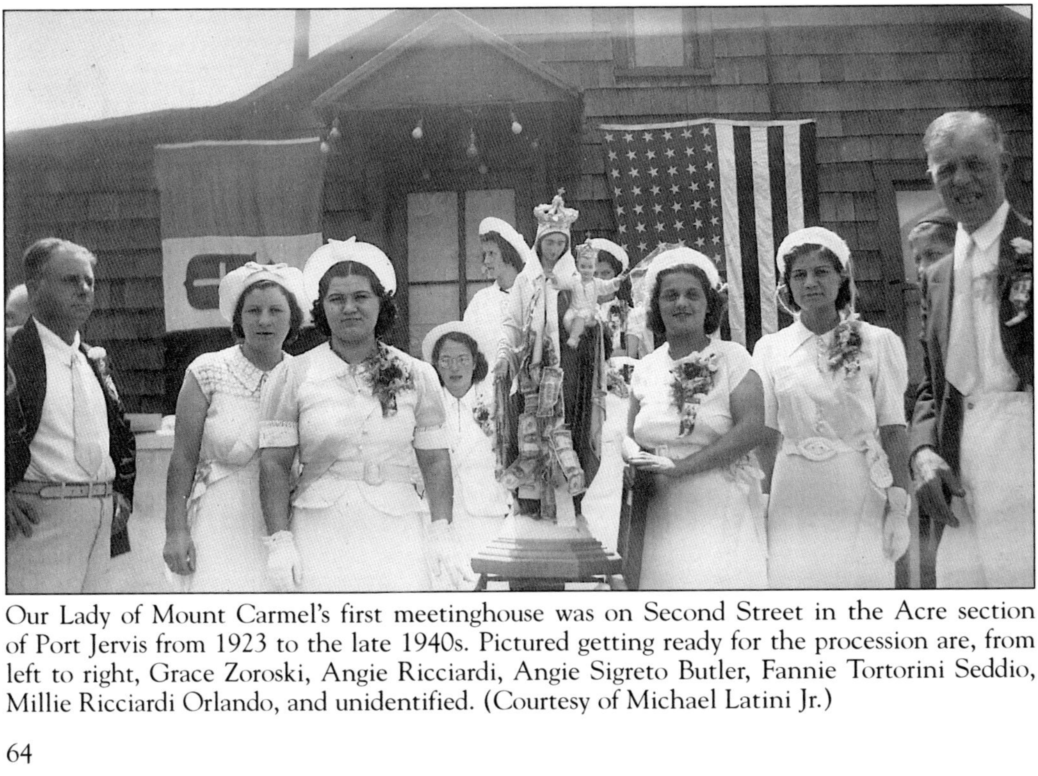

Our Lady of Mount Carmel's first meetinghouse was on Second Street in the Acre section of Port Jervis from 1923 to the late 1940s. Pictured getting ready for the procession are, from left to right, Grace Zoroski, Angie Ricciardi, Angie Sigreto Butler, Fannie Tortorini Seddio, Millie Ricciardi Orlando, and unidentified. (Courtesy of Michael Latini Jr.)

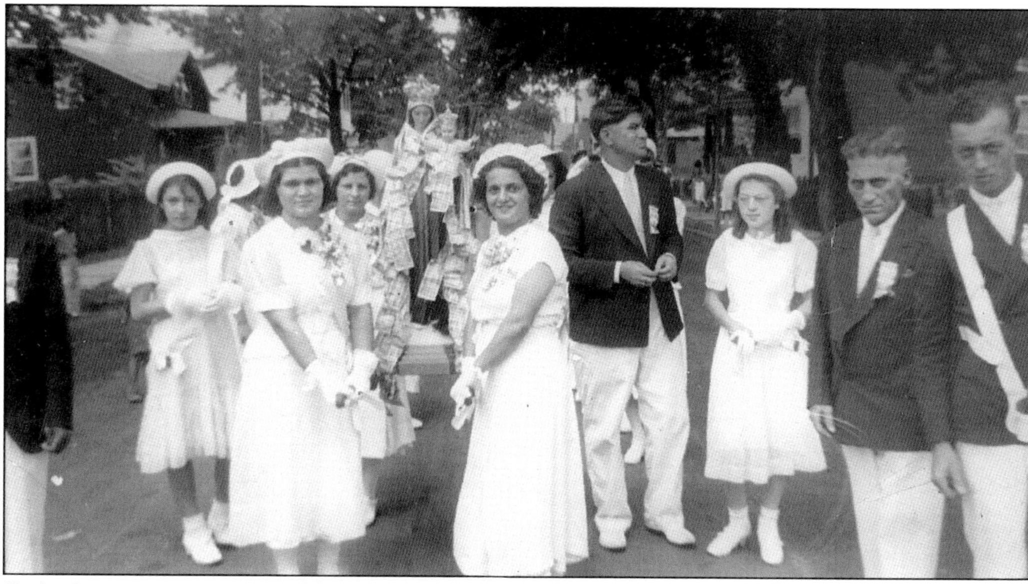

Onlookers pin money on a blue ribbon adorning the Blessed Mother during the feast parade of Our Lady of Mount Carmel. The money is used to help finance the celebration, for donations to charities and scholarship funds in the Port Jervis and Delaware Valley schools. Pictured from left to right are Millie Ricciardi Orlando, Grace Primavera, Fannie Tortorini Seddio, Mike Ricciardi, Angie Sigreto Butler, unidentified, and Mario Cordisco. (Courtesy of Michael Latini Jr.)

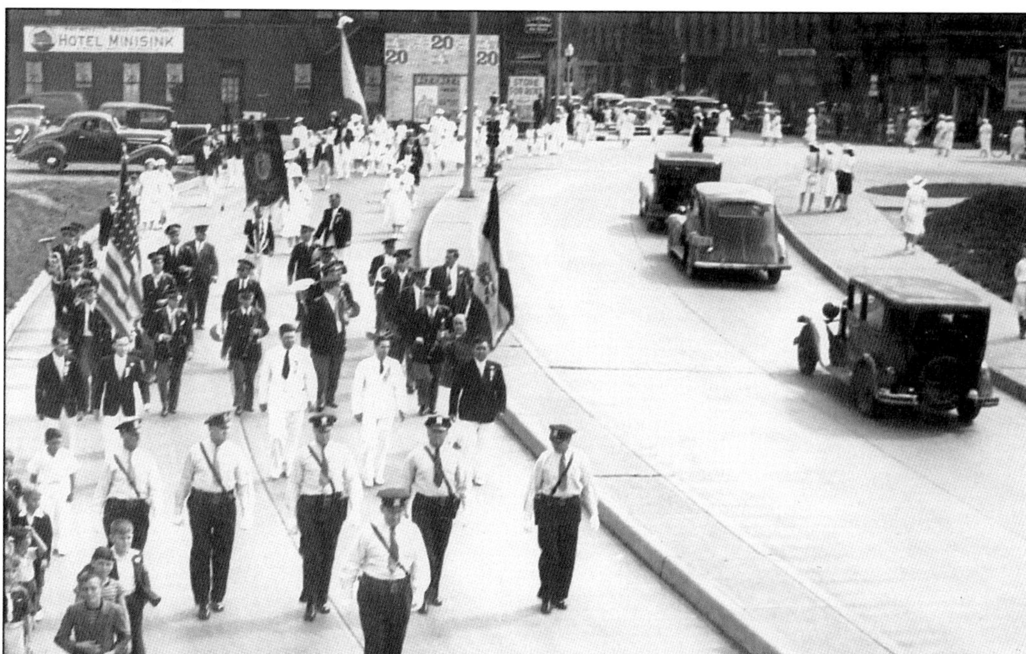

A procession of Our Lady of Mount Carmel proceeds through the underpass after celebrating mass at St. Mary's Church c. 1950. The parade was the beginning of the celebration that featured Italian foods, rides, concession stands, and spectacular fireworks. (Courtesy of Michael Latini Jr.)

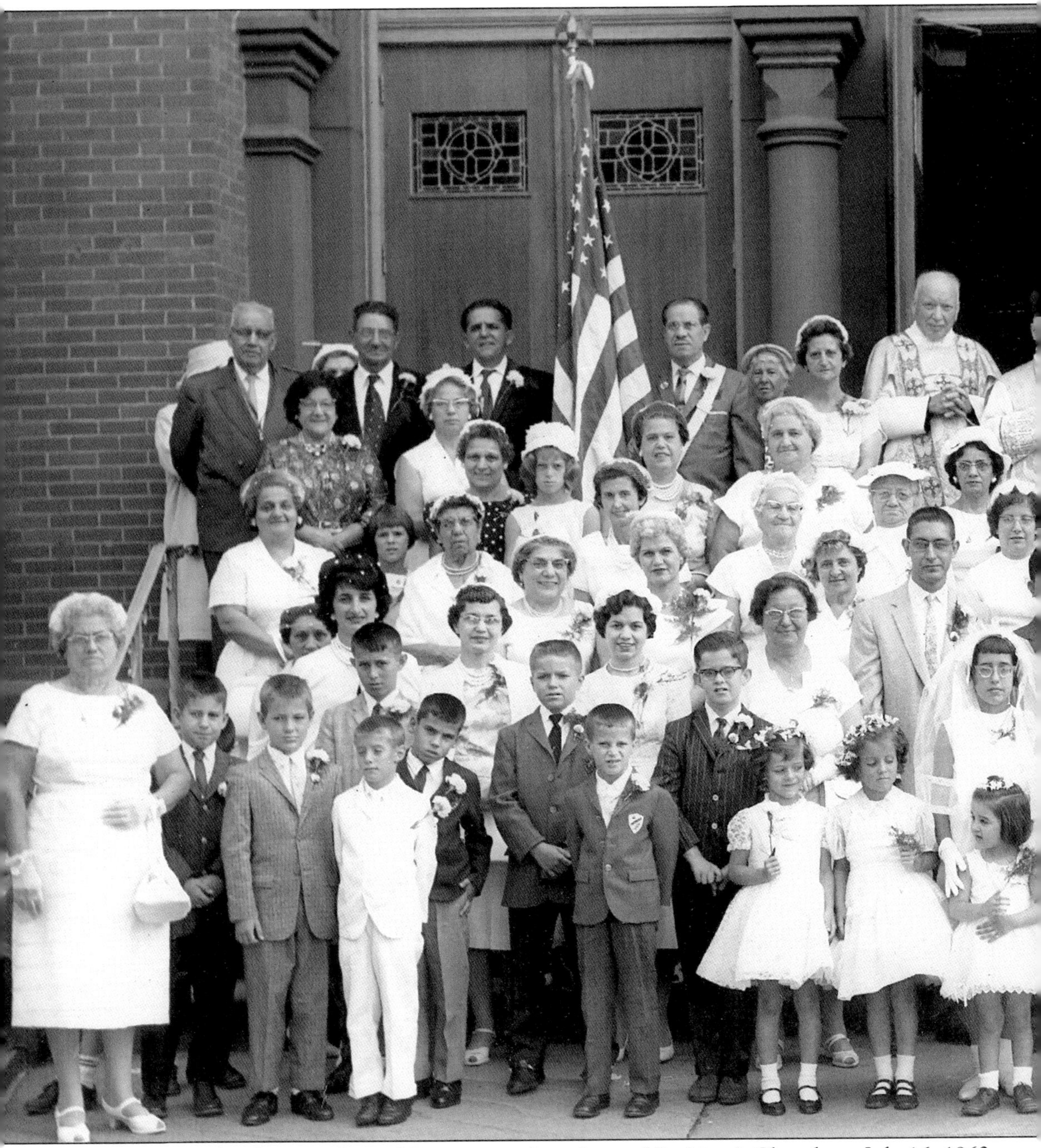

The Our Lady of Mount Carmel Society stands in front of St. Mary's Church on July 16, 1963. Shown from left to right are the following: (first row) L. Barbarino, N. Ogrodnick, J. Andriac, unidentified, C. Wilson, J. Latini, T. Masonatti, T. Rombousek, A. Andriac, M. Andriac, J. Colaiaco, C. Colaiaco, L. Trovei, S. Masonatti, unidentified, J. Seddio, P. Prestimonico, C. Wilson, J. DeLaney, A. Seddio, N. Amato, and S. Trovei; (second row) A. Osowick, F. Colaiaco, T. Rybak, N. Rybak, A. Masonatti, V. Petiti, J. Petiti, L. Prestimonico, M. Latini Sr., L. Latini, J. Piccolo, J. Cordisco, A. Stellato, B. Cordisco, C. Inella, and A. Caiafa; (third row) F. Seddio, M. Nason, M. Sigreto, A. Ricciardi, L. Biondi, M. Cordisco, A. Cordisco,

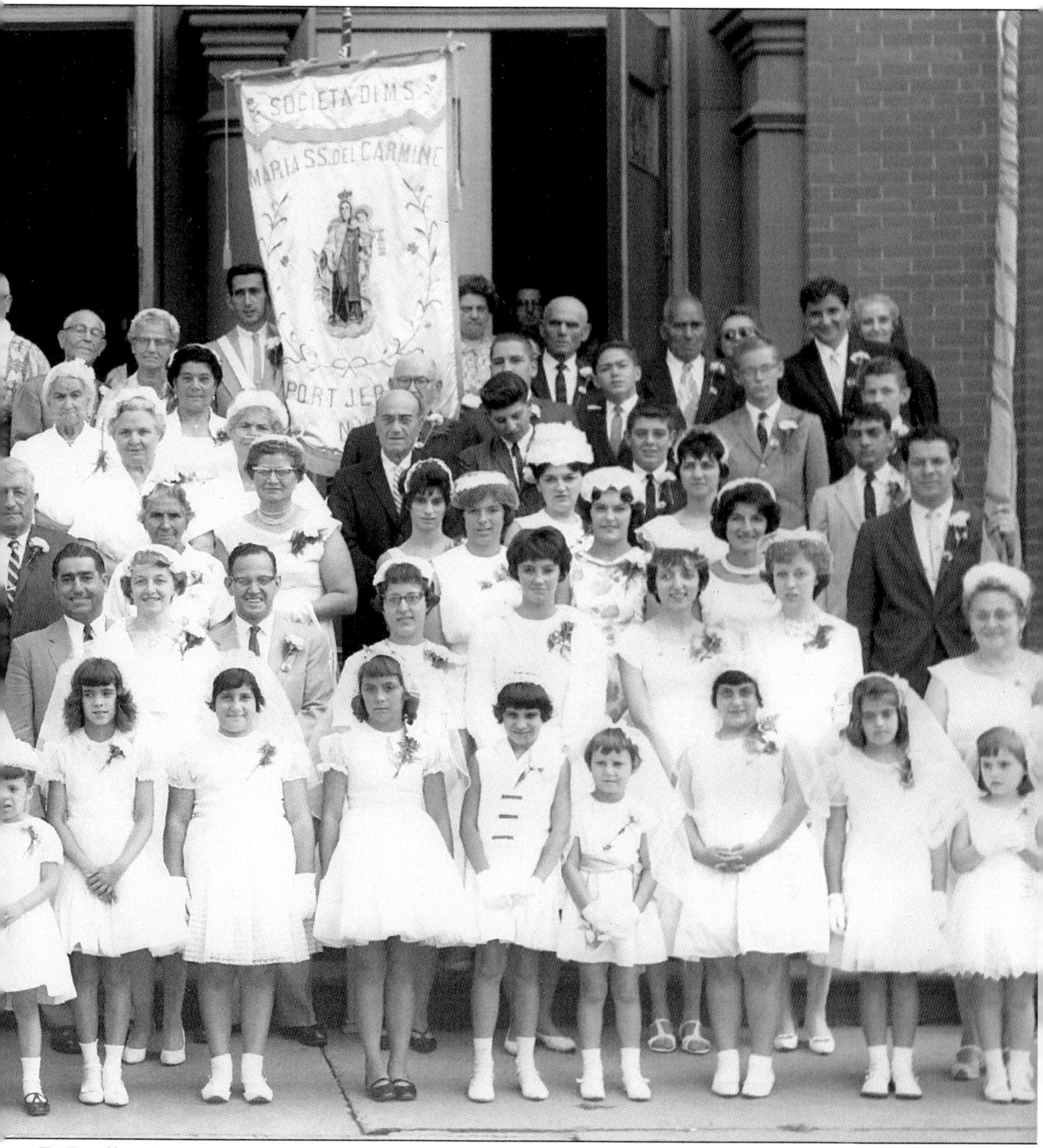

E. Faiello, G. Ingrassia, J. Caputo, R. Trotta, M. Ricciardi, T. Wilson, D. Faiello, M. Trovei, M. Calvario, J. Cordisco, C. Caputo, and C. Masonatti; (fourth row) F. Rubinitti, A. Salva, F. Decker, P. Piccarillo, F. Amato, S. Piccarillo, N. Tortorini, F. Fox, M. Masonatti, R. Mazzarro, T. Marino, M. DeAngelo, T. Viserta, T. Viserta, J. Colaiaco, M. Latini Jr., M. Innella, J. Cooper, L. Miglionico, N. Rybak, and A. Fanno; (fifth row) B. Tortorini, T. Petiti, A. Orlando, M. Masonatti, A. Calabria, Monsignor McNulty, A. Faiello, R. Viserta, J. Amato, J. Biondi, J. Trotta, and M. Trovei. (Courtesy of Michael Latini Jr.)

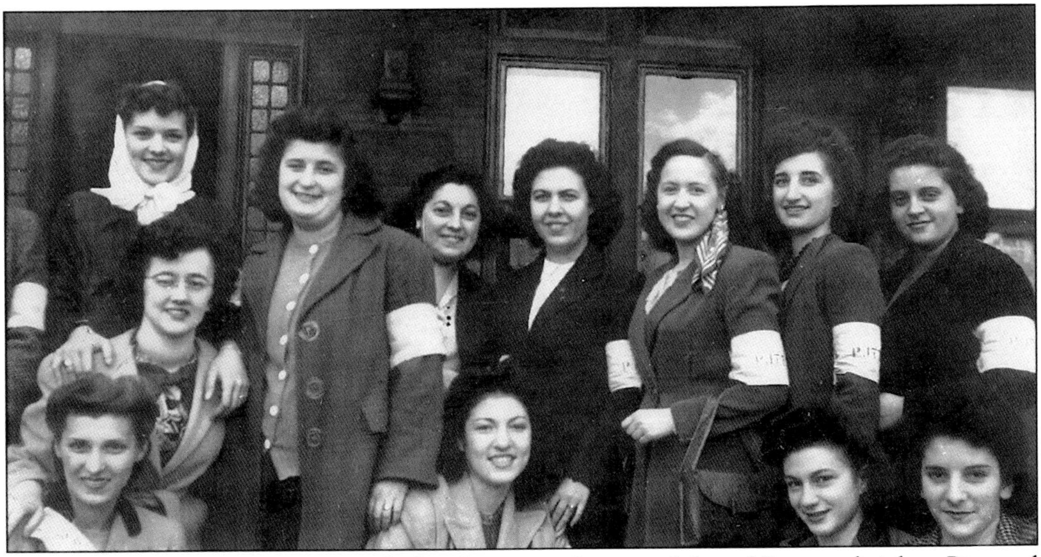

World War II troop trains were met by local women who served the soldiers sandwiches. Pictured from left to right are the following: (front row) Eleanor Semarano, Stella Hunter, and Julia Allen; (middle row) Maria Remlinger and Olga Pericone; (back row) Stella Taylor, Margaret Fahey, Ann Marino, Mary Calvario, Shirley Grady, Anna Trovei Kelly, Fannie Caputo Colaiaco, and Fannie Tortorini Seddio. (Courtesy of Anna and Bill Kelly.)

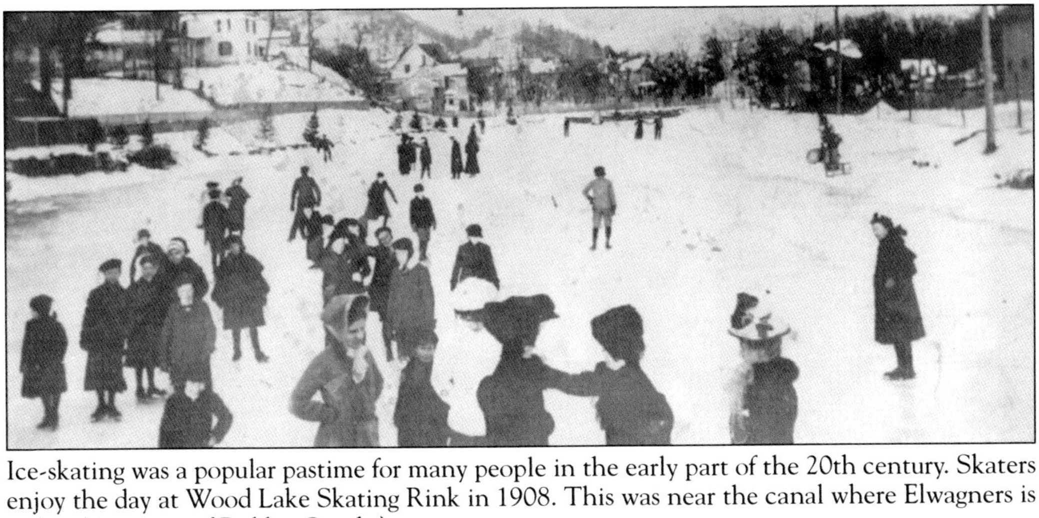

Ice-skating was a popular pastime for many people in the early part of the 20th century. Skaters enjoy the day at Wood Lake Skating Rink in 1908. This was near the canal where Elwagners is today. (Courtesy of Robbie Smith.)

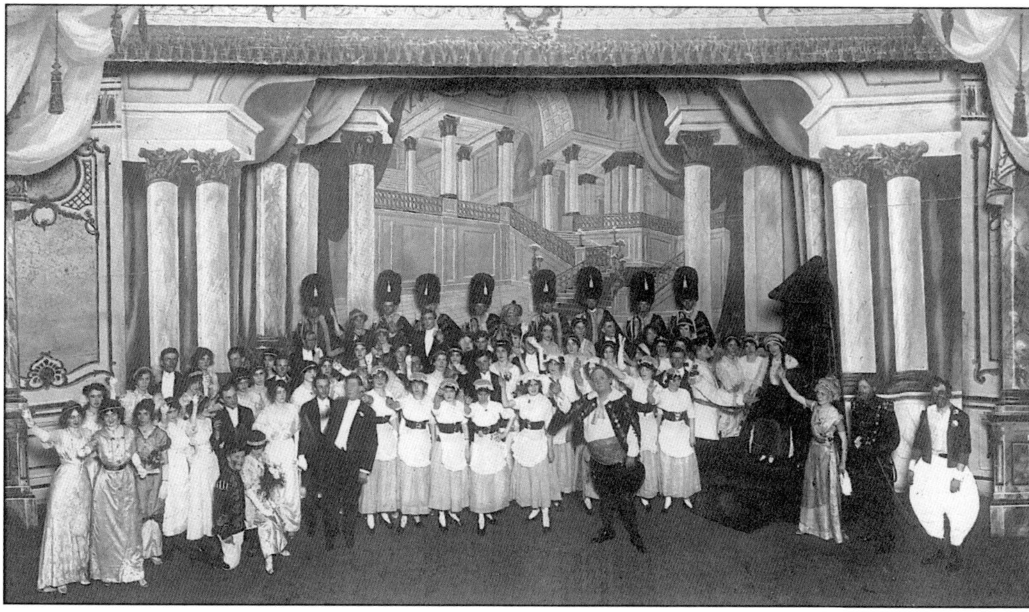

The Strand Theater stood on Pike Street. This popular movie house showed not only the latest movies but also plays and vaudeville acts. Years later, it was the State Theater; the building was demolished in the 1990s. (Collection of the Minisink Valley Historical Society.)

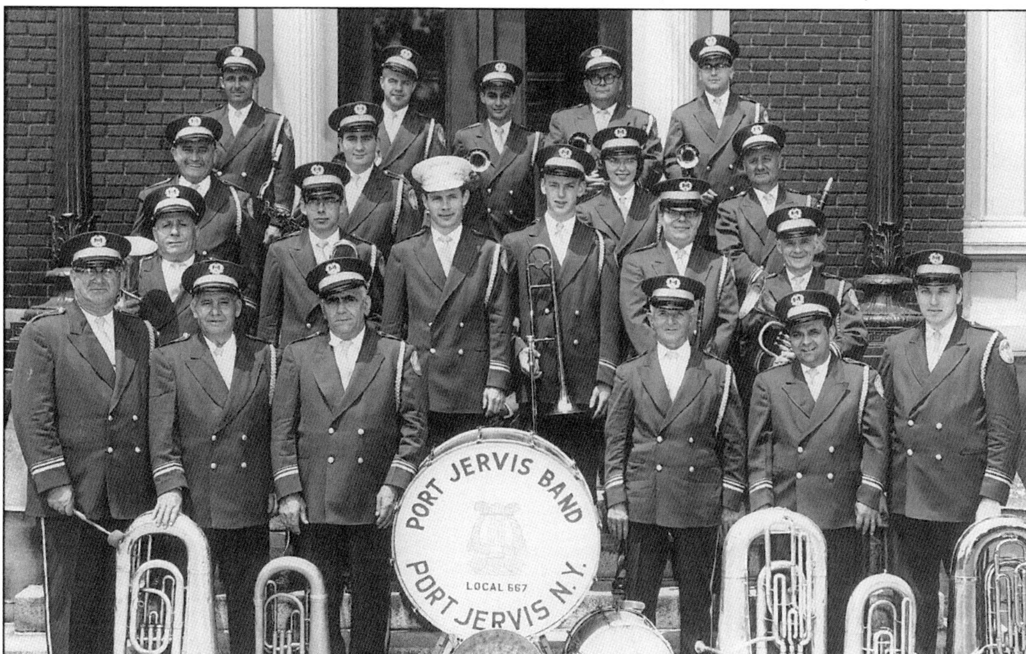

Members of the Port Jervis City Band pose c. 1950. They are, from left to right, as follows: (first row) Mike Ricciardi, Barney Tortorini, Carmen Acoveno, Frank Rombousek, Shorty Lombardo, and Denis Laizure; (second row) Angelo Stellato, Steve Fredricks, Buzz Neubert, ? Bachelder, Frank Schips, and Bill Wagner Sr.; (third row) Earl Cummings, unidentified, Lynn Ott, and Dominick Caliciotti; (fourth row) John K. Lewis, Bill Wagner Jr., Frank Seddio Jr., ? Acoveno, and ? Sakofsky. (Courtesy of Brian Lewis.)

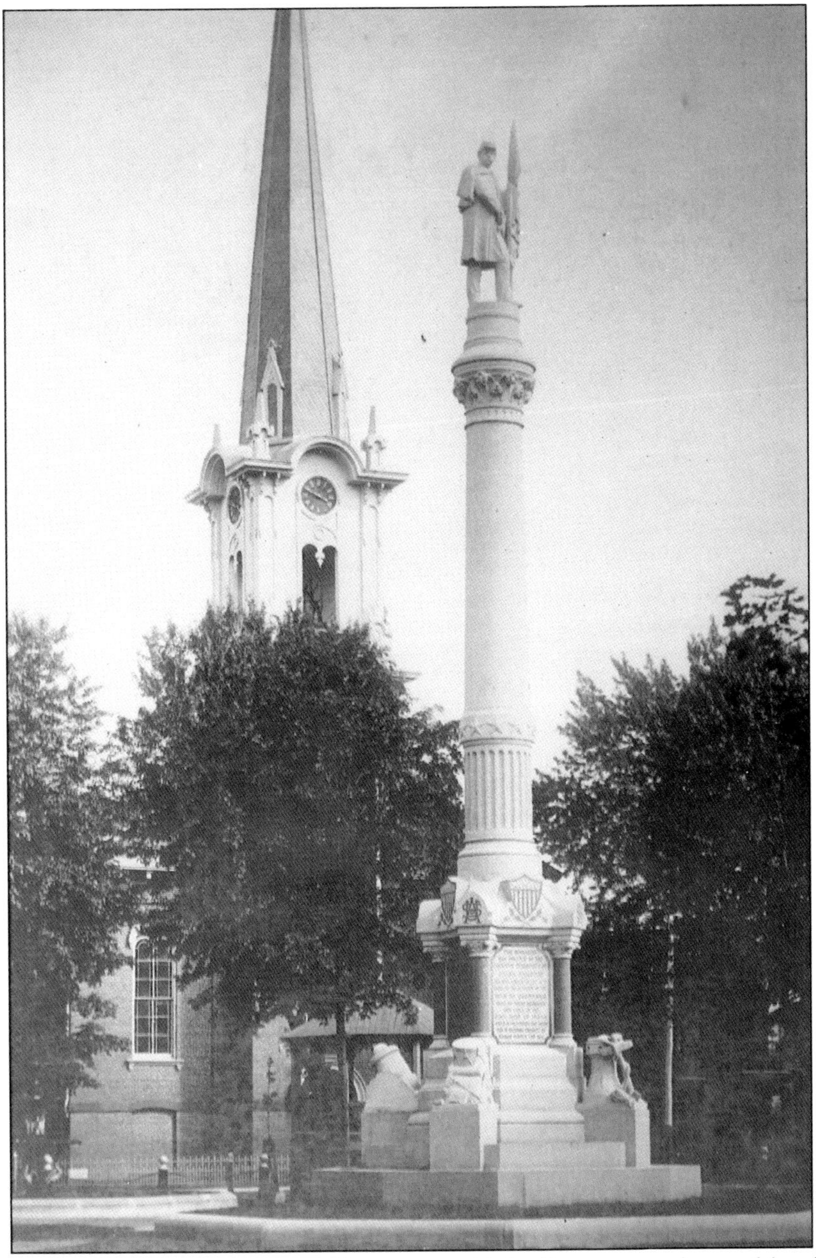

Orange Square, located at the corner of Broome and Pike Street, was donated by the D & H Canal Company in the early 19th century. In its center is the Civil War Monument, which was financed by the estate of Diana Farnum, who gave approximately $10,000 for the construction of the monument. The unveiling and dedication in July 1886 was marked with a three-mile-long parade and events attended by more than 10,000 people. This monument, 45 feet tall, is considered to be one of the finest monuments in southeastern New York State. Renowned American author Stephen Crane interviewed Civil War veterans at this monument and later wrote his masterpiece *The Red Badge of Courage* based on those interviews. The spire of the Drew Methodist Church on Sussex Street rises in the background. (Collection of the Minisink Valley Historical Society.)

Five

LODGING

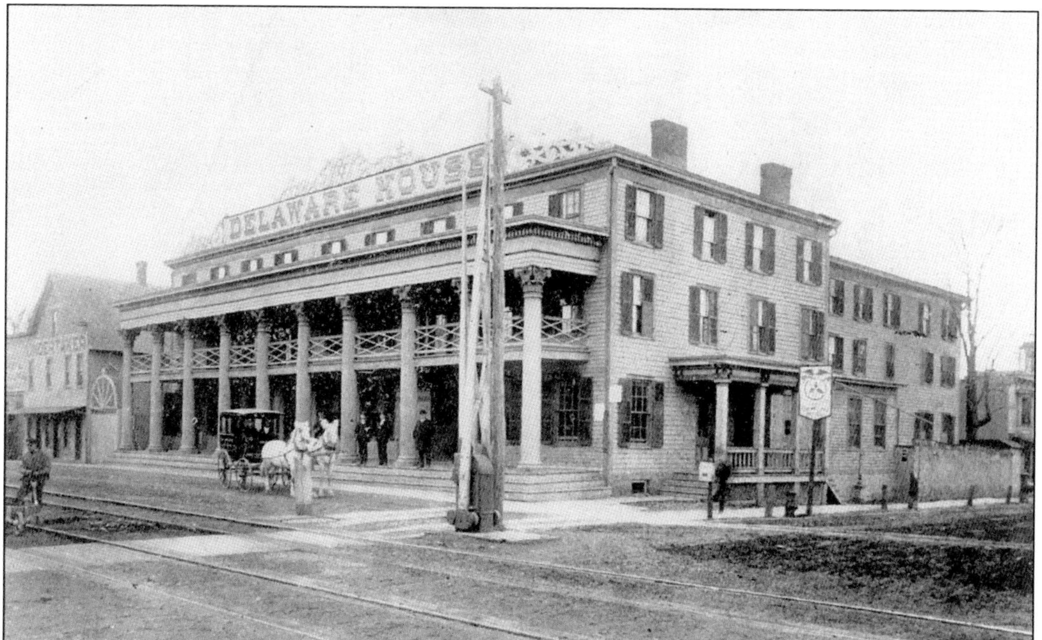

Built in 1847, the Delaware House on the corner of Railroad Avenue and Pike Street was one of the most exclusive hotels in Port Jervis. The 10-column building featured a balcony, a huge dining room, a large lobby, and fine guest accommodations. In one of the largest fires in the city's history, the Delaware House burned in 1902. (Collection of the Minisink Valley Historical Society.)

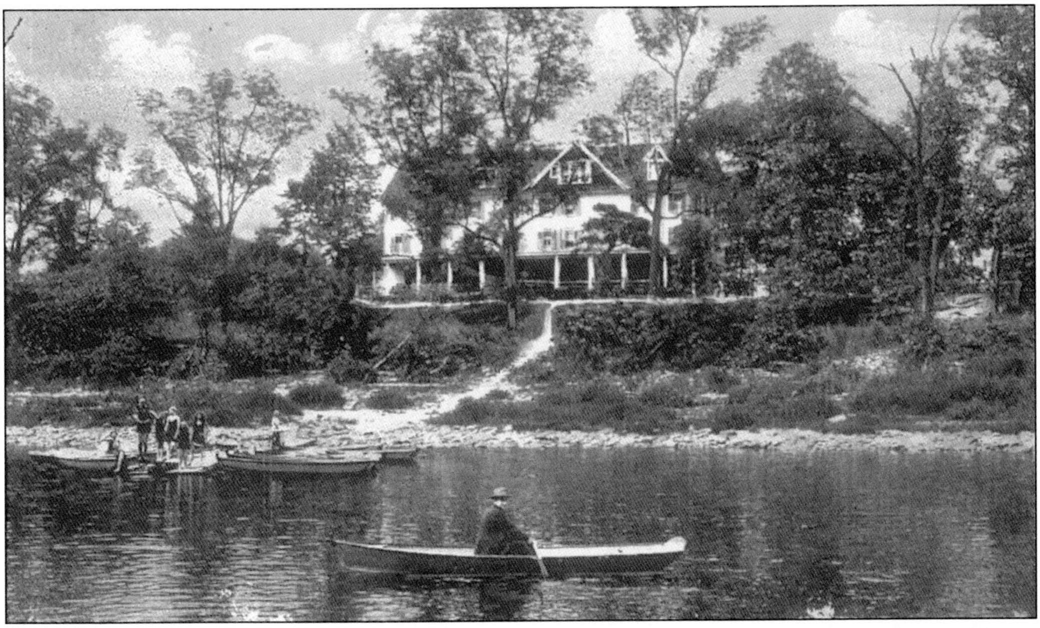

The Eddy Farm in Sparrowbush is a picturesque hotel along the banks of the Delaware River. The hotel was established in 1871 and was owned and operated by the Patterson family until the mid-1990s. A guest at the hotel named this resort after observing an eddy in the river. At one time, it was a place frequented by sport enthusiasts. Later, guests began to arrive from New York City with their families for summer vacations. As each year went by, more guests came to stay. Buildings were added to accommodate the growth and popularity of the resort. This postcard shows the main house *c.* 1907. (Collection of the Minisink Valley Historical Society.)

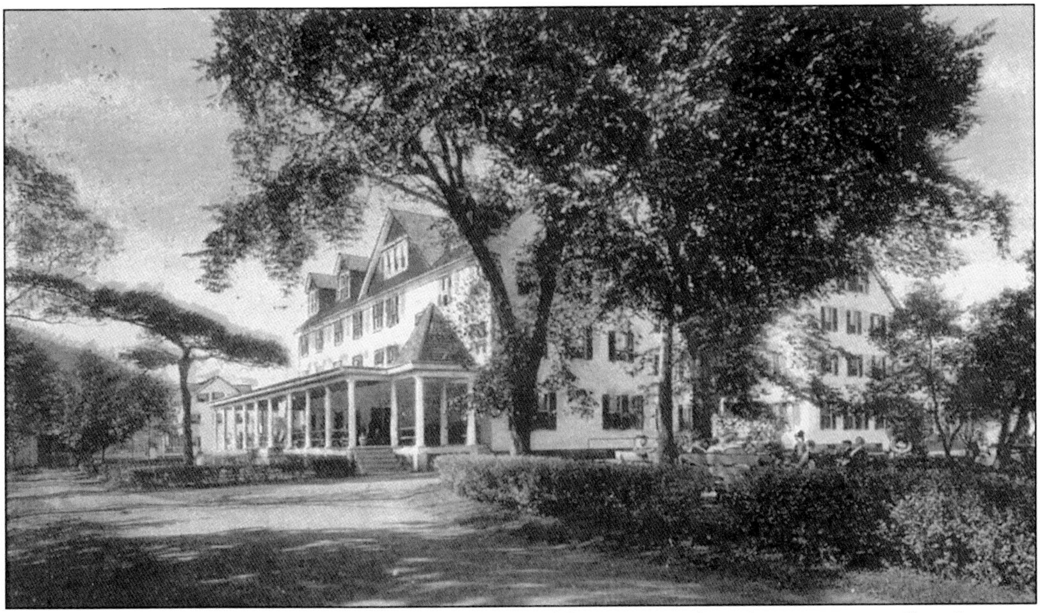

By 1923, Eddy Farm Resort boasted a par-three golf course. Today, the resort is still a thriving business. (Collection of the Minisink Valley Historical Society.)

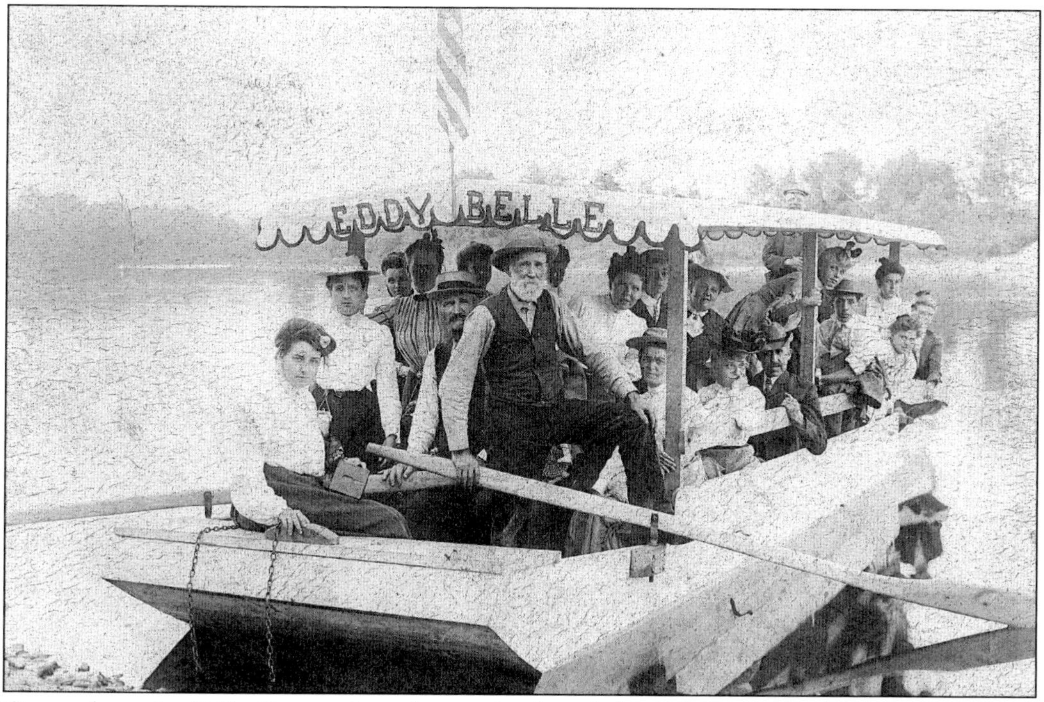

Guests from the Eddy Farm enjoy a boat ride aboard the *Eddy Belle* on the Delaware River. (Collection of the Minisink Valley Historical Society.)

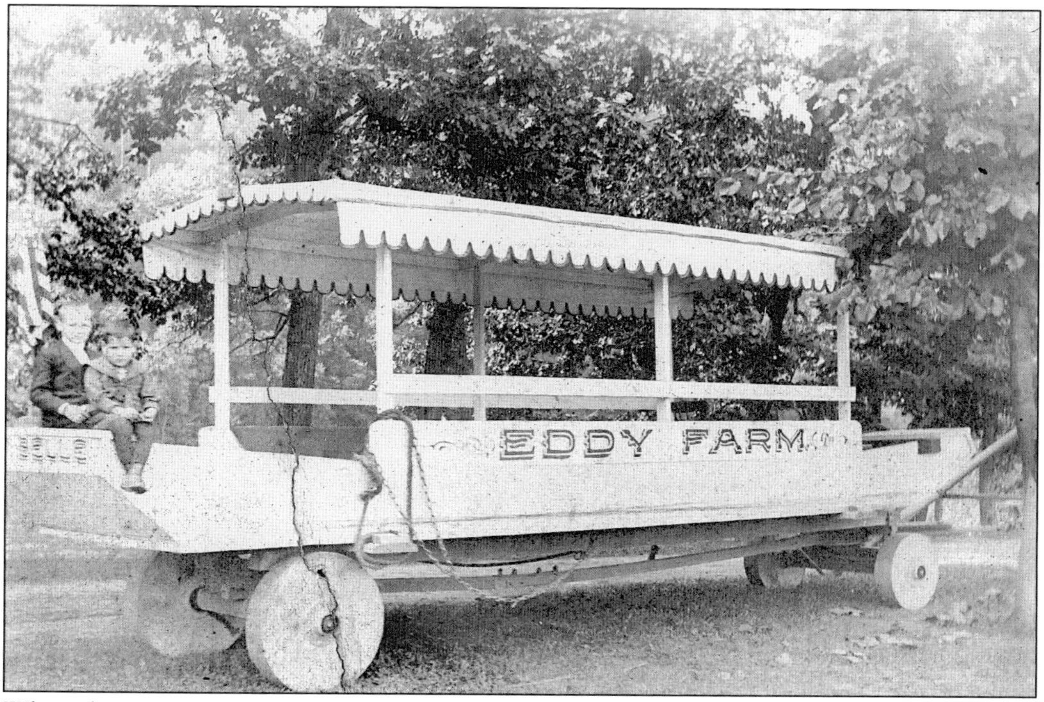

When the guests arrived from New York at the Sparrowbush train station, this wagon, owned by Eddy Farm, transported them to their vacation at the resort. (Collection of the Minisink Valley Historical Society.)

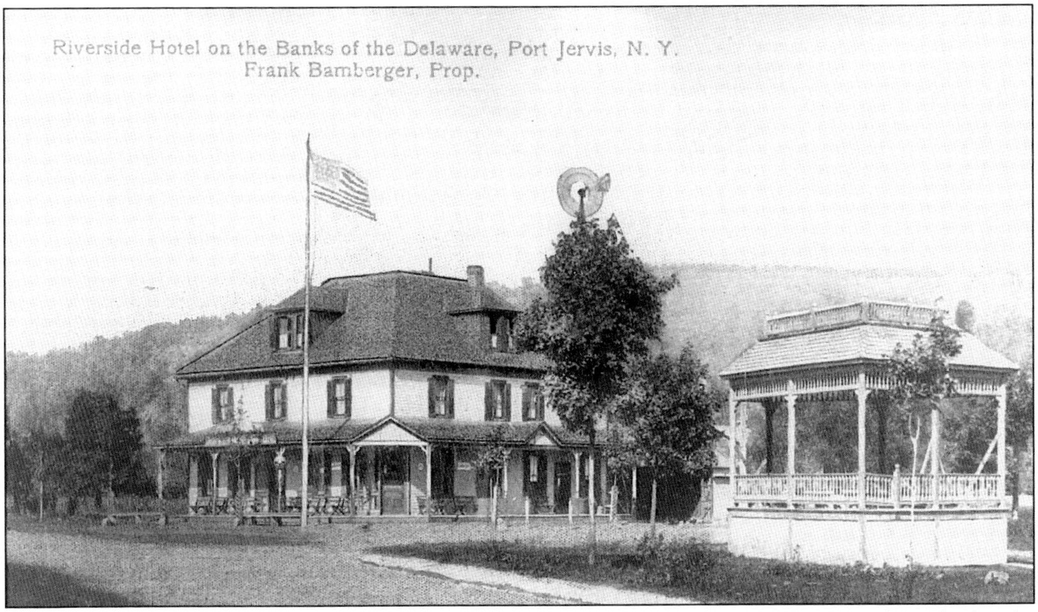

The Riverside Hotel, *c*. 1900, was one of many hotels in Port Jervis. It was situated on the banks of the Delaware River on West Main Street. Charles Bamberger was the proprietor of this hotel, which in later years was known as Buffalo Bills. This building was destroyed by fire in the 1990s. (Collection of the Minisink Valley Historical Society.)

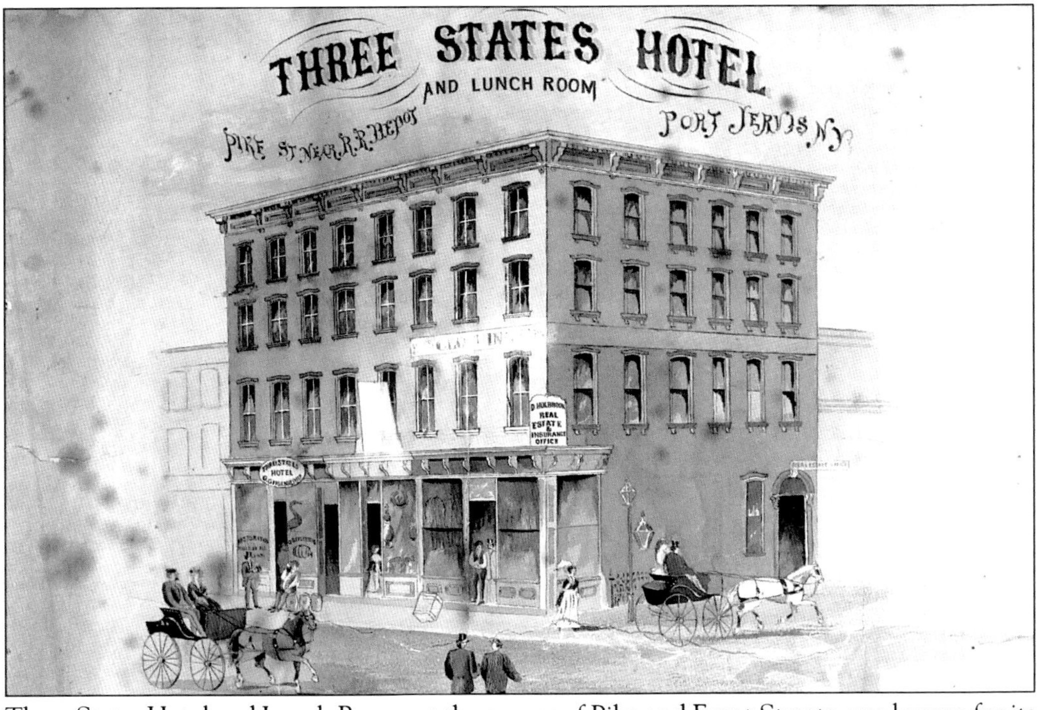

Three States Hotel and Lunch Room, at the corner of Pike and Front Streets, was known for its fine beers, wines, and liquors. It also claimed to have the best accommodations, complete with meals served at all hours. George Geisenheimer was the proprietor. (Collection of the Minisink Valley Historical Society.)

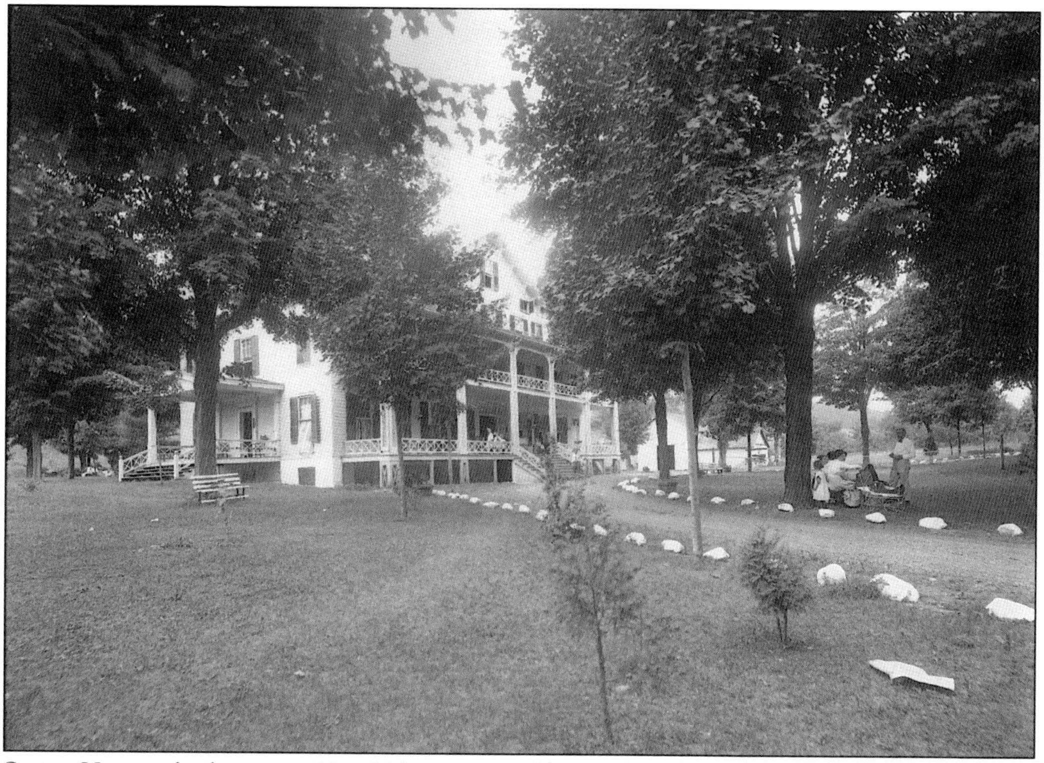

Spring House, also known as Hotel Huguenot and located on Route 209, was a popular vacation spot for tourists. Local bands entertained guests at the hotel. This building burned in the late 1970s. (Collection of the Minisink Valley Historical Society.)

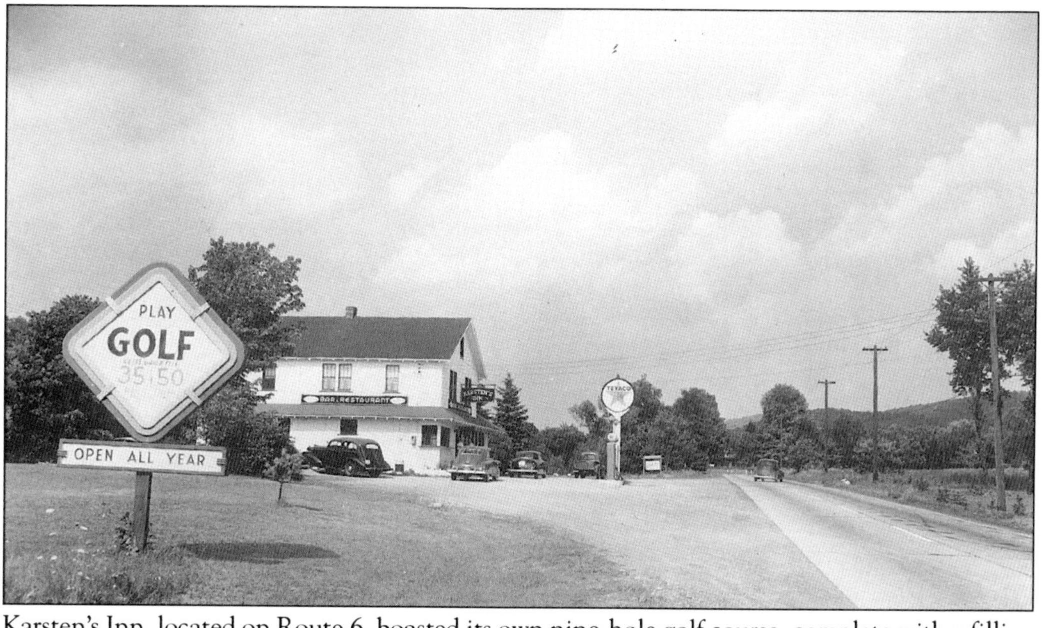

Karsten's Inn, located on Route 6, boasted its own nine-hole golf course, complete with a filling station. The inn is shown here in the 1940s. Today, this is the home of the Port Jervis Elks Club. (Collection of the Minisink Valley Historical Society.)

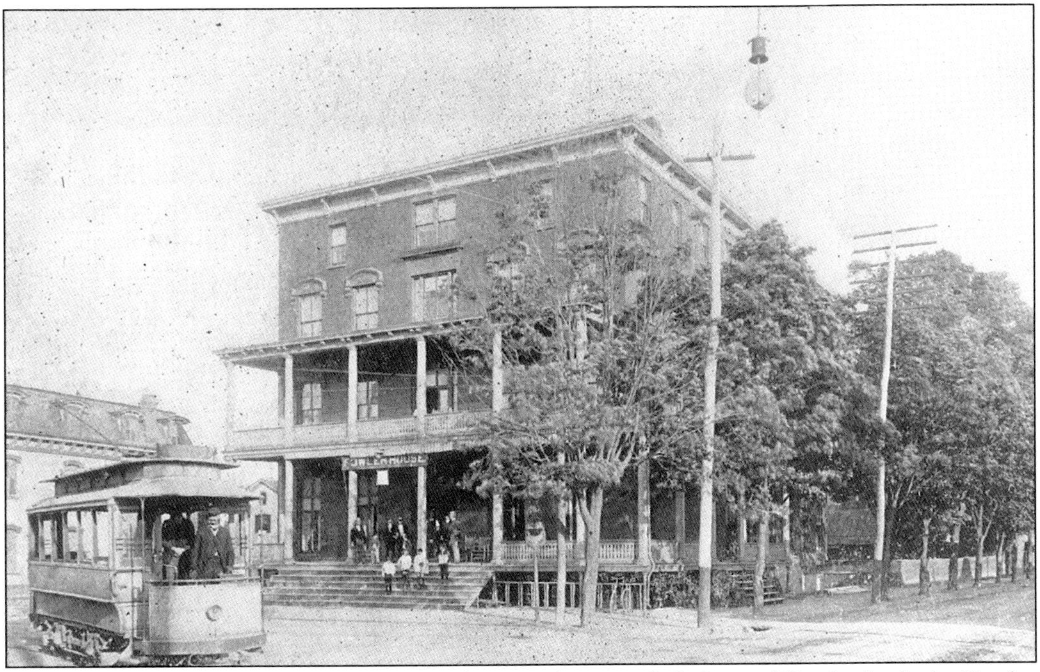

In 1855, on the corner of Fowler Street and Jersey Avenue, Col. Samuel Fowler built the Fowler House at a cost of nearly $50,000. It became one of the leading hotels of its day. (Collection of the Minisink Valley Historical Society.)

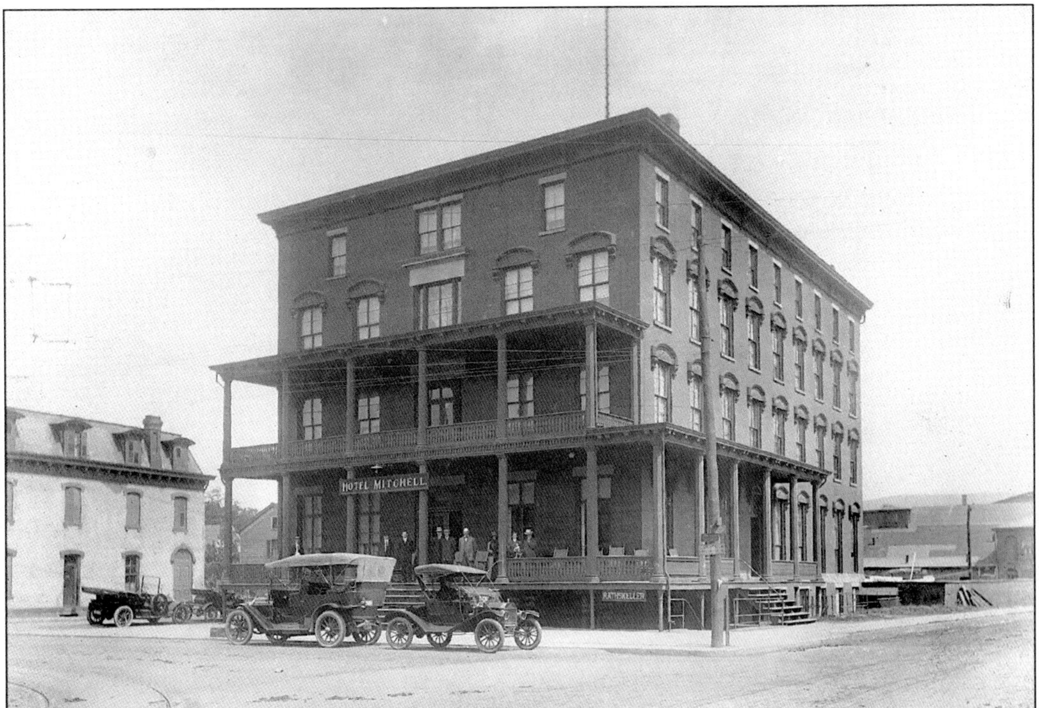

The Fowler House later became the Mitchell Inn. The building stood on this site until it was condemned and demolished in the 1940s. (Collection of the Minisink Valley Historical Society.)

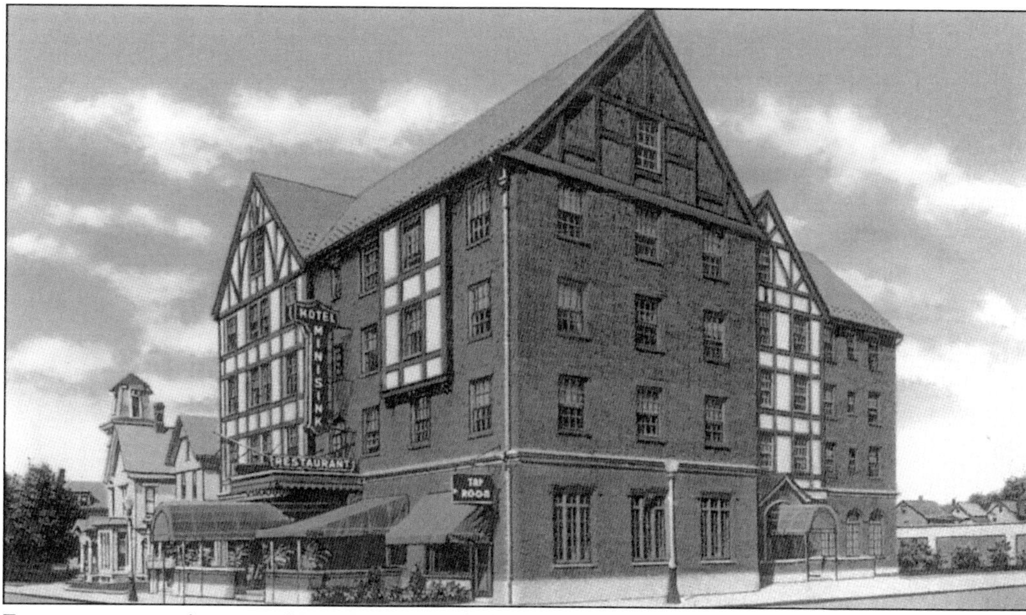

For many years, the city of Port Jervis needed a modern hotel large enough to handle the many tourists. In 1924, the businessmen of the city erected Hotel Minisink on Pike Street. After many renovations, it is now the home to many professional offices and private apartments. (Courtesy of Robbie Smith.)

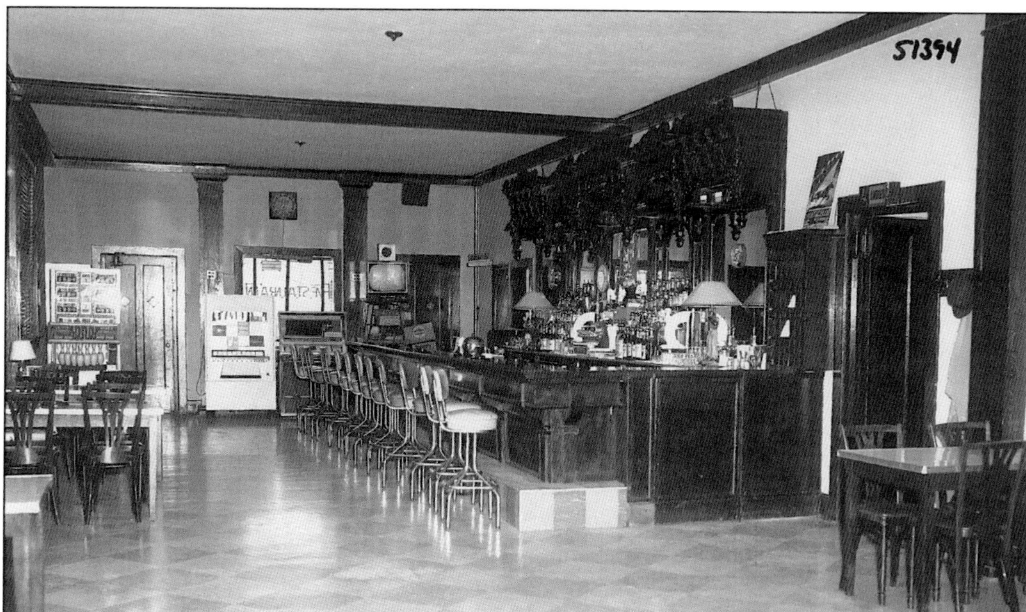

Built in the 1890s next to the depot, the Erie Hotel has always been a popular inn, restaurant, and tavern. This interior *c.* 1960s photograph shows the beautiful hand-carved bar. In recent years, the building has been totally renovated and has become one of the most popular restaurants in the city. (Courtesy of the Erie Hotel.)

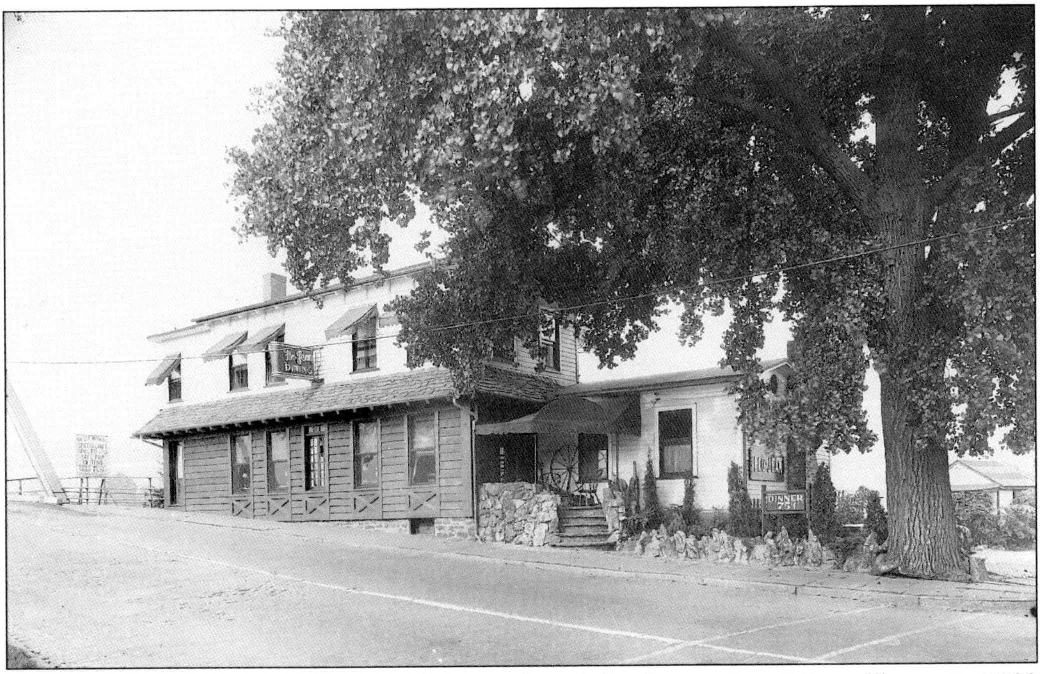

Florence K. Dalrymple and her sister Jean purchased the former site of the tollhouse in 1929 from George McGory. The Dalrymple sisters established a restaurant and named it the Flo-Jean. (Courtesy of Lynne Wallace.)

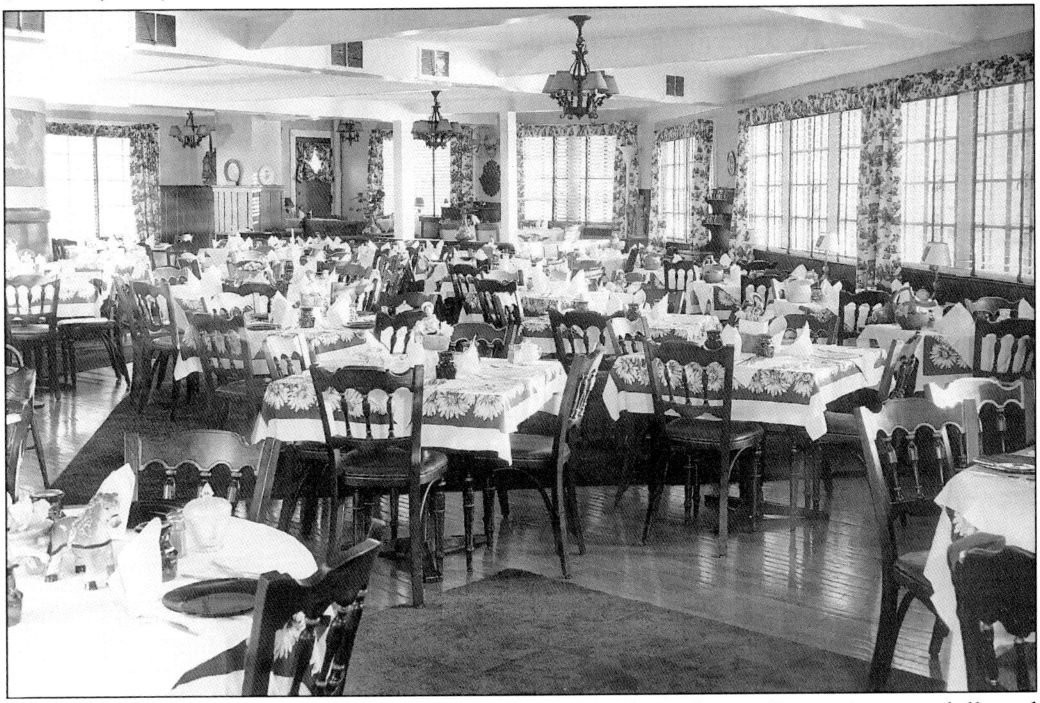

The dining room of the Flo-Jean has spectacular views of the Delaware River. Antique dolls and carriages were on display along with other fine antique furnishings. After 72 years, the world-famous restaurant is still a jewel of Port Jervis. (Courtesy of Lynne Wallace.)

Six

WORKING

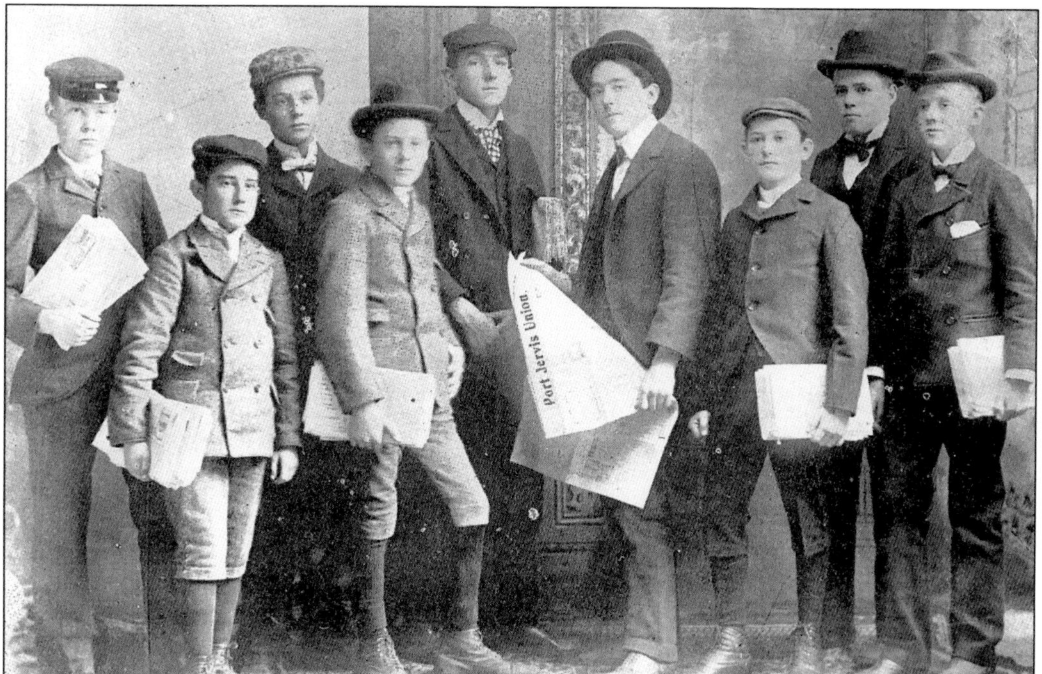

There has been a newspaper in Port Jervis since the 1850s. Through the years, the names of the local paper have been the *Tri-State Union*, the *Port Jervis Daily Union*, the *Union Gazette*, and the *Gazette*. These young men helped deliver newspapers throughout the city and the surrounding communities in the 1890s. (Collection of the Minisink Valley Historical Society.)

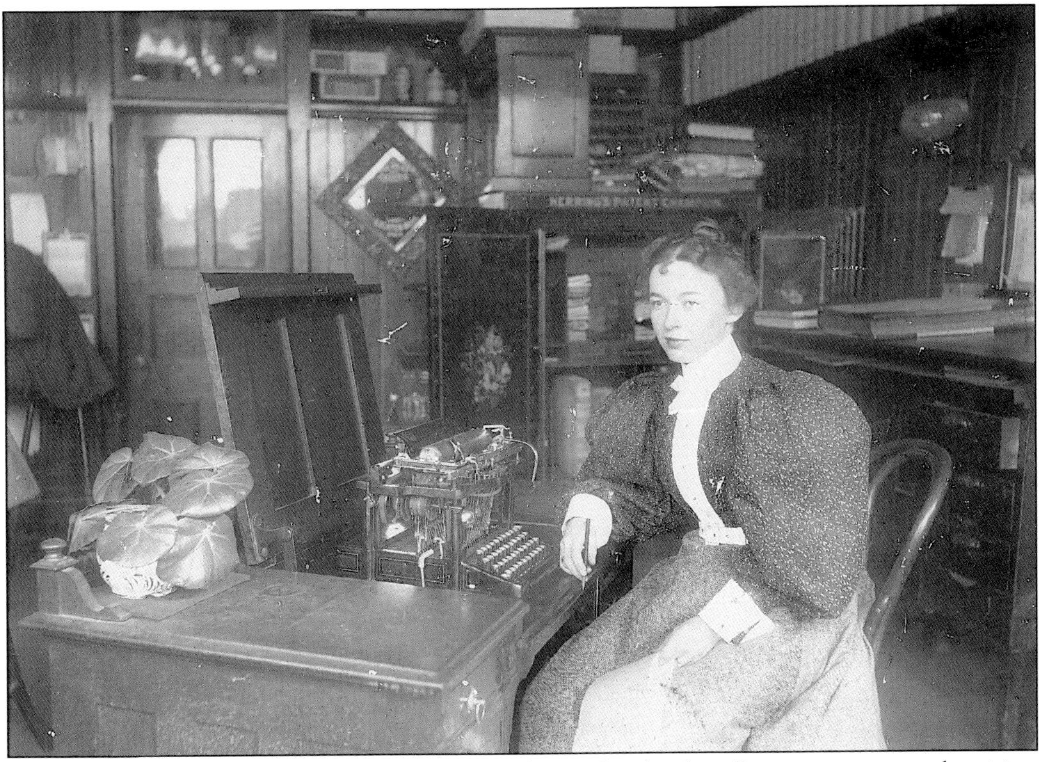

The Erie Depot was a grand building inside and out. On the first floor were a general waiting room, a smoking room, a ladies' waiting room, and a ticket office. This rare photograph shows the office on the second floor *c.* 1890. (Courtesy of Brian Lewis.)

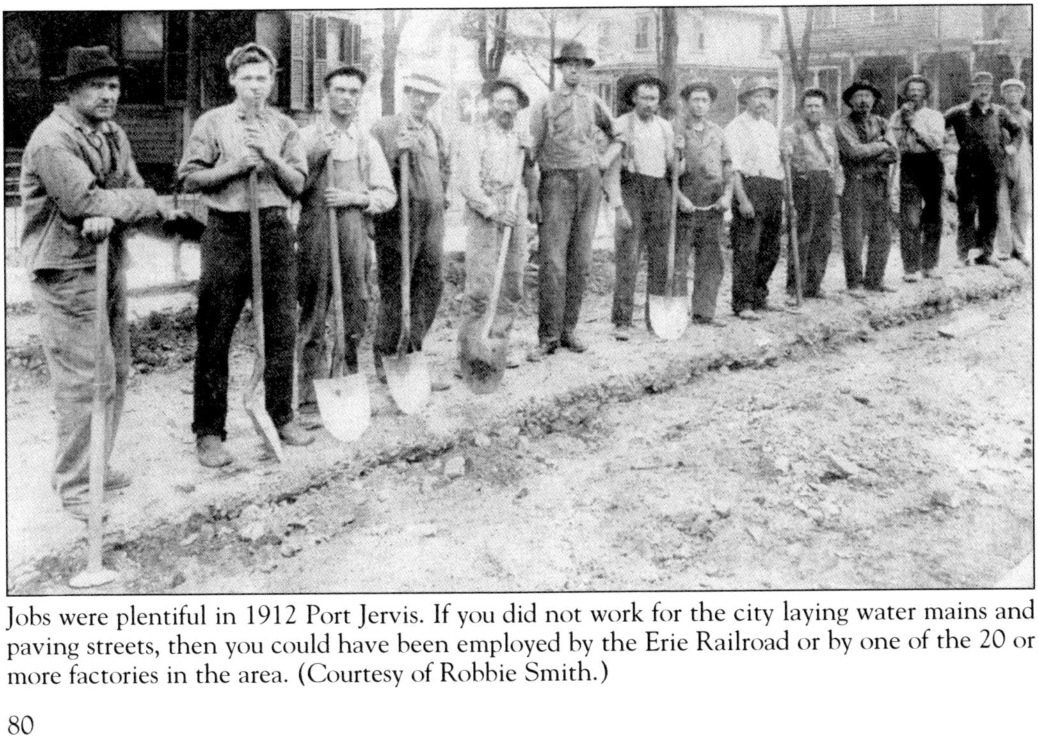

Jobs were plentiful in 1912 Port Jervis. If you did not work for the city laying water mains and paving streets, then you could have been employed by the Erie Railroad or by one of the 20 or more factories in the area. (Courtesy of Robbie Smith.)

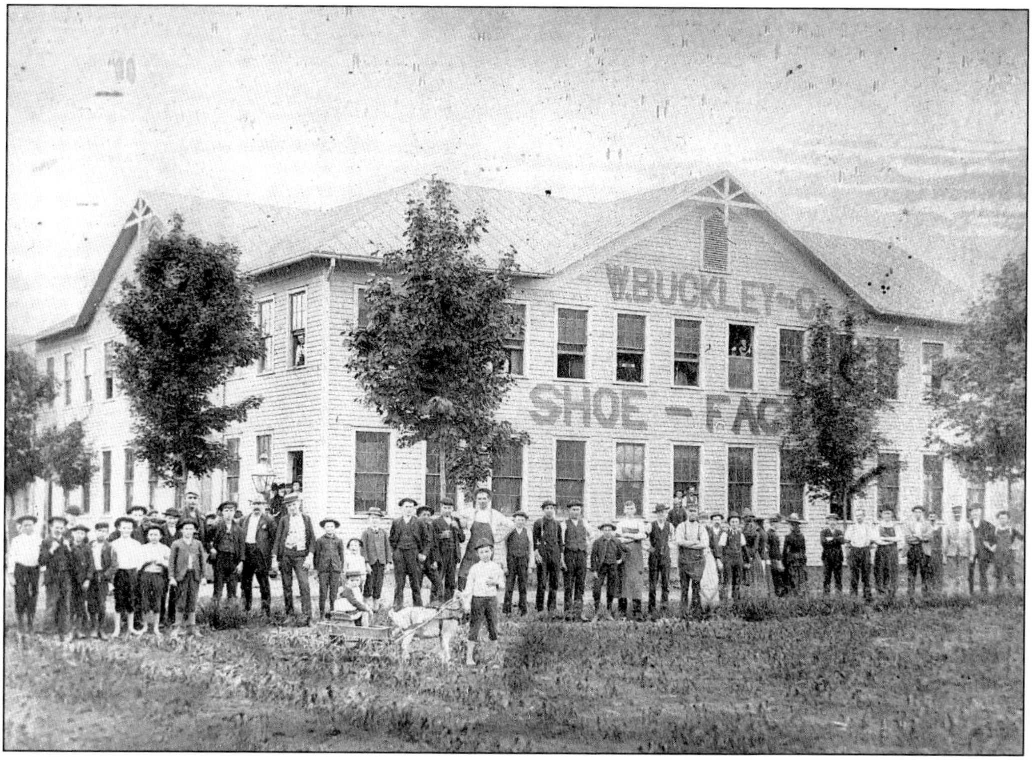

The manufacturing of shoes prospered in Port Jervis. The W. Buckley & Company Shoe Factory operated in West End. The shoe-making business employed many area residents until the mid-20th century. (Collection of the Minisink Valley Historical Society.)

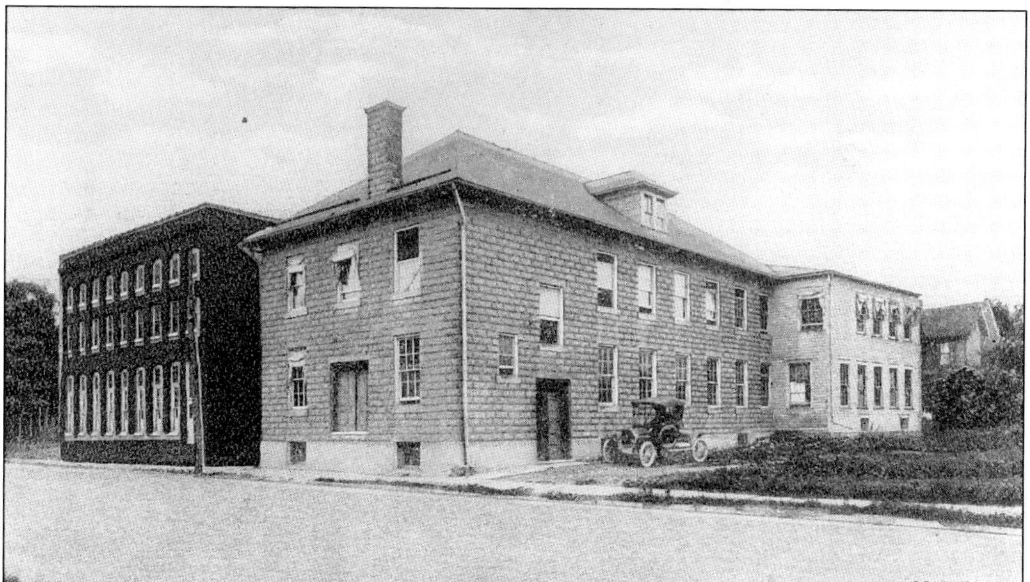

For more than 75 years, gloves were manufactured in Port Jervis. Chant Glove Factory produced most of them in its two factories in the area. This factory did business on Hammond Street until the mid-1950s. (Collection of the Minisink Valley Historical Society.)

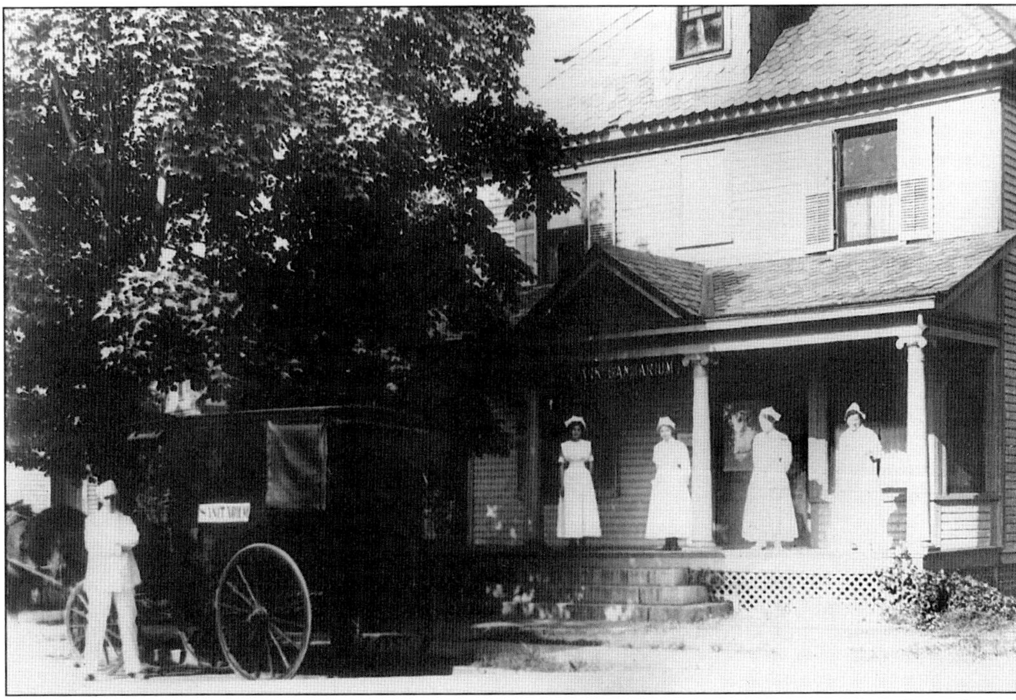

The first Port Jervis Ambulance, established in 1904, was on Prospect Street in Port Jervis. (Collection of the Minisink Valley Historical Society.)

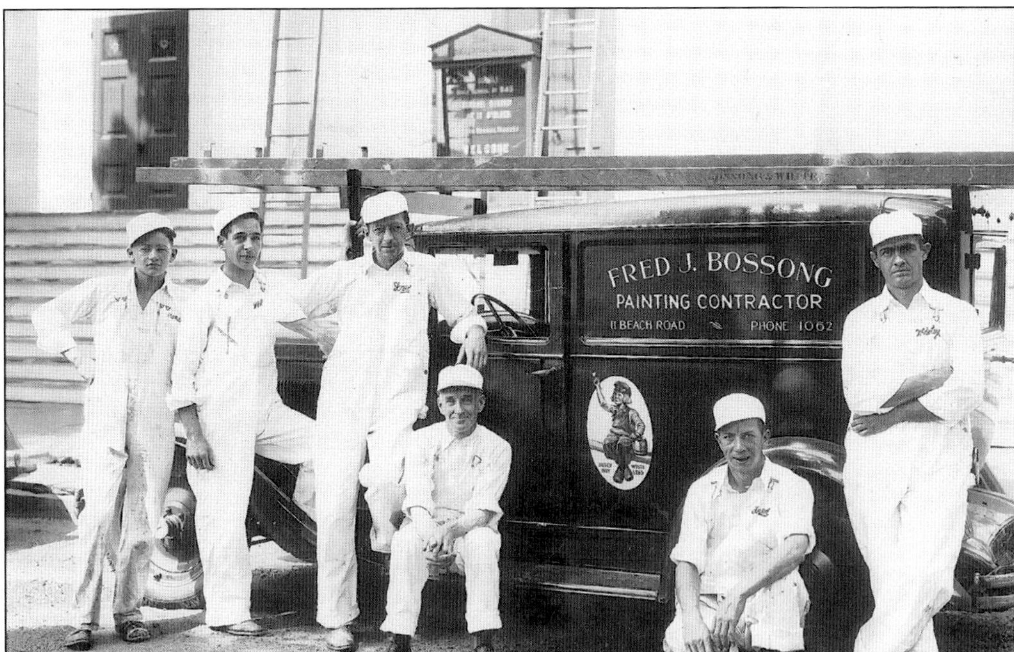

The crew of Fred J. Bossong Painting & Contractor takes a break from painting the Presbyterian church. Shown from left to right are unidentified, Fred White Jr., unidentified, Fred White Sr., Fred Bossong, and Frank DePietro. Dutch Boy was the paint of choice. (Courtesy of Fred White III and Joseph White.)

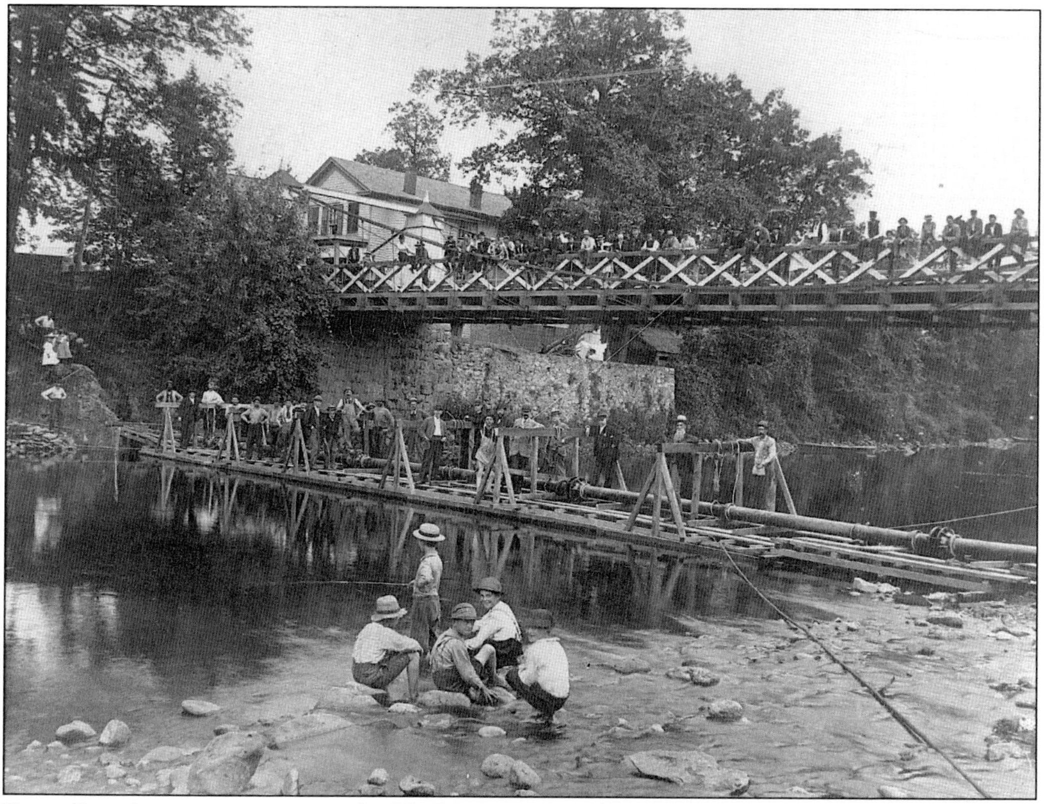

Extending the water main into the Tri-States section (Carpenter's Point) in the 1890s seemed to attract plenty of attention and interest. In 1869, the central water system was established and operated privately. It was not until 1928 when the city purchased it for $600,000. (Collection of the Minisink Valley Historical Society.)

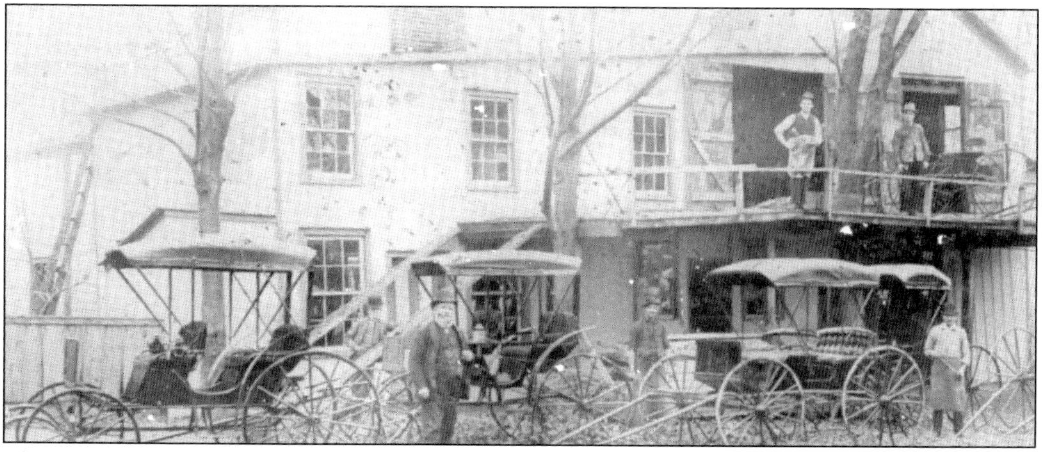

The Nathan Skinner Wagon Factory, shown *c.* the 1880s, occupied the property behind the Hotel Minisink, on the corner of Canal and West Broome Streets. (Collection of the Minisink Valley Historical Society.)

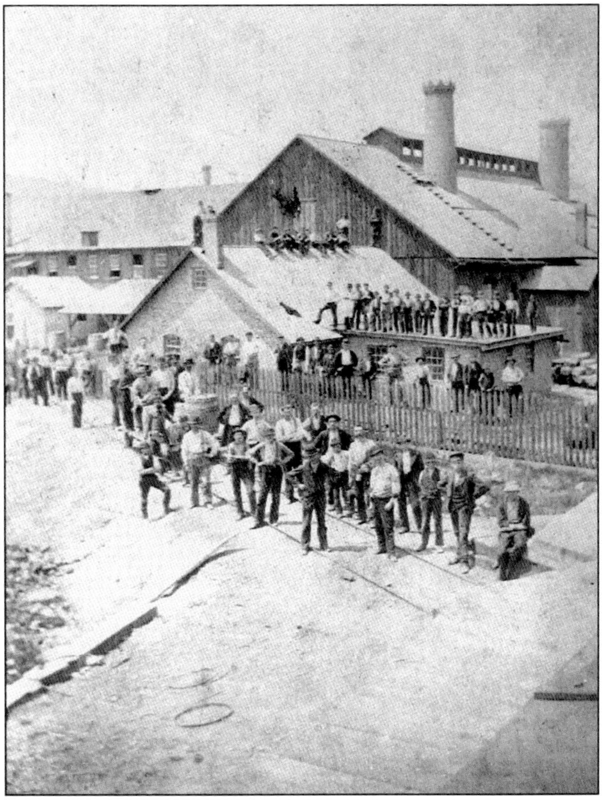

The Poutney Glass Factory was one of the first in the industry to come to Port Jervis. It was established in 1873 near the D & H Canal on Hamilton Street. (Collection of the Minisink Valley Historical Society.)

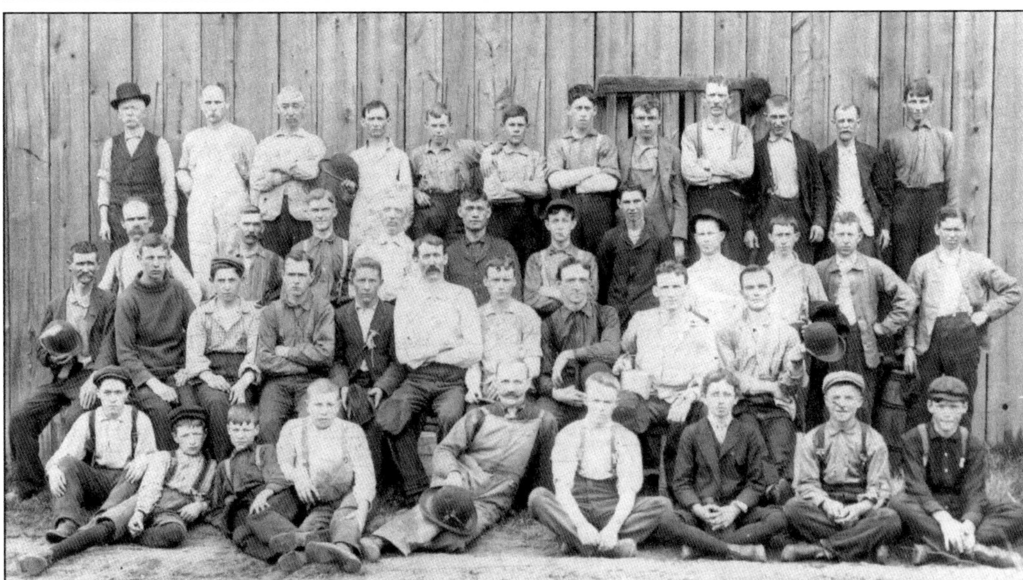

Glass factories have been in Port Jervis for more than 120 years. One of the first plants was known as Brox & Buckley. These two people did more than just operate a glass factory. Brox's family made a financial donation to the city in 1932 toward the development of Elks-Brox Park. Mr. Buckley's contribution was as a landowner and developer in West End. Buckley Street is named after him. Pictured here are glassworkers *c.* 1880. (Courtesy of Gillinder Glass Archives.)

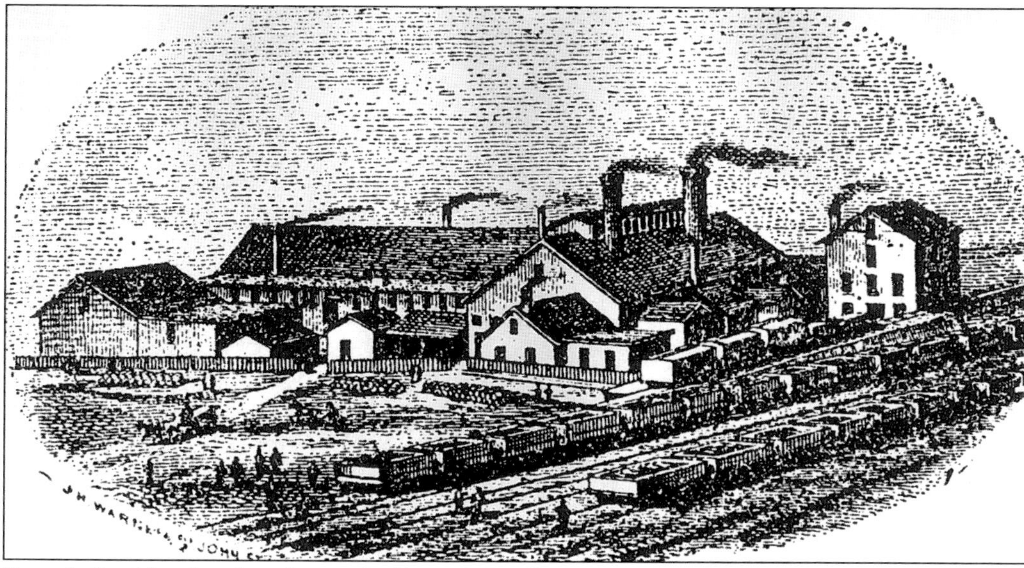

Brox & Buckley developed into the Brox & Ryall Company and later the Orange County Flint Glass Works. In 1911, the factory closed down and, a year later, was purchased by Gillinder Brothers. It reopened in January 1913. The plant burned in 1919 and was rebuilt in its present form in 1920. (Courtesy of Gillinder Glass Archives.)

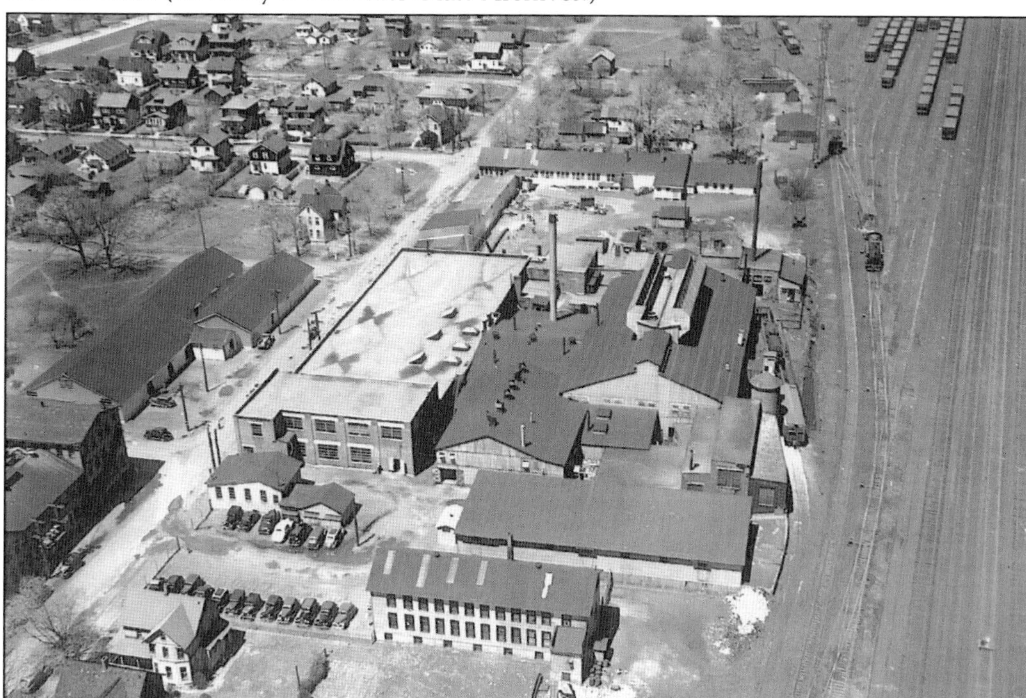

This photograph shows the three companies operating here at the same time. The multistory wooden building in the front was the Edward W. Moyer Company, a glasscutter. The center section of buildings is Gillinder Brothers. The one-story building at the top was the Foskett Company, a glass-decorating plant. All three were in business until the 1930s. As the companies closed, Gillinder Brothers purchased the buildings. (Courtesy of Gillinder Glass Archives.)

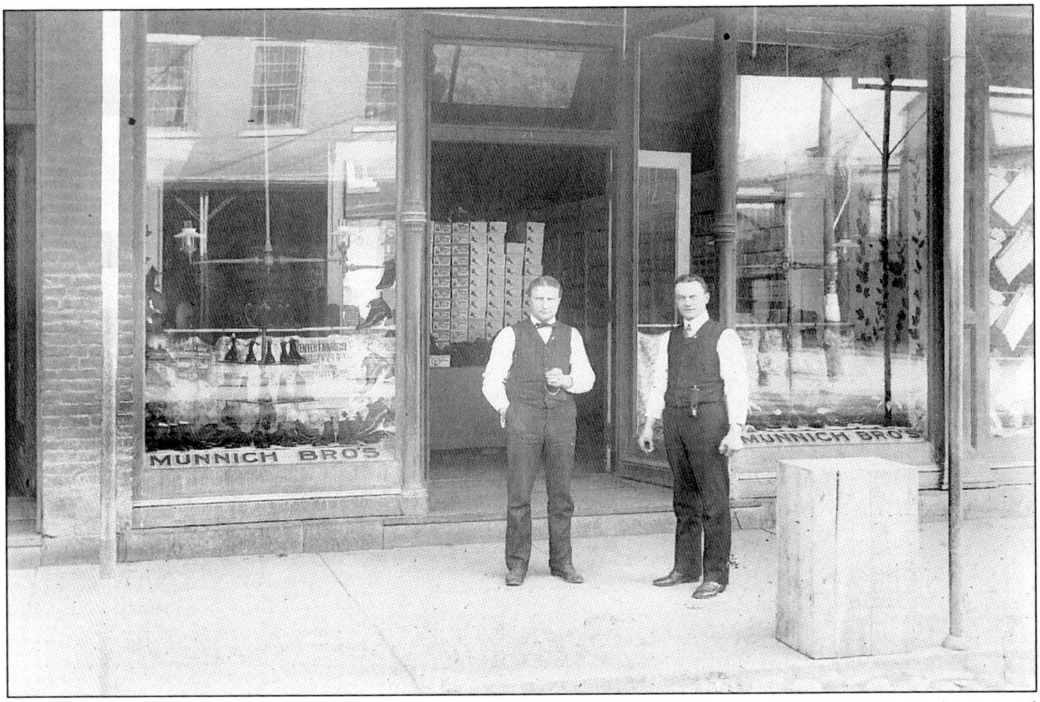

The Munnich family ran a shoe store on Pike Street for many years. Henry Munnich started a shoe factory in the city in 1863 and continued until 1895. This store, shown c. 1900, was at 21 Pike Street. (Courtesy of the Minisink Valley Historical Society.)

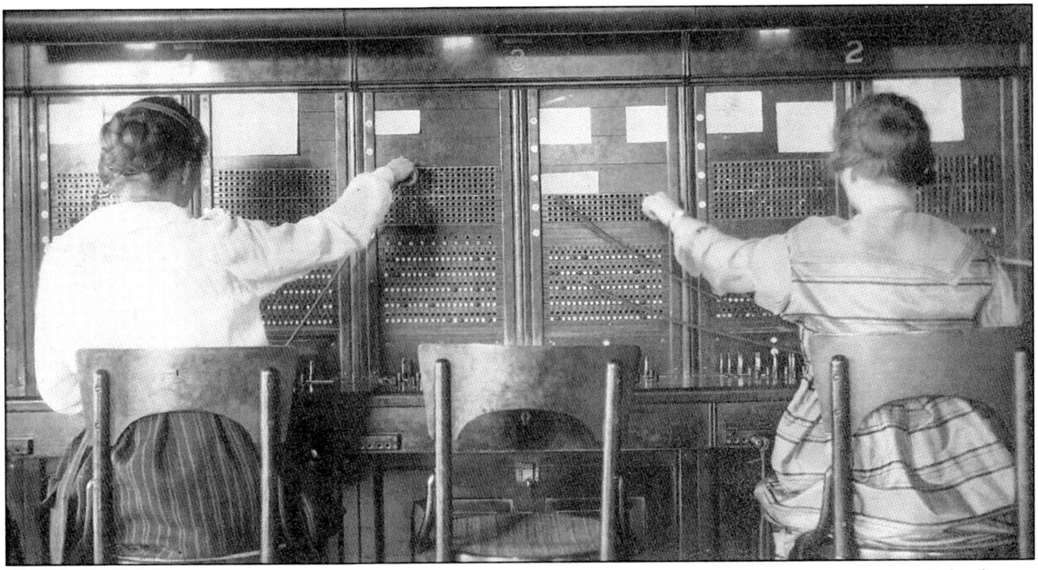

The first telephone was used in the village of Port Jervis in 1878. The Port Jervis Telephone Company organized 20 years later. In its first year of existence, there were 420 paid subscribers for telephone service. By 1915, operators connected many more friends and families in the surrounding communities. (Courtesy of Ted Willers.)

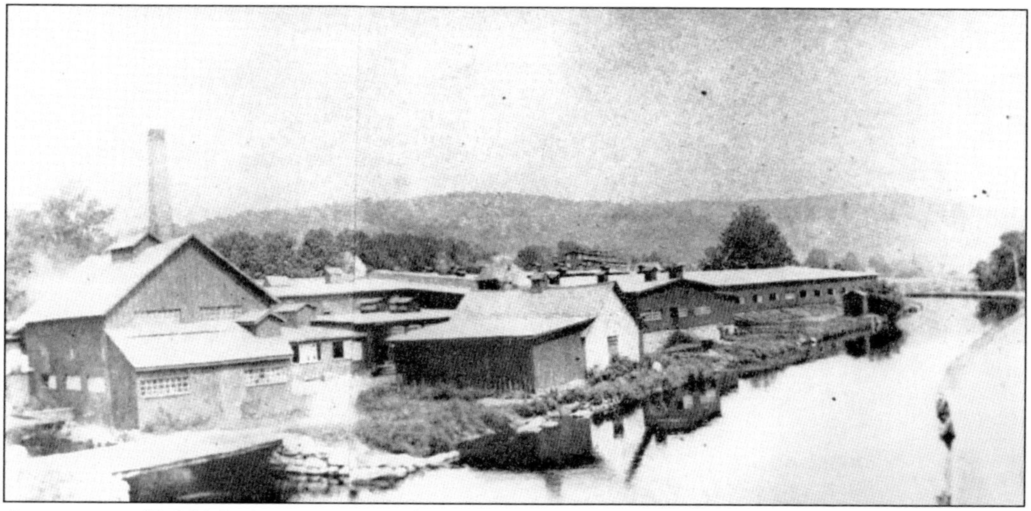

As many as 50,000 hides were tanned annually at the Sparrowbush Tannery and shipped via of the D & H Canal. The tannery is shown in the late 1800s. (Collection of the Minisink Valley Historical Society.)

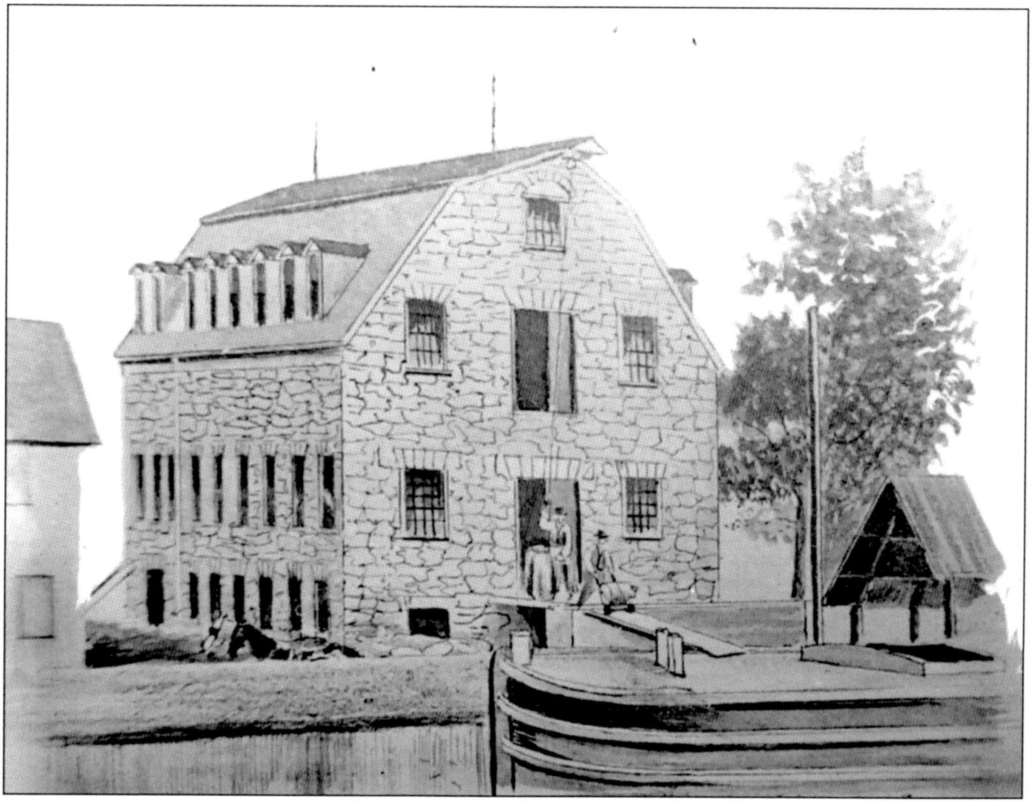

The Old Stone Mill, a grain mill, was erected in 1832 and stood behind the Port Jervis Free Library. The mill was powered by the flow of water in the canal. Sadly, the building burned in recent years. (Collection of the Minisink Valley Historical Society.)

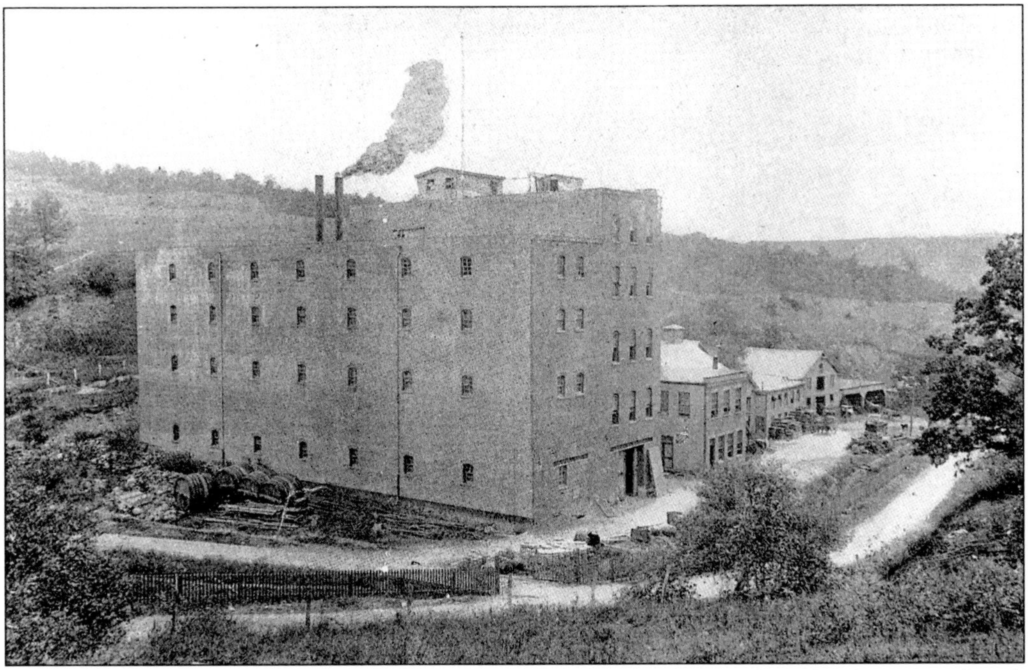

The Deerpark Brewery once stood near the No. 1 Reservoir. After the brewery closed, the building was used by the Tri-State Bottling Company in the late 1950s. (Courtesy of Robbie Smith.)

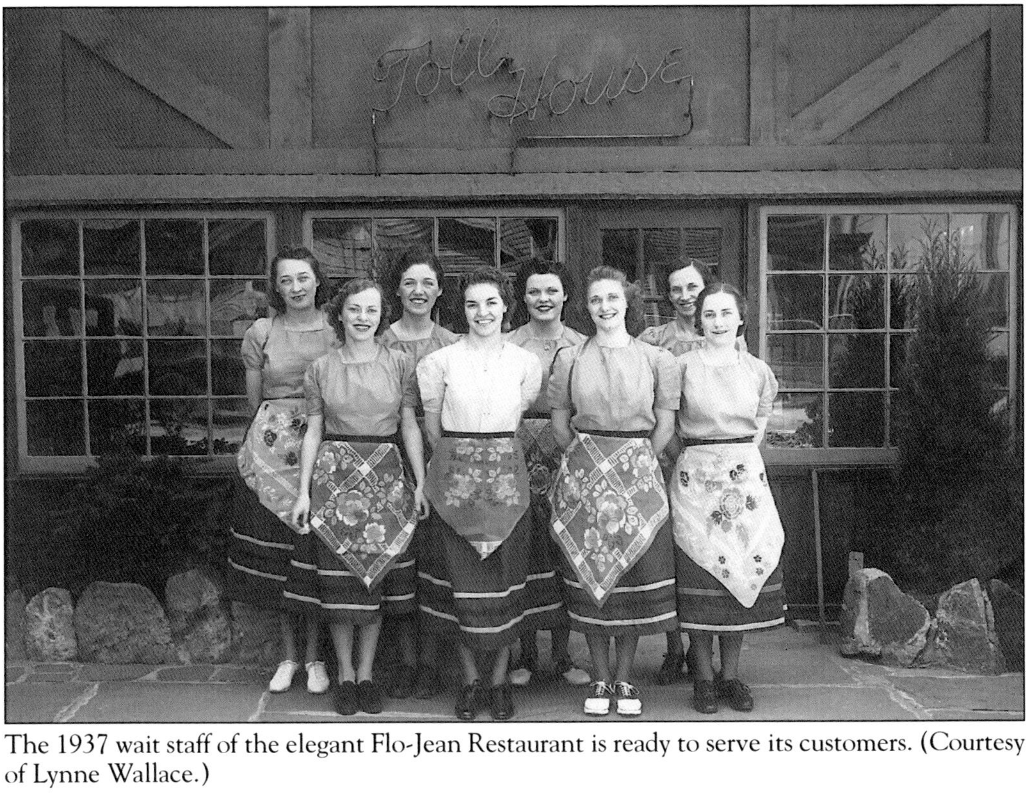

The 1937 wait staff of the elegant Flo-Jean Restaurant is ready to serve its customers. (Courtesy of Lynne Wallace.)

Seven

THE BUSINESS DISTRICT

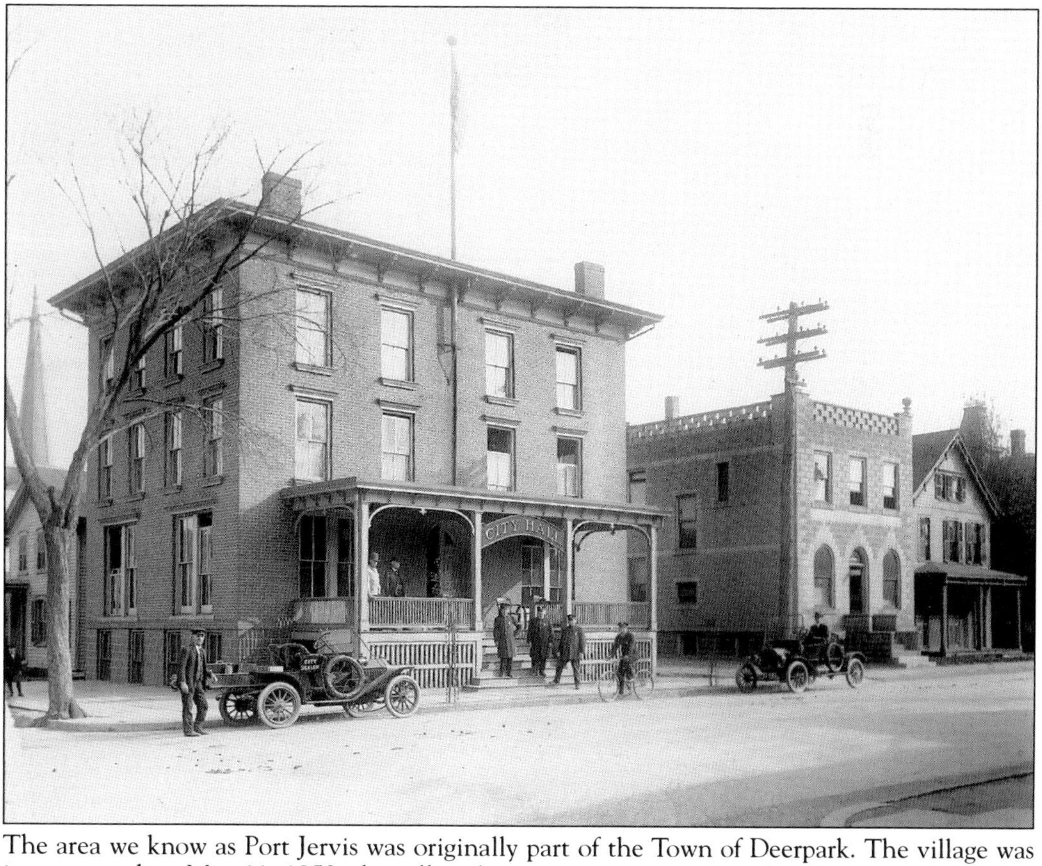

The area we know as Port Jervis was originally part of the Town of Deerpark. The village was incorporated on May 11, 1853; the village became a city in 1907. A headquarters was needed to conduct business in the new city. The former Imperial Hotel, on the corner of Hammond and Sussex Streets, was purchased from Isaac T. Edwards. During the urban renewal period, this row of buildings was demolished. The city hall sign on the building in this *c.* 1920 photograph now hangs in the Common Council Chambers. The building on the right was the Tri-State Telephone Company offices. (Collection of the Minisink Valley Historical Society.)

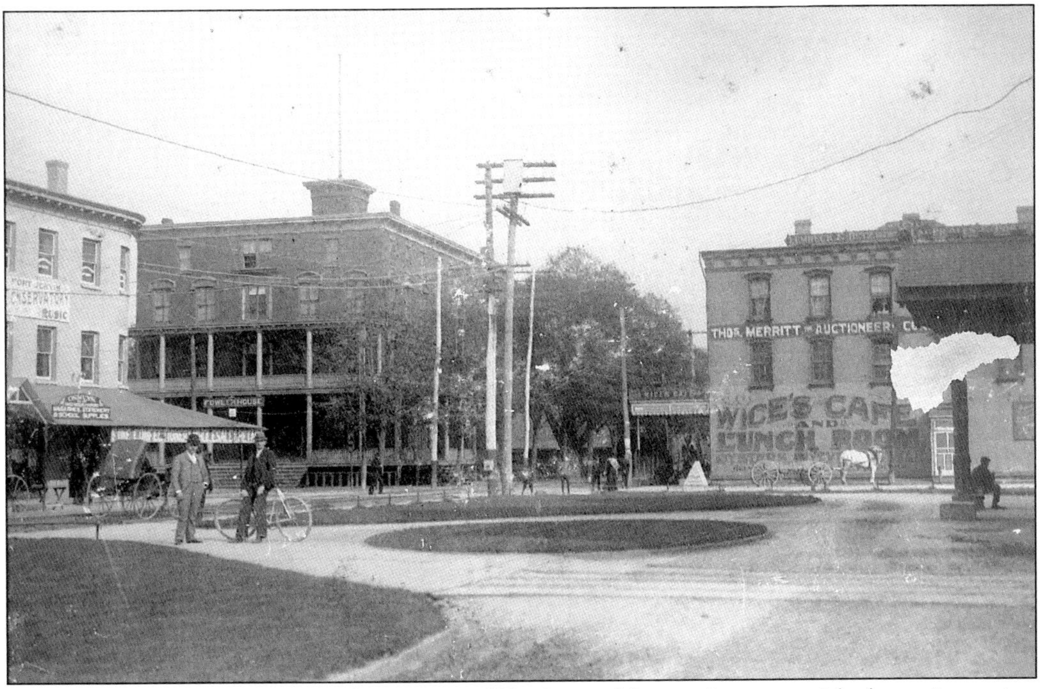

Commerce thrived c. 1890 on the corners of Fowler and Jersey Avenues with the train station on one corner, Colonel Fowler's newspaper store on a second corner, his hotel on a third corner, and Wice's Café and Lunchroom on the fourth corner. This is the present Hockenberry's Furniture Store. (Collection of the Minisink Valley Historical Society.)

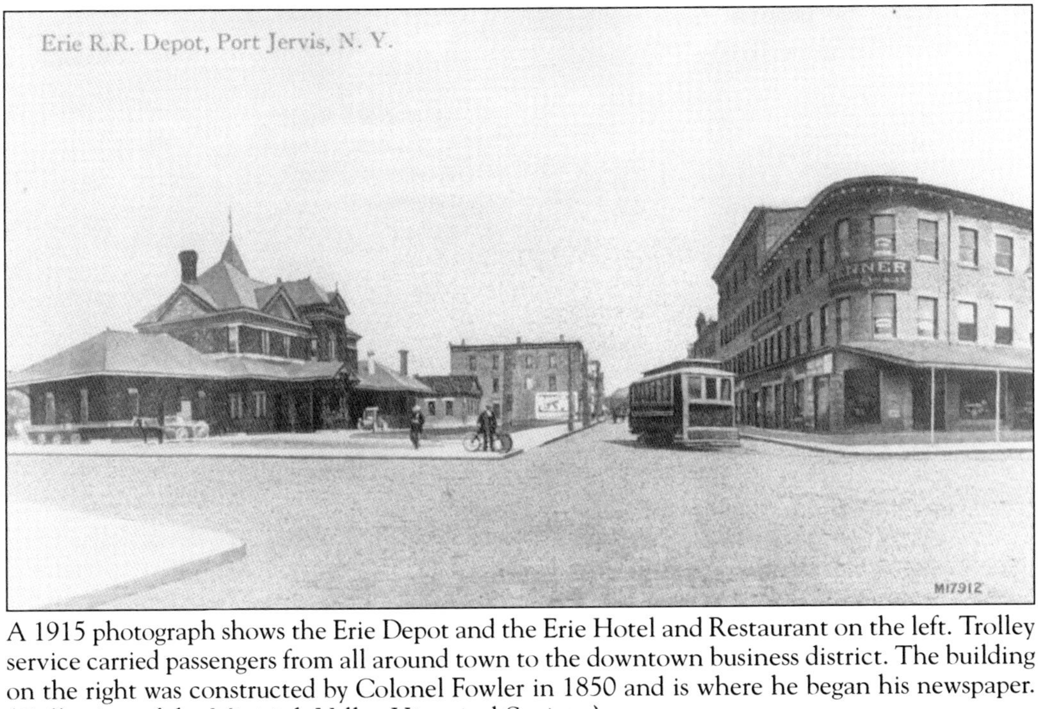

A 1915 photograph shows the Erie Depot and the Erie Hotel and Restaurant on the left. Trolley service carried passengers from all around town to the downtown business district. The building on the right was constructed by Colonel Fowler in 1850 and is where he began his newspaper. (Collection of the Minisink Valley Historical Society.)

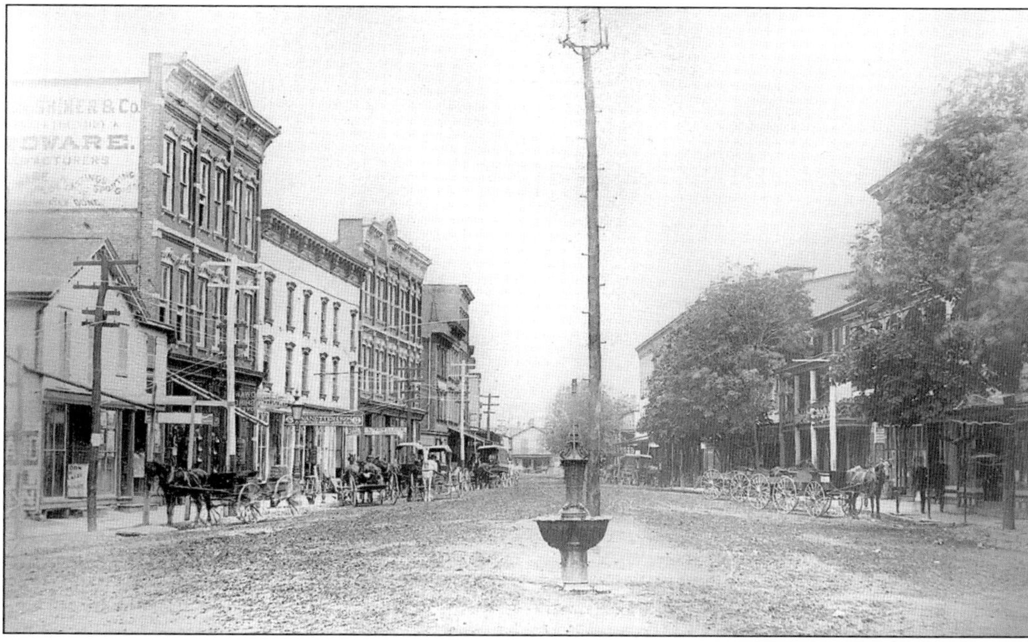

Around the 1890s, drinking fountains were placed in two spots in the city: one at the intersection of Pike and Main and this one at Graeb Point on Front Street. These were favorite spots for citizens to gather and talk over local events. (Collection of the Minisink Valley Historical Society.)

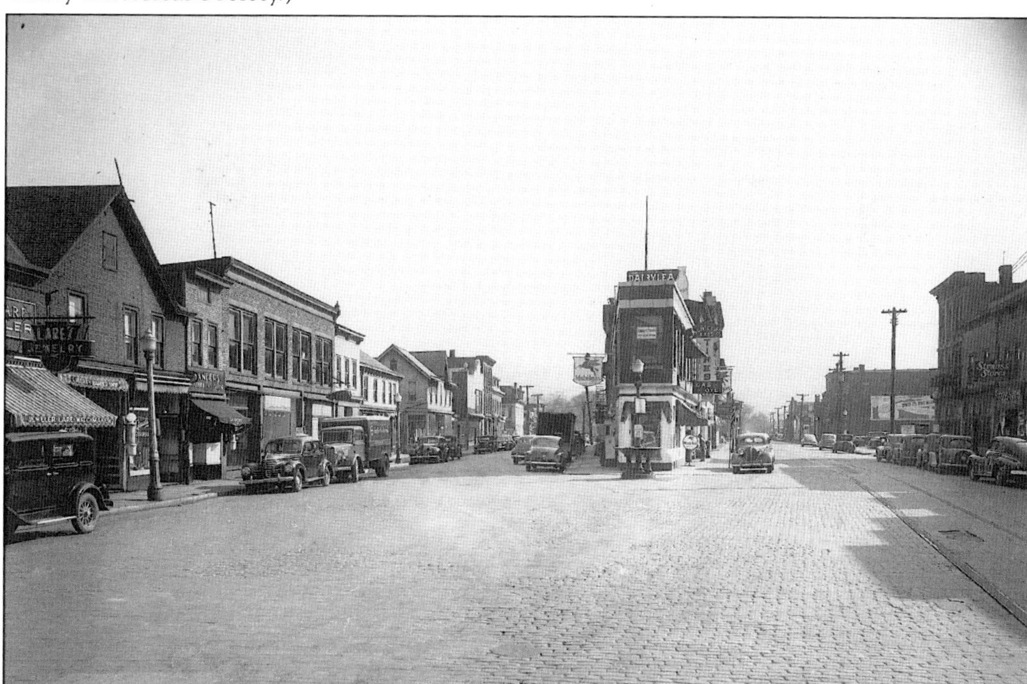

The scene changed by the 1940s at Graeb Point. The drinking fountain became a planter, and streets were paved. Schields Brothers Tire Service opened for business at this location. (Courtesy of John Hess.)

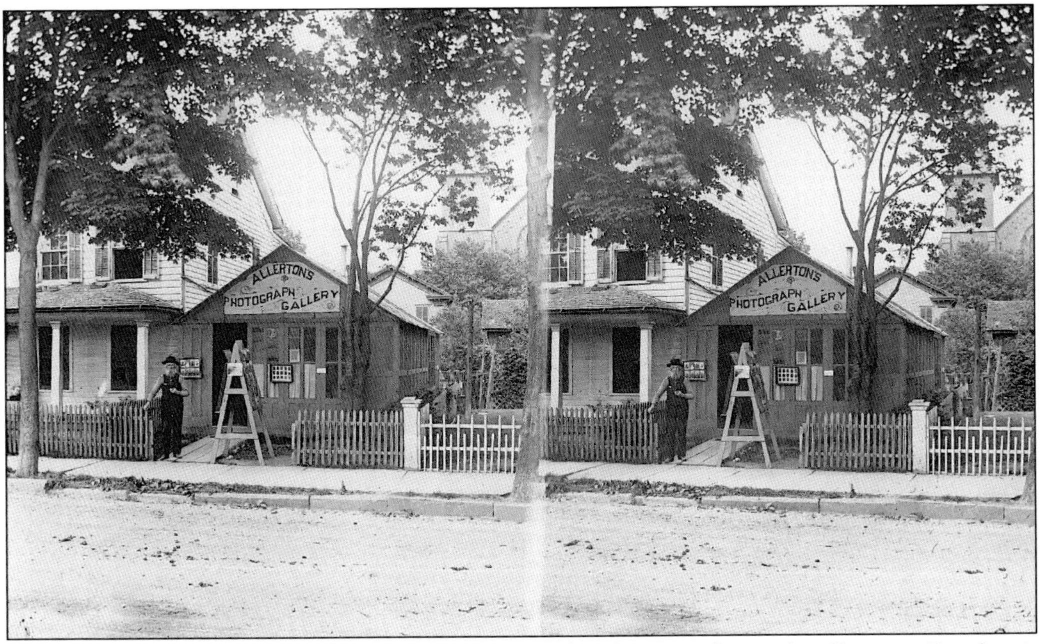

William Allerton, seen in this stereo view, was a popular photographer with galleries in Port Jervis and Dingmans Ferry, Pennsylvania. This studio was on Front Street; St. Mary's Church is in the background in this *c.* 1890s picture. (Collection of the Minisink Valley Historical Society.)

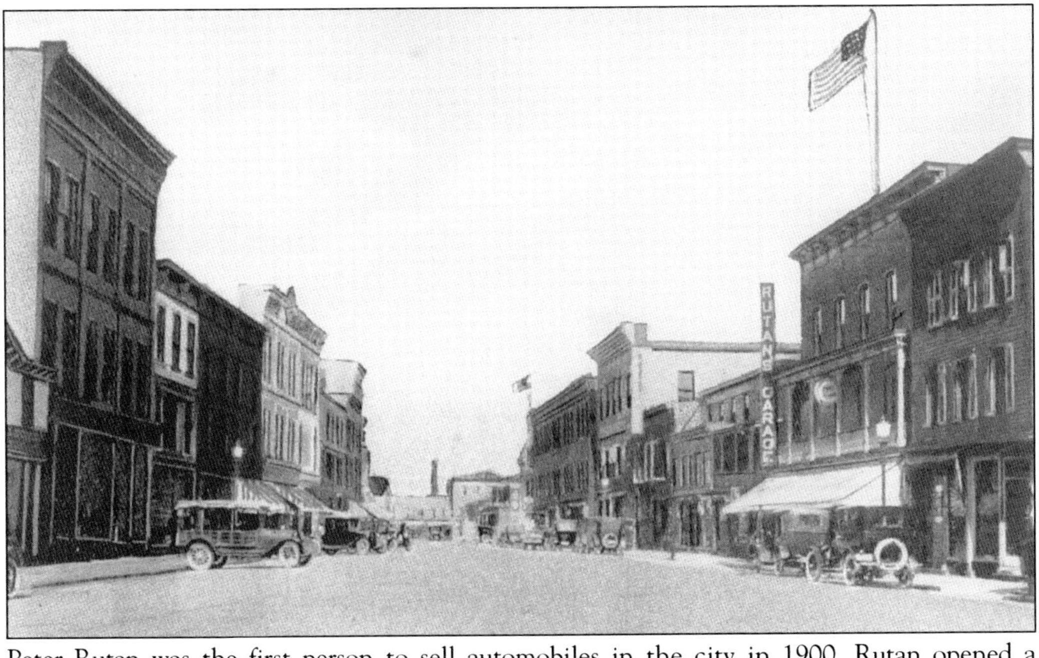

Peter Rutan was the first person to sell automobiles in the city in 1900. Rutan opened a modern facility on Front Street where cars were raised to the second floor for viewers down below. His name can still be seen on the facade of the building. (Collection of the Minisink Valley Historical Society.)

The first gaslights were installed along the business district in 1863. Later, an additional 25 were placed randomly throughout the village. At that time, Port Jervis was only the second village in Orange County illuminated with these objects of wonder. These lights lasted for 24 years. On January 21, 1887, they were replaced by new electric lights. (Collection of the Minisink Valley Historical Society.)

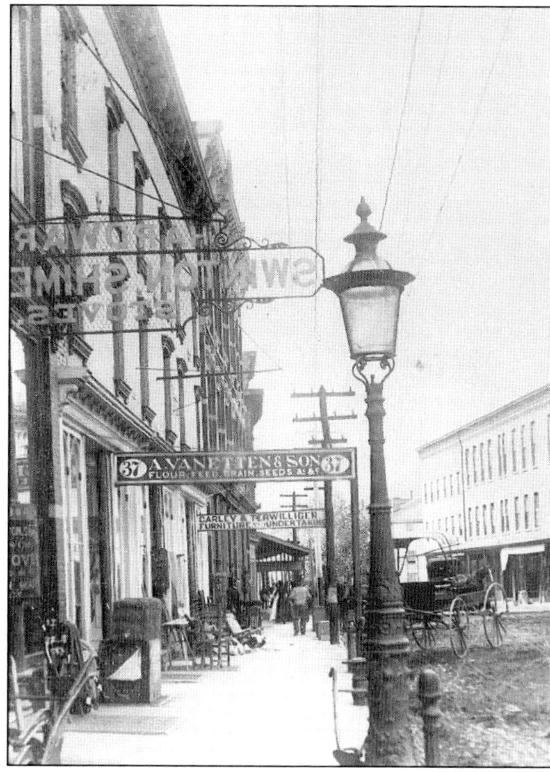

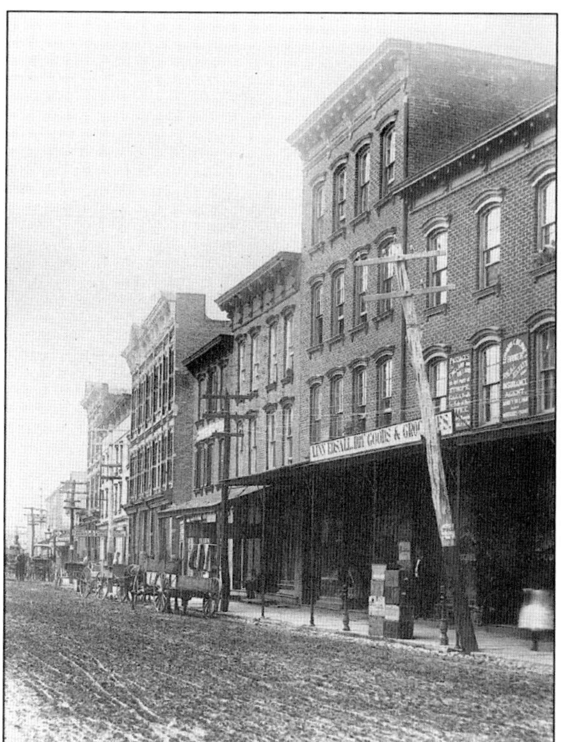

In 1895, Front Street had many three- and four-story commercial buildings. Some still survive today with beautiful ornate facades. In 1890, Port Jervis residents complained about the conditions of the roads, which were dirt and either muddy or very dusty. It was years before all the roads were paved. (Collection of the Minisink Valley Historical Society.)

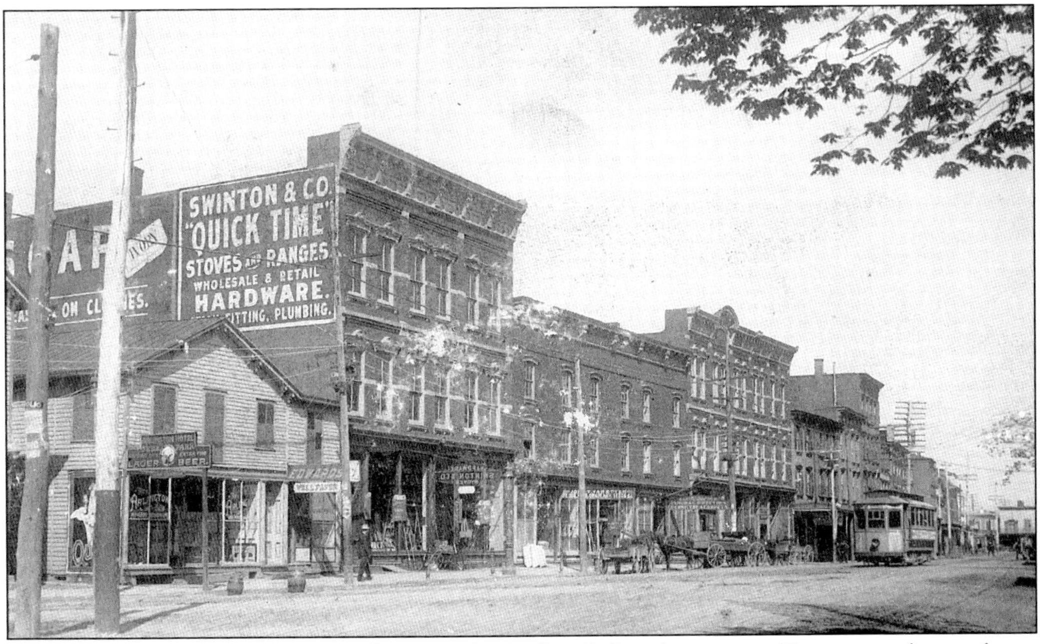

As seen in this c. 1910 photograph, Front Street bustled with activity. Customers shopped at a variety of stores. Swinton & Company, at 47–60 Jersey Avenue, produced stoves that were sold worldwide. It was one of the most important products created locally in the late 19th and early 20th centuries. (Collection of the Minisink Valley Historical Society.)

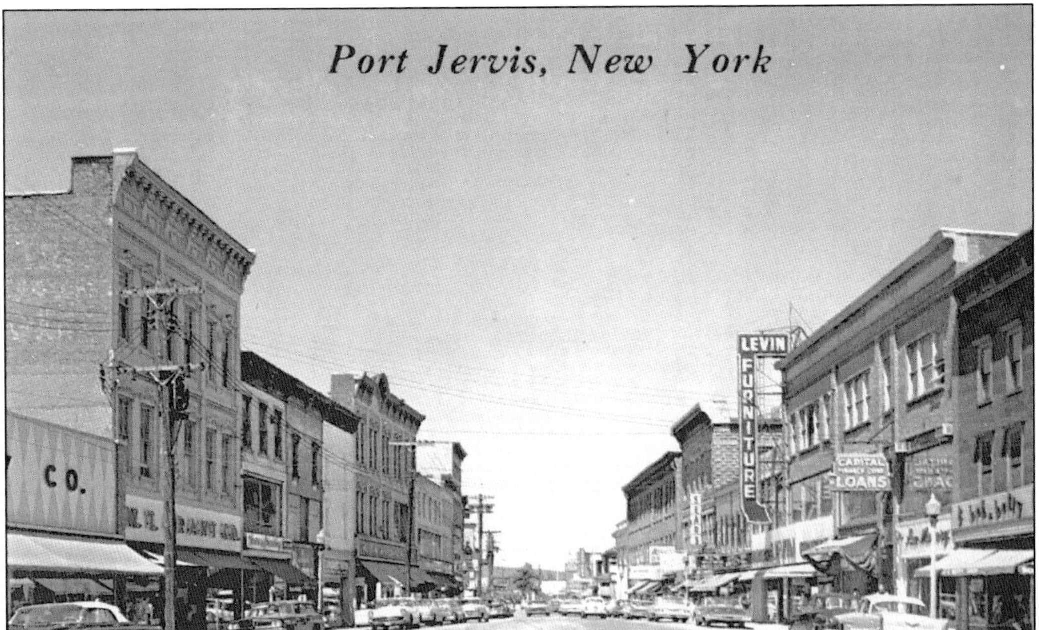

This 1960s postcard of Front Street shows new stores on the block. On the left are J.C. Penney, W.T. Grant, J.J. Newberry, and F.W. Woolworth. On the right are Bob and Betty (a children's clothing store), Levin Furniture, and Sears. (Collection of the Minisink Valley Historical Society.)

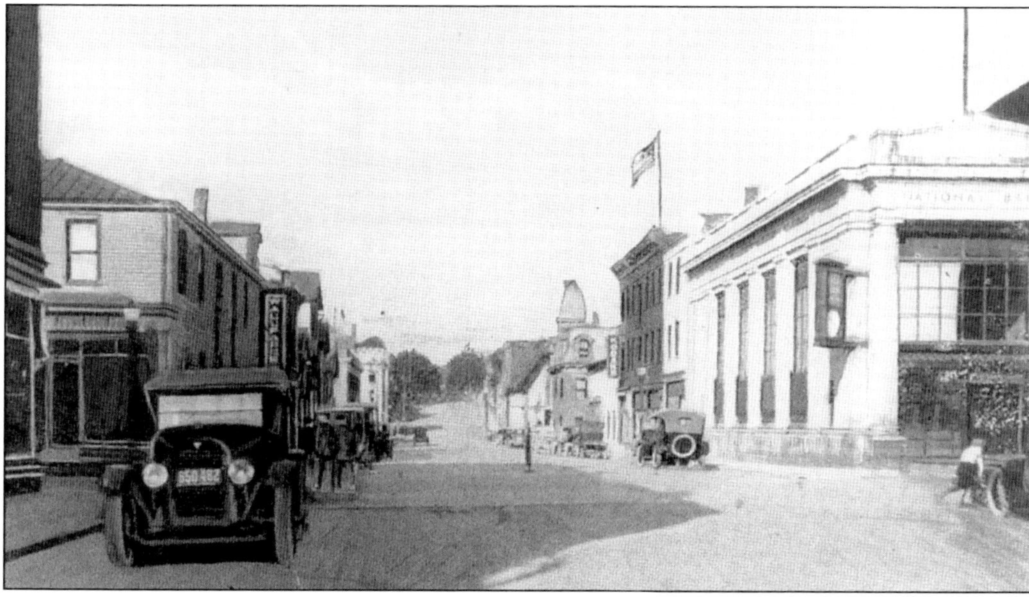

This view looks north on Sussex Street in the 1920s. The building on the right was the National Bank of Port Jervis, later known as the National Bank & Trust Company, first established at the Delaware House in 1853. Up a little farther is a Kodak sign, marking the spot where Gus Krauss opened a larger store to meet the photography needs of his customers. Krauss was a leader in preserving the history of the city with his thousands of photographs. He was in business from 1907 until he retired in 1961, turning over his shop to Don Cole. The Cole family ran the business until the 1990s. (Collection of the Minisink Valley Historical Society.)

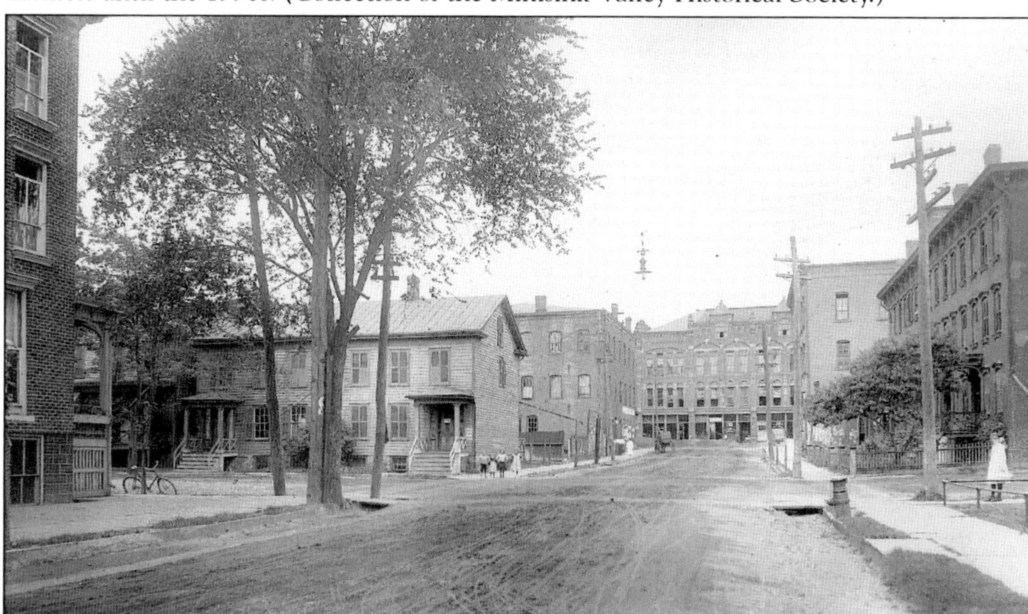

In 1900, the view down Hammond Street was very different. The post office had not yet been built. Looking directly across the center of this photograph, we can see probably one of the most impressive buildings in Port Jervis: the Masonic-Farnum Building. (Collection of the Minisink Valley Historical Society.)

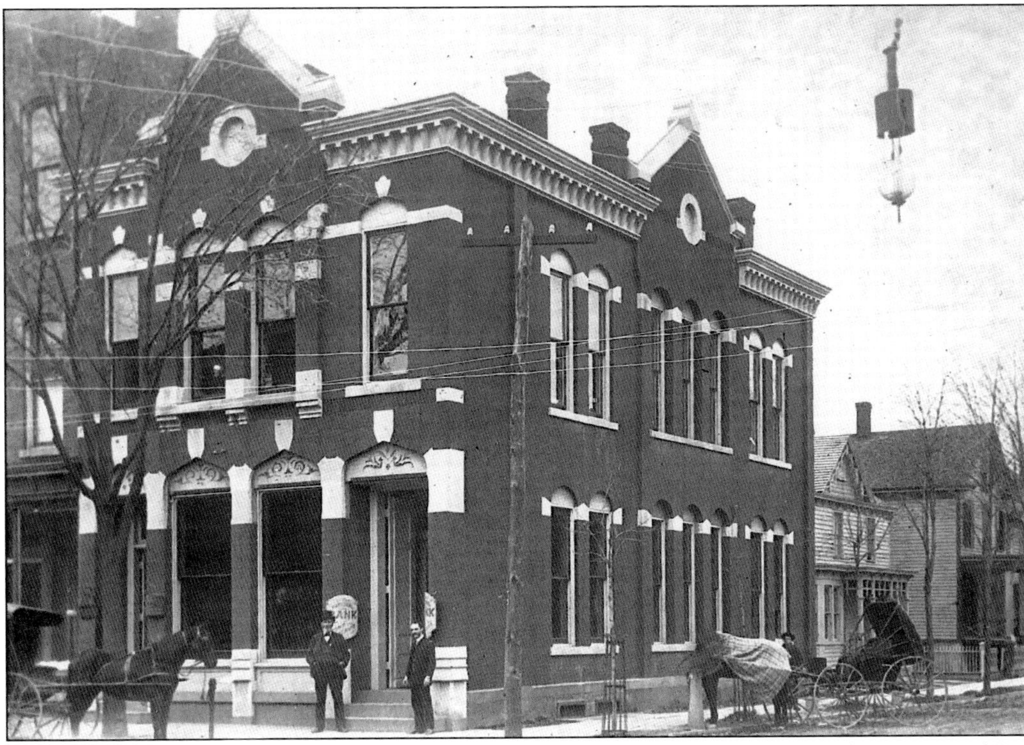

The First National Bank of Port Jervis, established in 1870, was located at the corner of Ball and Sussex Streets. This was demolished in 1912. (Courtesy of Robbie Smith.)

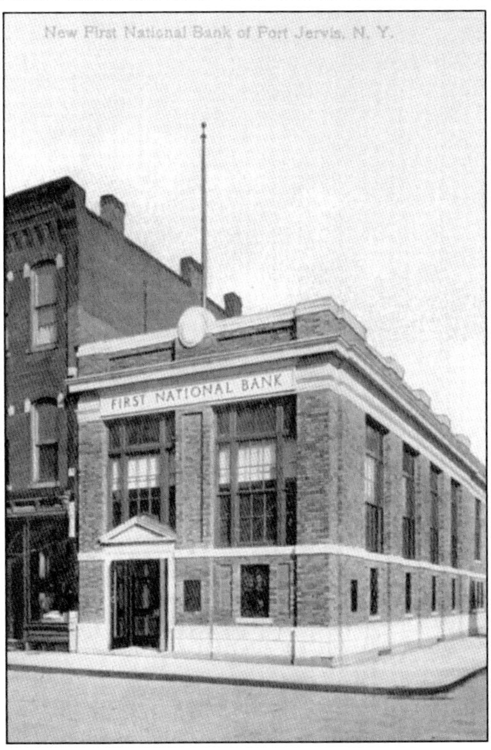

The new First National Bank of Port Jervis is shown years later. This bank stood for many years on this corner. The site is now the parking lot for Aliton's Pharmacy. (Collection of the Minisink Valley Historical Society.)

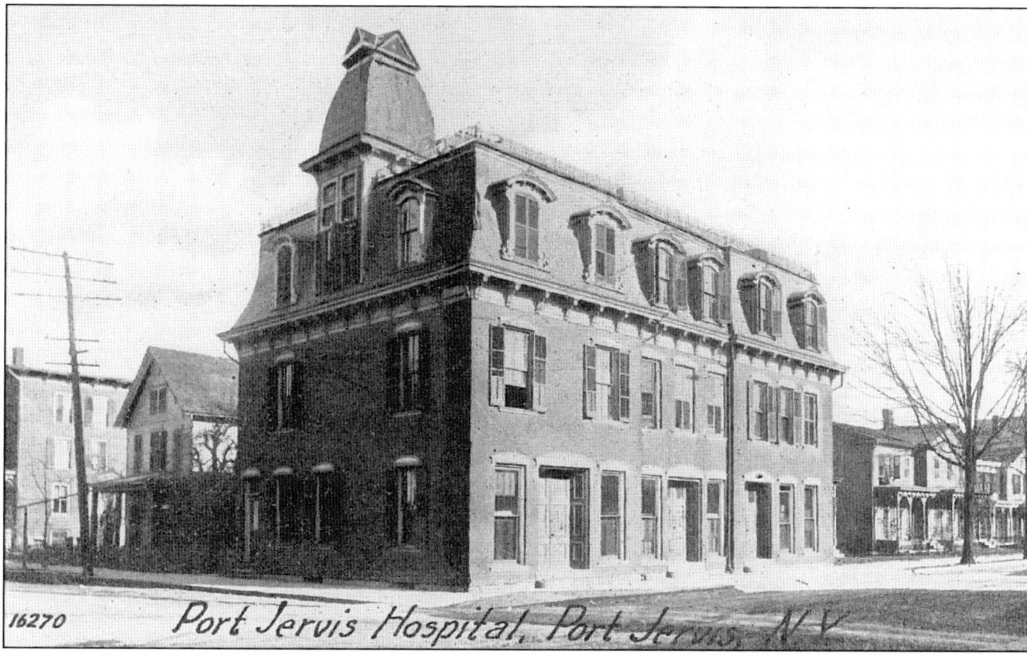

Dr. J.H. Hunt opened the first hospital in Port Jervis in 1889. A 25-bed facility called the Hunt Memorial Hospital stood on the corner of Ball and Sussex Streets. In 1892, Dr. W.L. Cuddeback and Dr. Henry B. Swartwout took over the facility, renaming it the Port Jervis Hospital. Today, the Salomon Smith Barney Building stands at this location. (Collection of the Minisink Valley Historical Society.)

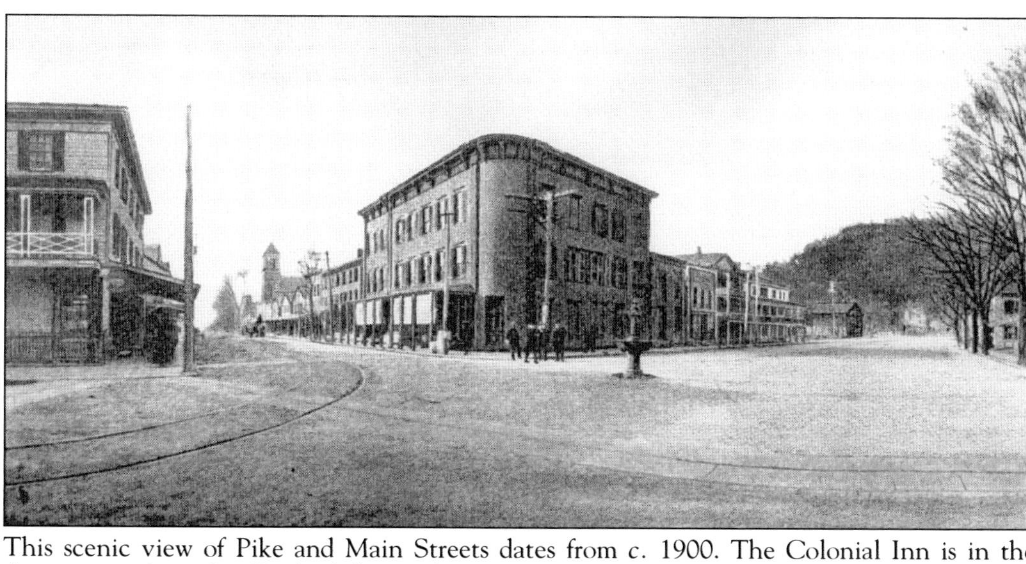

This scenic view of Pike and Main Streets dates from *c.* 1900. The Colonial Inn is in the distance on the right. To the left on Pike Street is the steeple of the Baptist church, later the Deerpark Club. (Collection of the Minisink Valley Historical Society.)

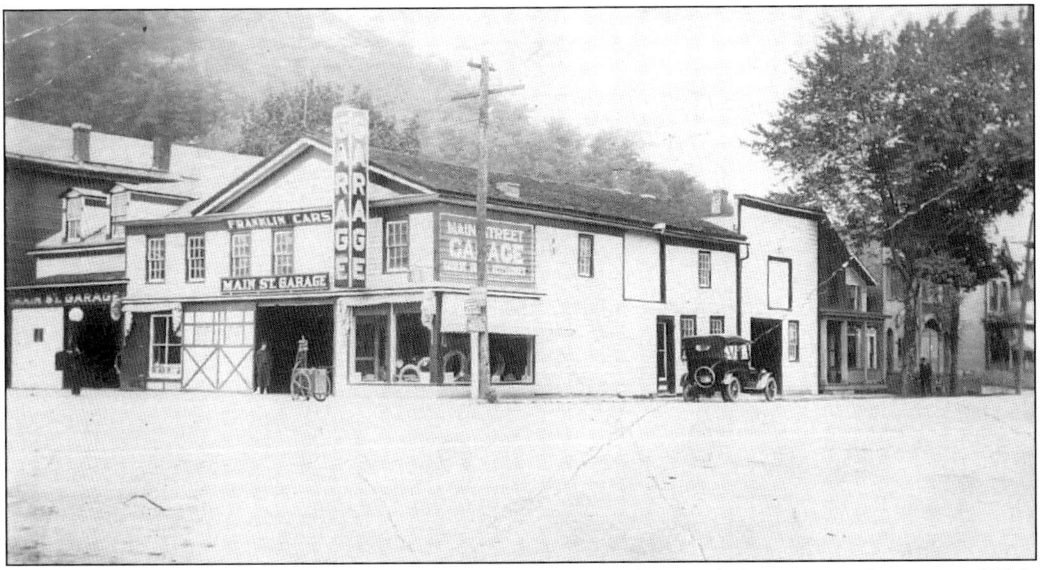

Main Street Garage, on the corner of West Main and Canal Streets, is shown *c.* 1920. (Collection of the Minisink Valley Historical Society.)

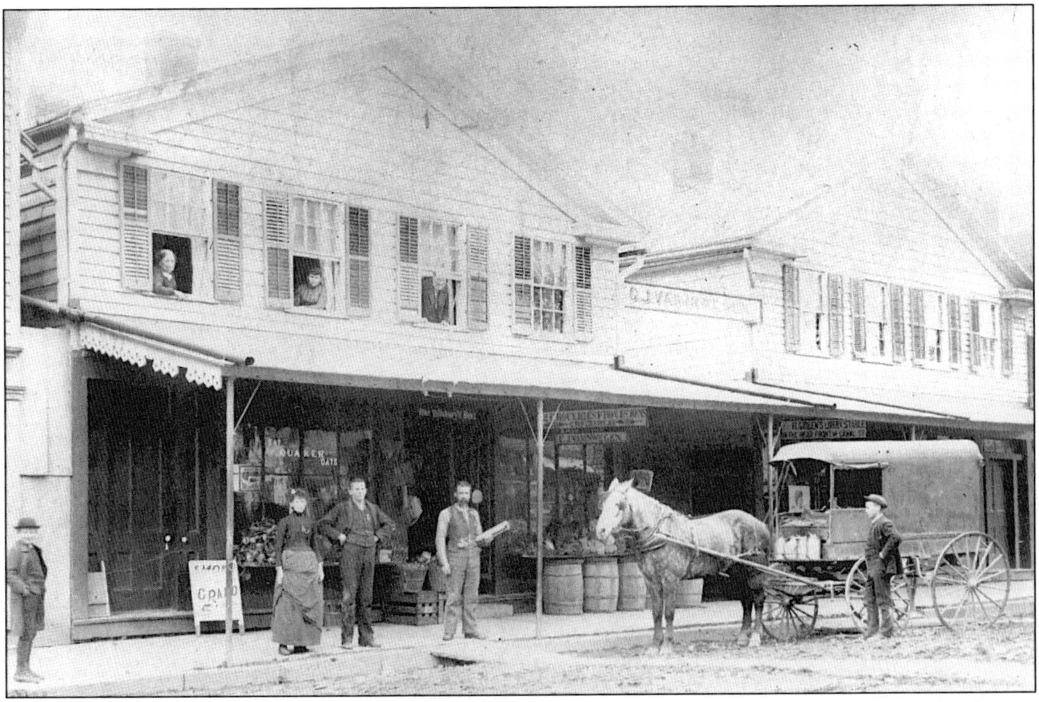

"Remember to eat your Quaker Oats," advertised a sign in the grocery store at 174 Pike Street in the 1890s. (Collection of the Minisink Valley Historical Society.)

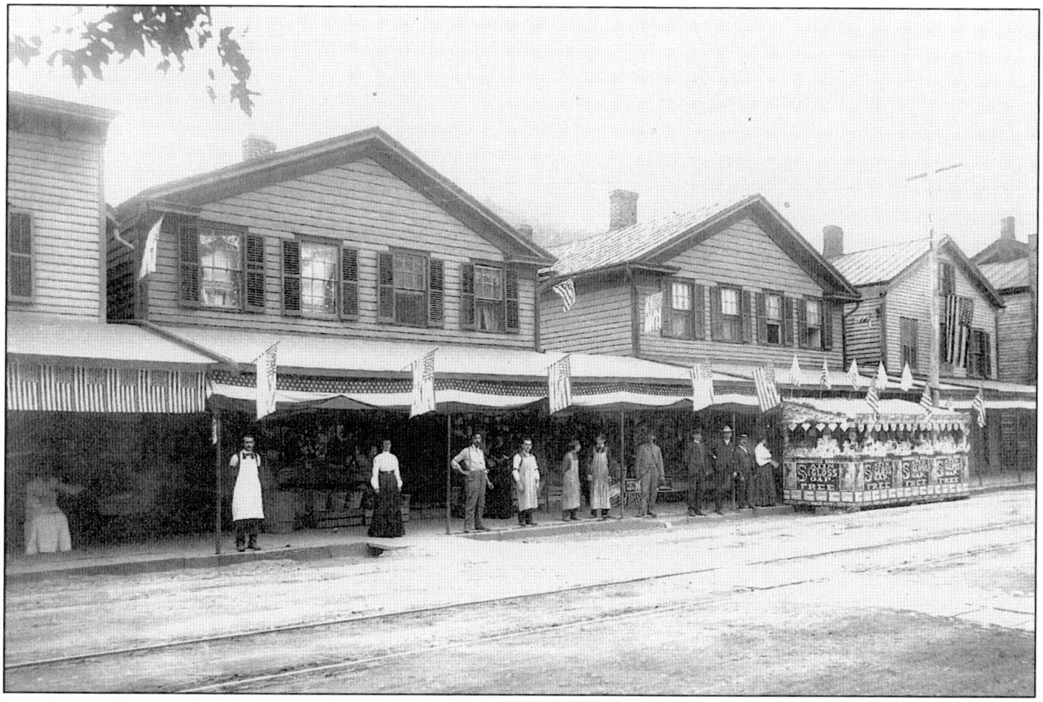

In the early 1900s, upper Pike Street had a totally different appearance. The shop owners stopped to pose for a photograph in the area known as the Banner Market Block. (Collection of the Minisink Valley Historical Society.)

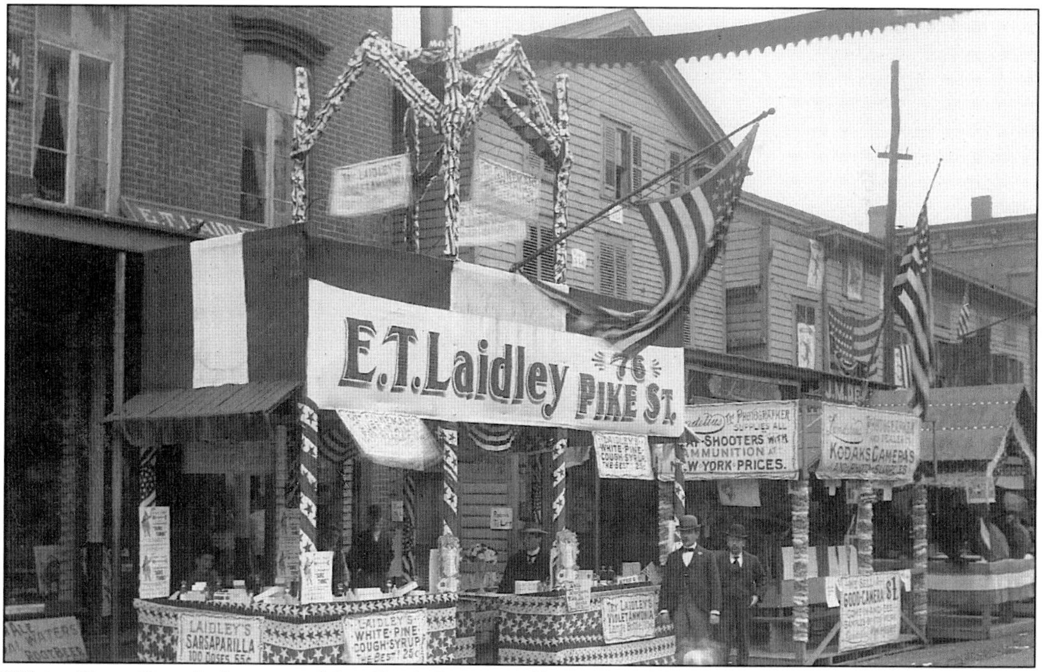

White Pine Cough Syrup and Laidley's Sarsaparilla were sold at E.T. Laidley's at 76 Pike Street. This is the present site of Joe's Coffee Shop on the corner of Hammond and Pike Streets. (Collection of the Minisink Valley Historical Society.)

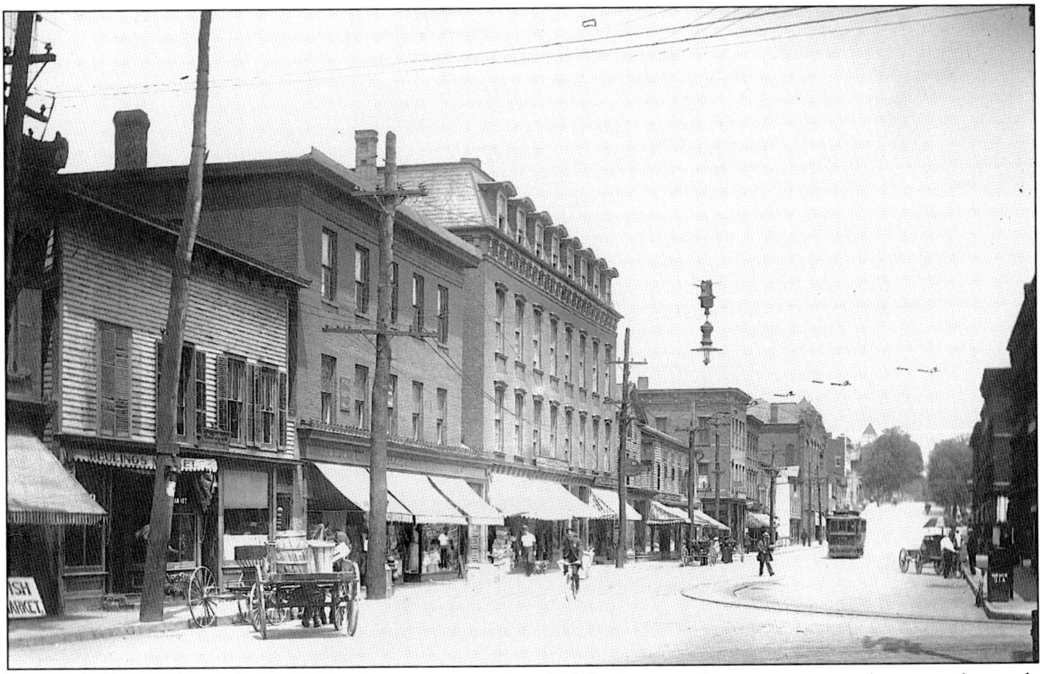

Pike Street, shown in a view looking east c. the 1920s, has undergone many changes through the years, starting with the building of the underpass in 1936. The area on the left shows where the underpass is and the road leading toward Front Street. (Collection of the Minisink Valley Historical Society.)

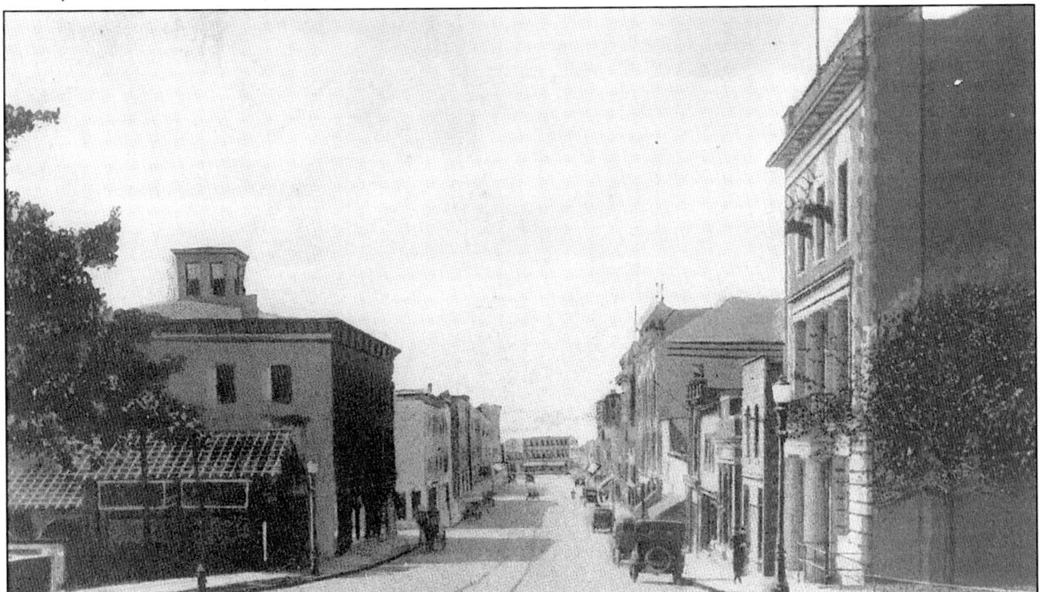

This 1920 view of Pike Street shows the Elks Club on the right. A large brick building stood on the corner of Hammond Street, on the left. Disaster struck in February 1971 when heavy snows on the roof caused the buildings to collapse onto Pike Street. This caused serious concerns for the safety of the older buildings in the city. About 50 buildings were demolished during urban renewal. (Collection of the Minisink Valley Historical Society.)

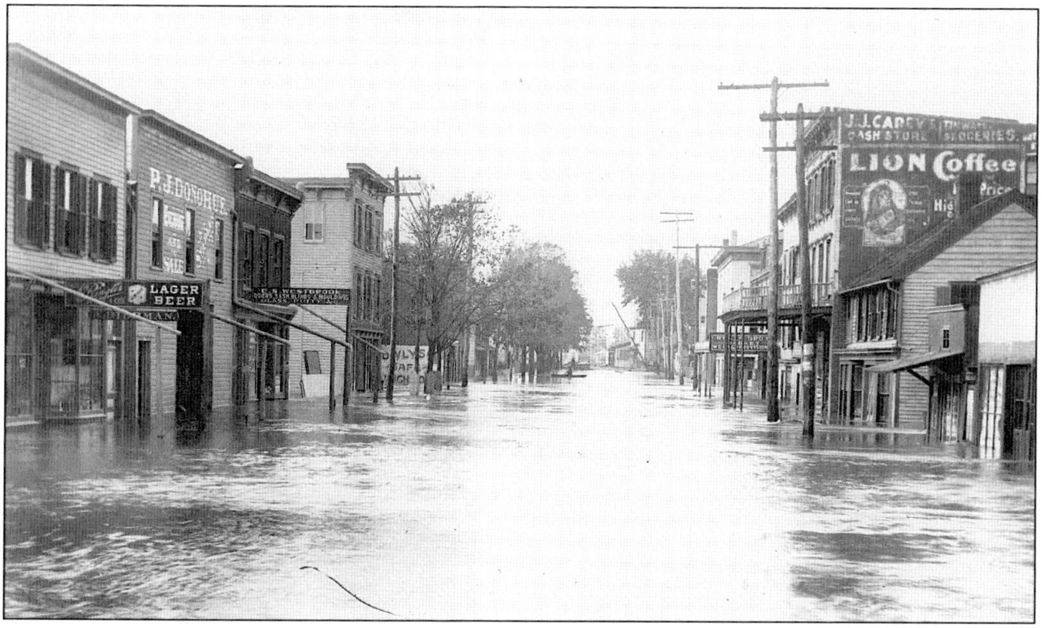

Businesses on Pike Street at the beginning of the 20th century included P.J. Donohue, a lager beer store, at 37 Pike Street. Next door was E.S. Westbrook at 35 Pike Street, which sold building supplies. On the right side was J.J. Carey, a grocery store. Farther down the street was a meat market. (Collection of the Minisink Valley Historical Society.)

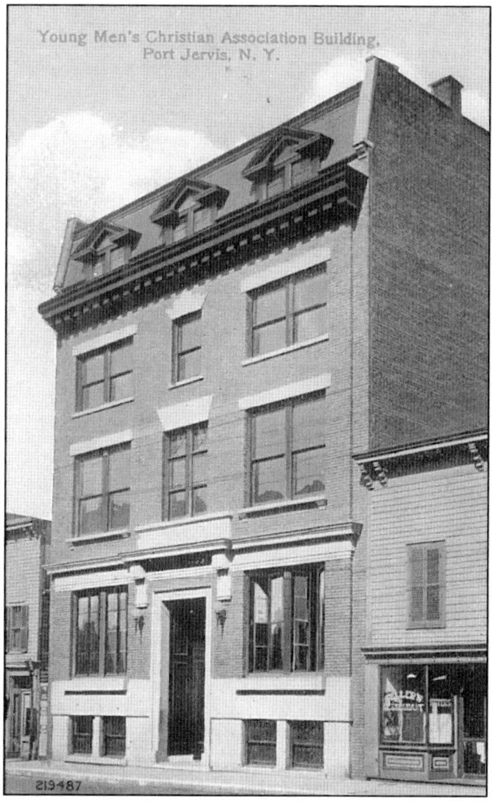

The YMCA Building was erected in 1912. Its uses included housing railroad employees and running community programs. It had been constructed so well that, during its demolition years later, a wrecking crane was needed to knock it down. (Collection of the Minisink Valley Historical Society.)

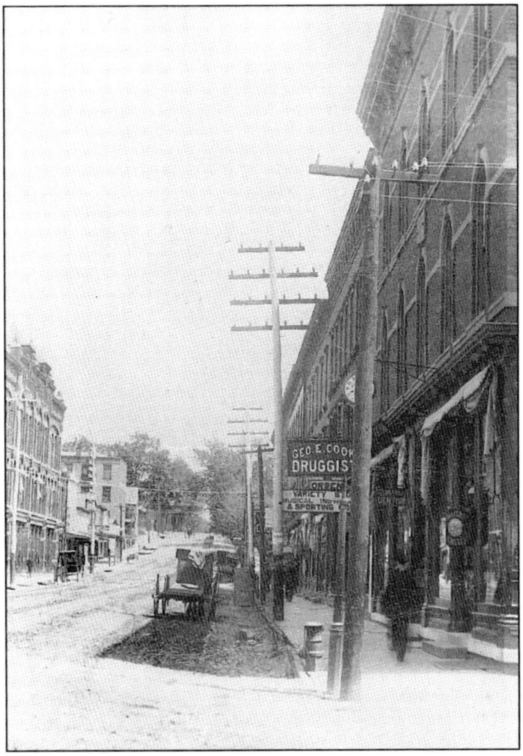

Pike Street, seen in a view looking toward East Main Street, is where George E. Coon's drugstore was located. Coon sold sundries and sporting goods. The large building on the left is the Farnum Building. The Port Jervis Library is in the distance. (Collection of the Minisink Valley Historical Society.)

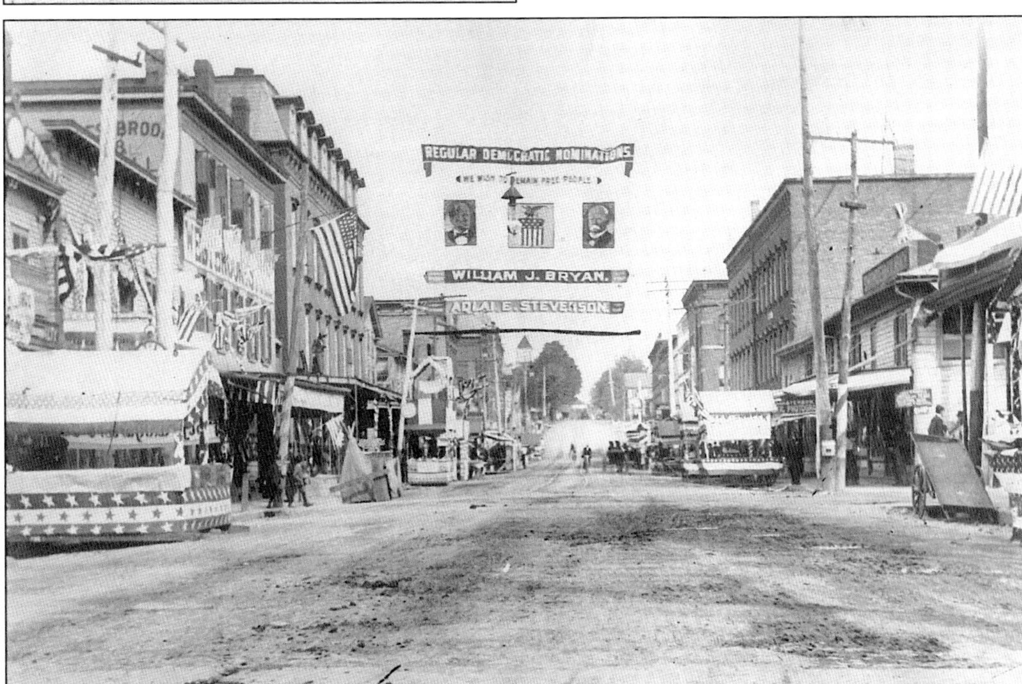

A patriotic scene on Pike Street shows the political support for William Jennings Bryant and Adalai Stevenson during the 1896 presidential election. (Collection of the Minisink Valley Historical Society.)

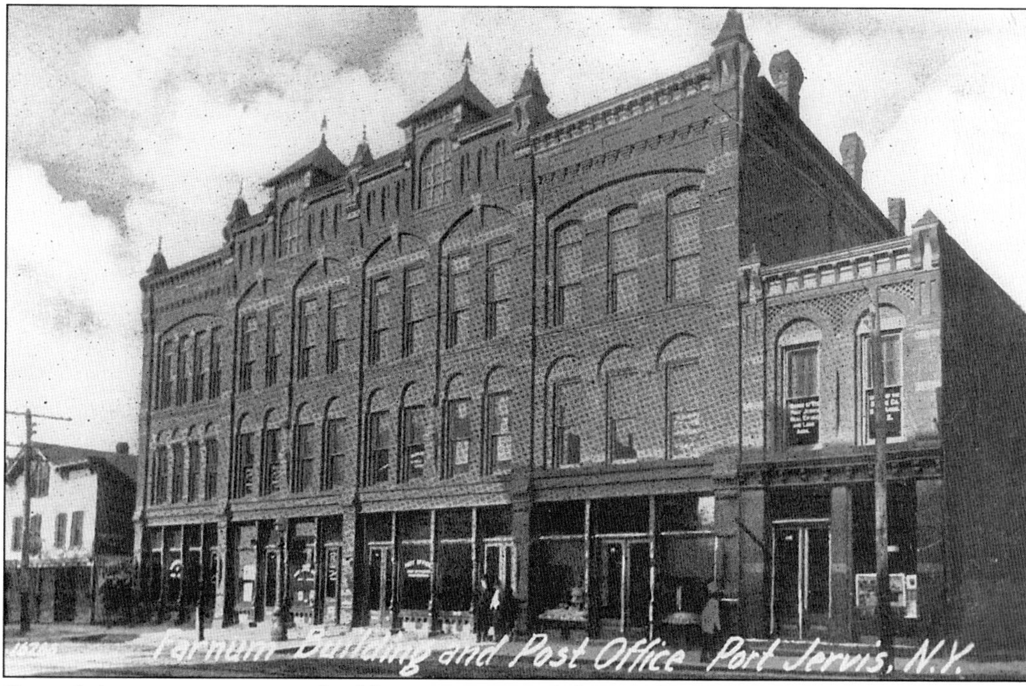

One of the most impressive buildings constructed during the Victorian era was the Masonic Farnum Building. Built in 1882, it housed the post office until 1914, when the current post office was built. This incredible building was demolished during urban renewal. (Collection of the Minisink Valley Historical Society.)

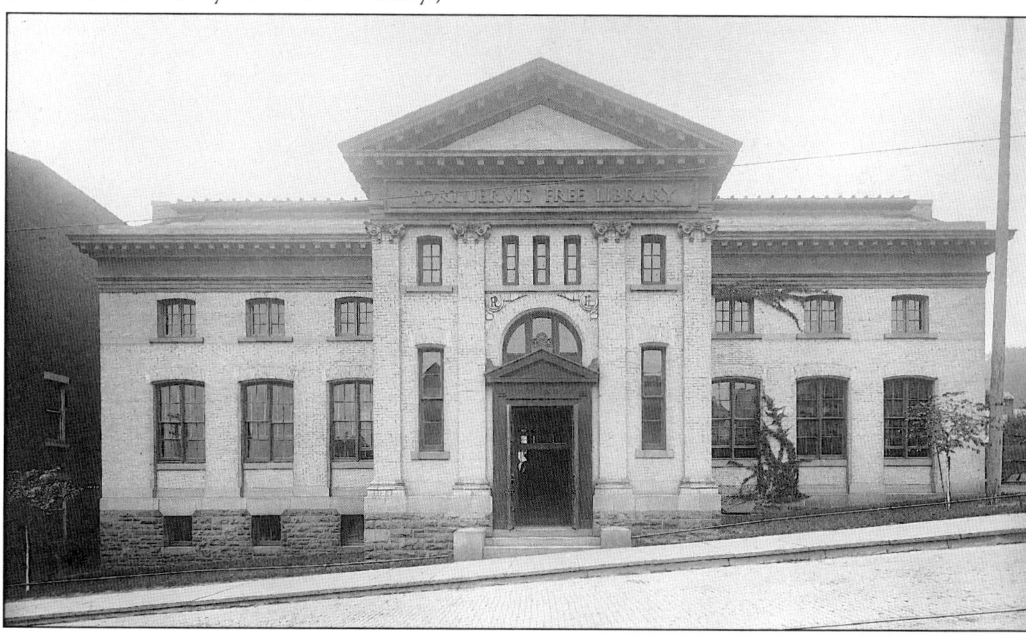

The Carnegie Library, on Pike Street, was built from donations by steel magnate Andrew Carnegie and local businessman Peter Farnum in 1902. The Carnegie Foundation built it as one of 1,600 during this time. Today, only a few hundred of such libraries are still standing. This is also the home of the Minisink Valley Historical Society archives. (Courtesy of Robbie Smith.)

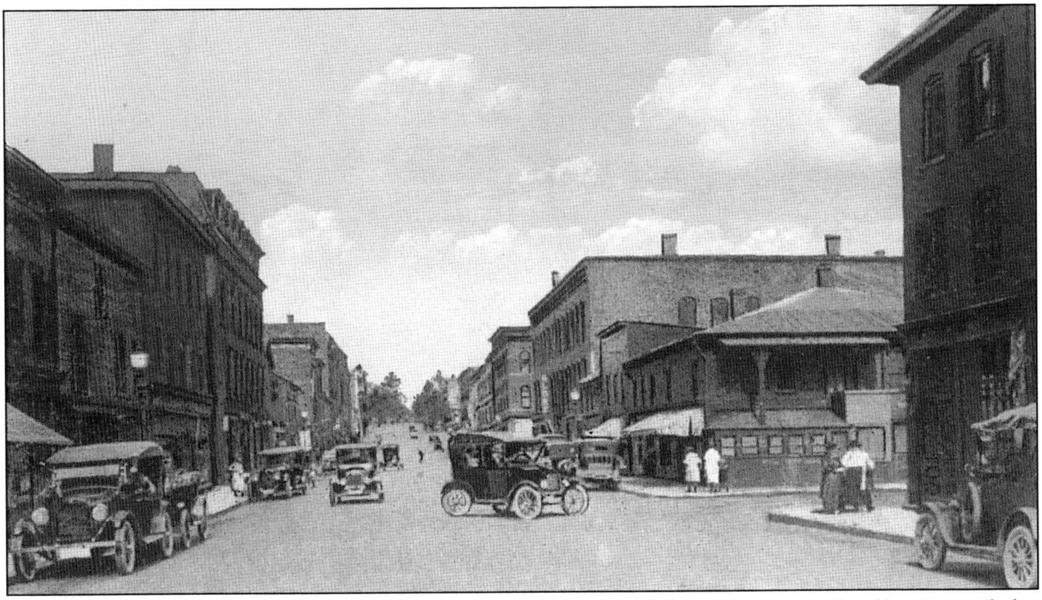

A busy intersection *c.* 1920s was the corner of Pike and Front Streets. (Collection of the Minisink Valley Historical Society.)

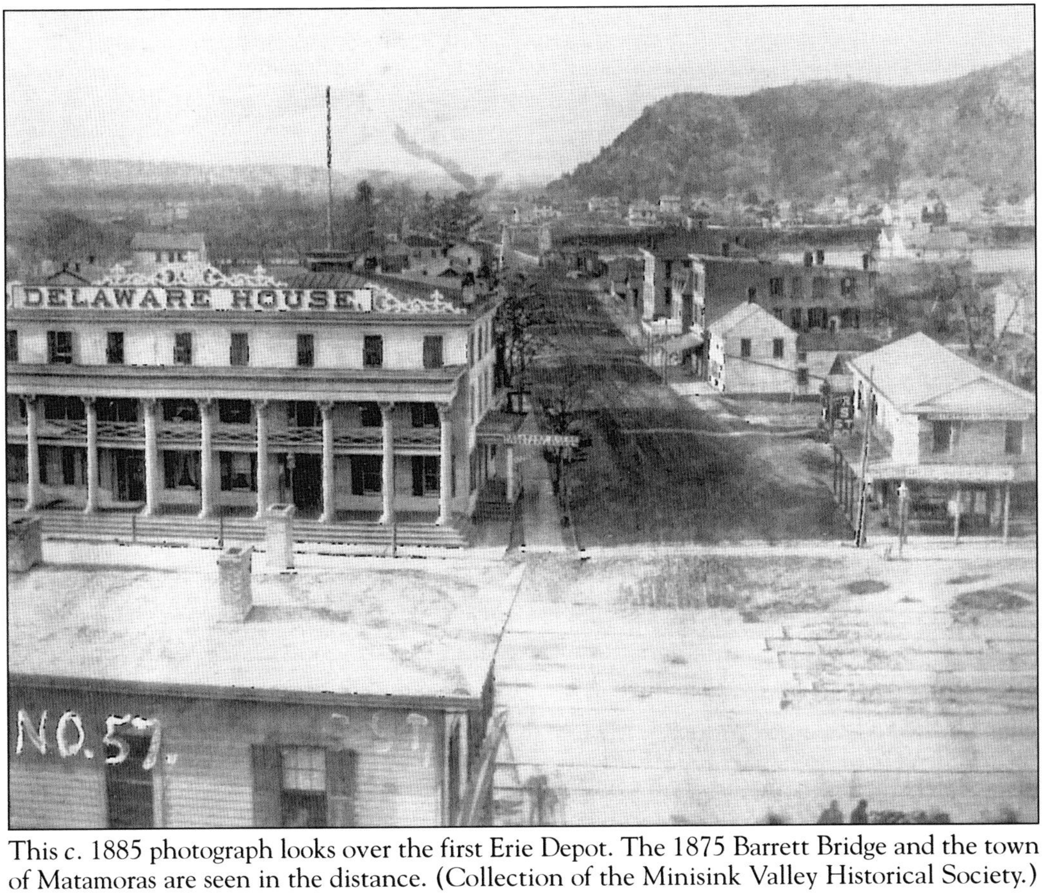

This *c.* 1885 photograph looks over the first Erie Depot. The 1875 Barrett Bridge and the town of Matamoras are seen in the distance. (Collection of the Minisink Valley Historical Society.)

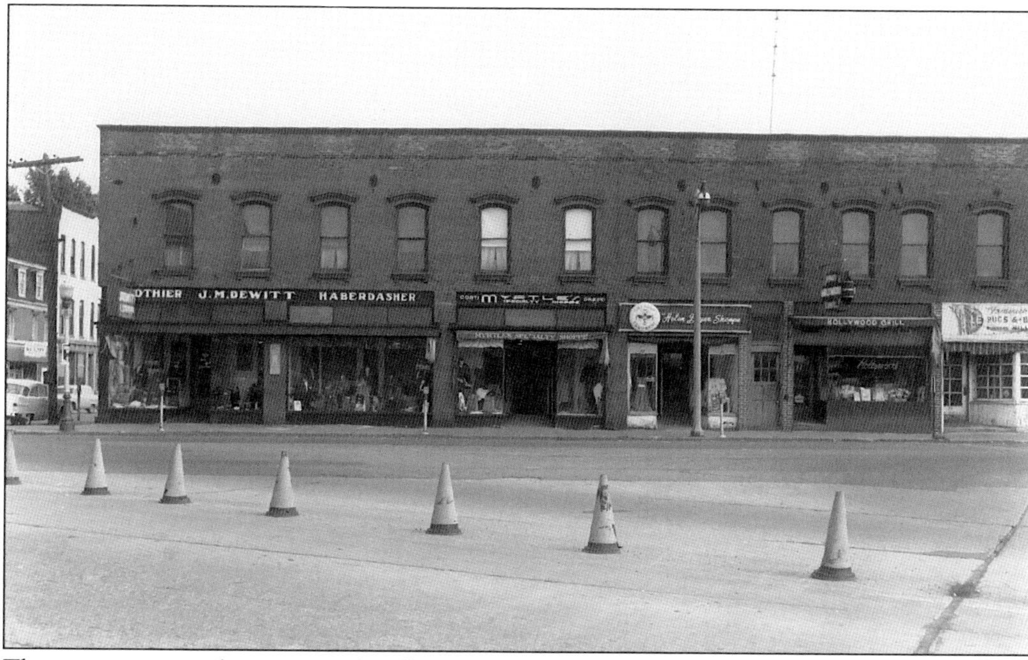

These stores near the corner of Ball and Pike Streets were very popular in the late 1950s. J.M. Dewitt had been in business in and around the city for more than 55 years, starting first in Matamoras, Pennsylvania. (Courtesy of John Hess.)

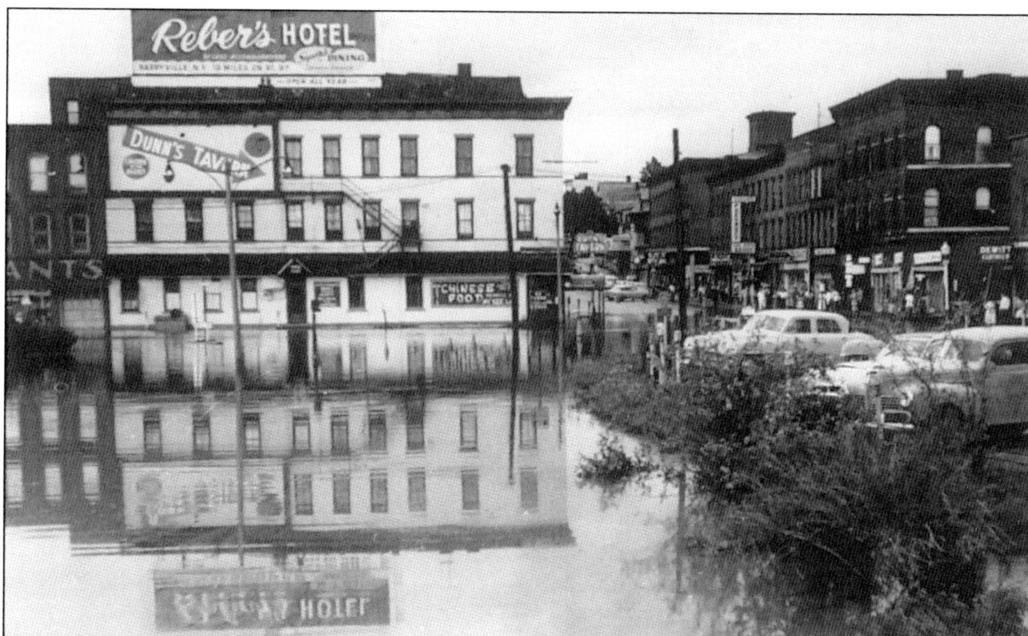

For many years, as vehicles drove out of the underpass to go up toward Pike Street, Dunn's Tavern was the first business that people noticed. The sign above the restaurant is an advertisement for Reber's, another eating establishment on Route 97 in Barryville. This photograph was taken during the Flood of 1955. (Collection of the Minisink Valley Historical Society.)

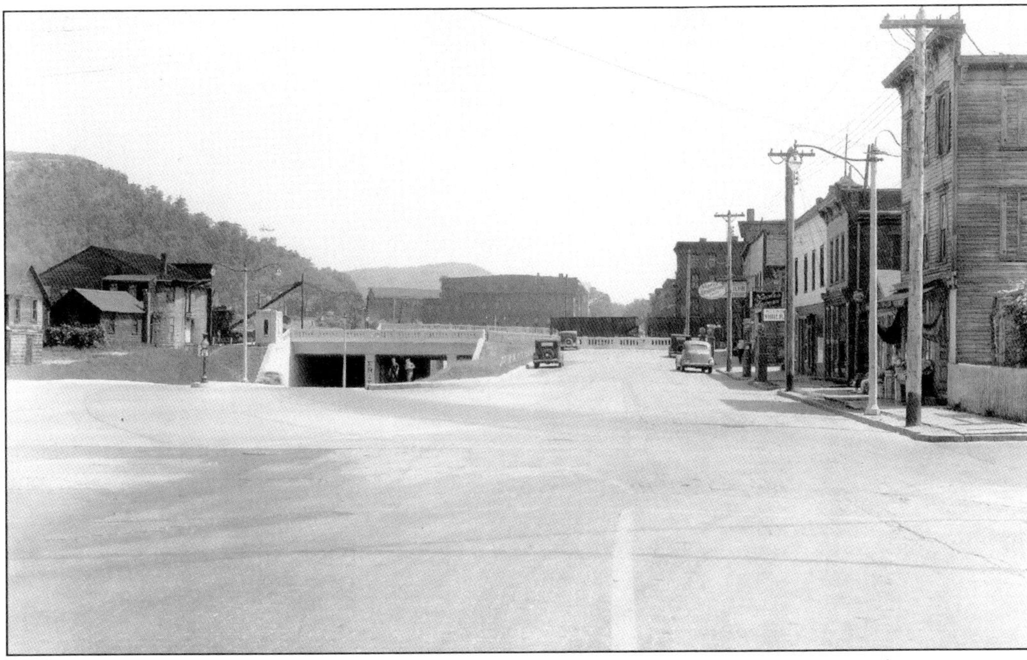

After the underpass was completed in 1937, these few stores were somewhat separated from the main business district, yet they still thrived. (Collection of the Minisink Valley Historical Society.)

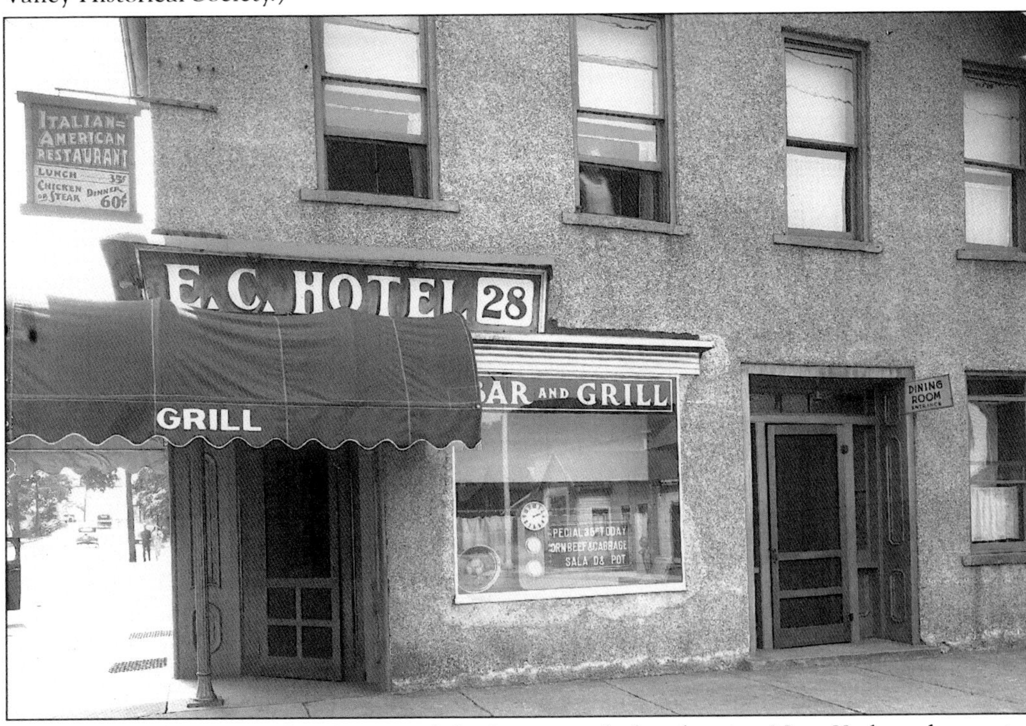

Today, this is known as Gino's, one of the last stops before leaving New York and entering Pennsylvania. In the 1940s, it was the E.C. Hotel, named for its founder, Encino Codichini. The business is still owned and operated by the Codichini family. (Courtesy of John Hess.)

Eight

STREET SCENES

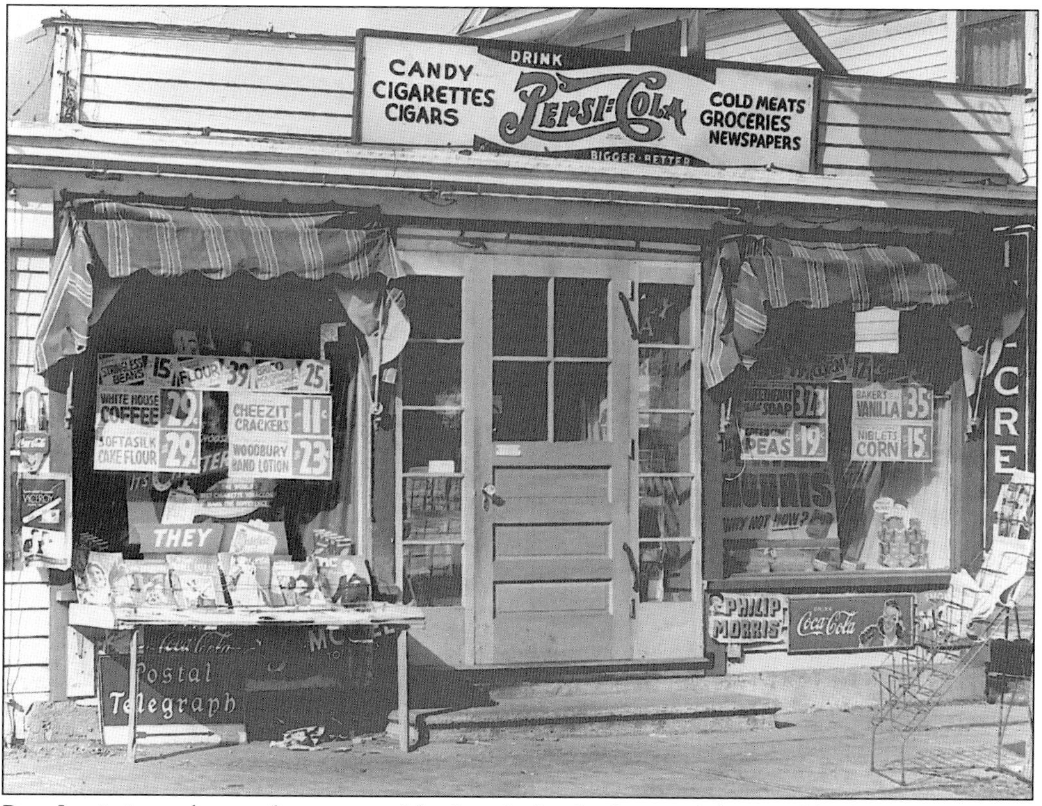

Port Jervis is made up of many neighborhoods. In the heart of the neighborhood were many candy stores. The shops and the people who ran them contributed to the sense of community. In the Acre, there was Trovei's and Colaiaco's; in the Kingston Avenue area, there was Hoppey's. These stores are long gone, but the children growing up in those areas will always remember the fond memories of going to the candy store. In 1940, Hess' Candy Store opened on Kingston Avenue. After a few years, it moved just down the street. The store, which is still open, has been part of that community ever since. (Courtesy of John Hess.)

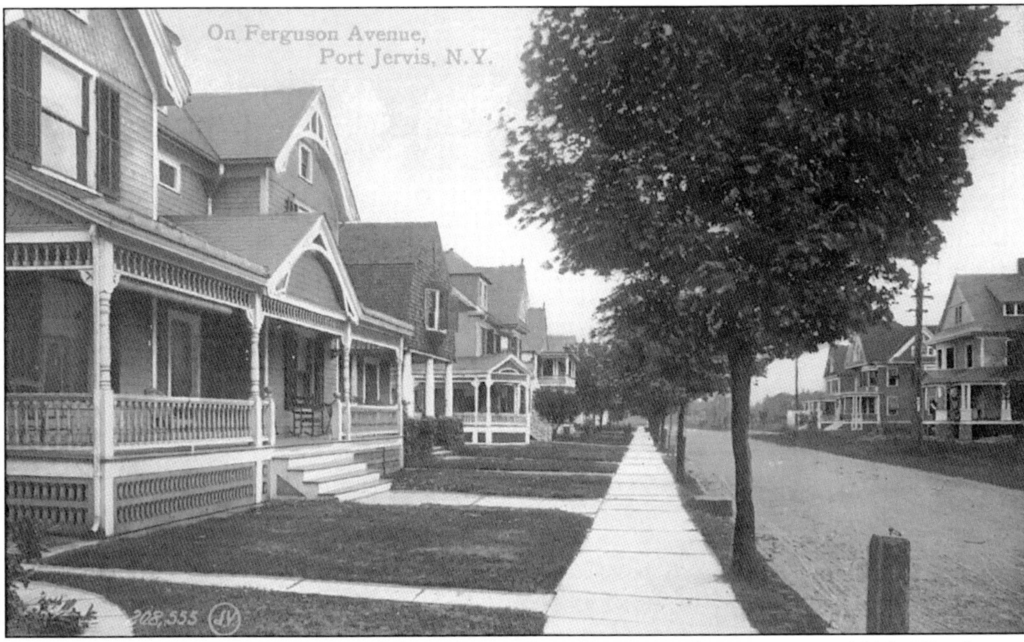

This postcard shows that not much has changed on Ferguson Avenue since 1910. The homes are still just as elegant. (Courtesy of Matt and Carol Osterberg.)

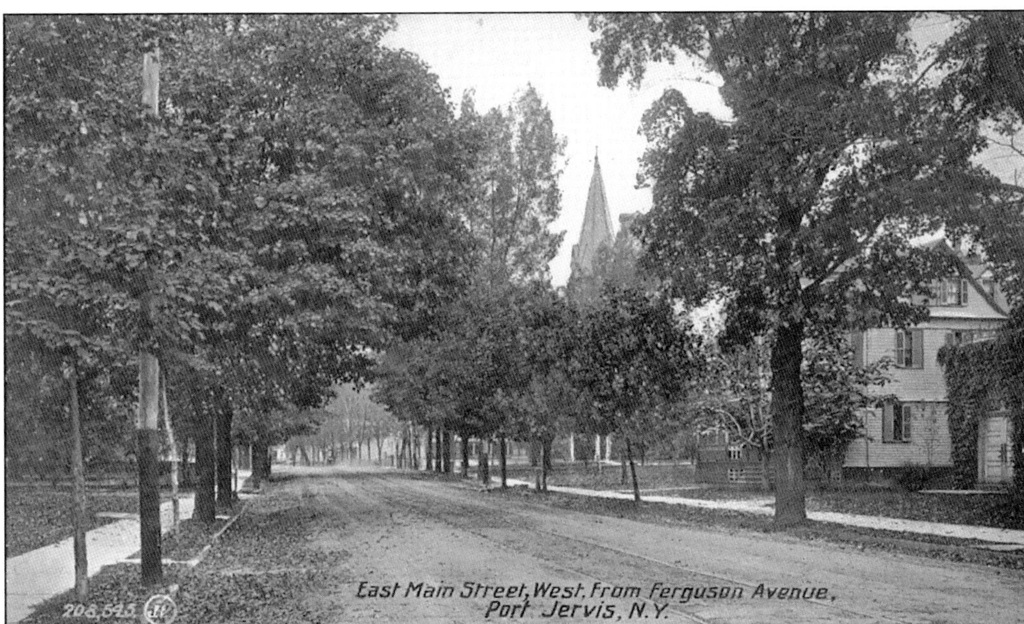

East Main Street was still unpaved when this postcard was produced in 1919. On the right can be seen a corner of the Baptist church. Farther up in the distance is the Deerpark Reformed Church. (Courtesy of Matt and Carol Osterberg.)

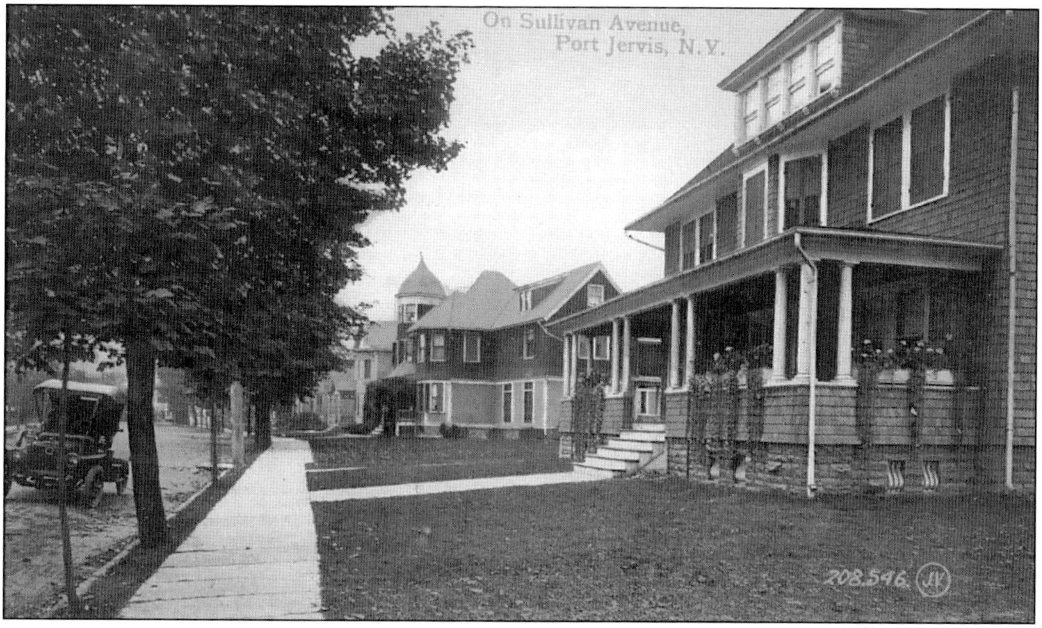

So many sections in Port Jervis have such grand homes. This 1912 postcard of Sullivan Avenue proves what a grand city Port Jervis really was and continues to be. (Courtesy of Matt and Carol Osterberg.)

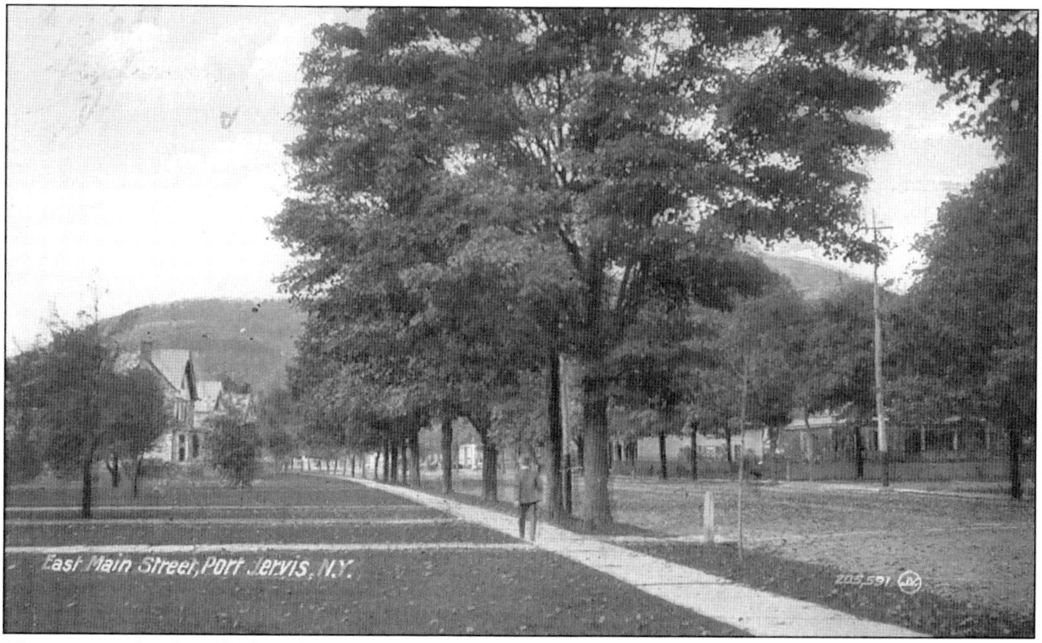

This view of sidewalk-lined East Main Street in 1908 shows the block between Elizabeth and Sussex Streets. (Courtesy of Ed Nikles Jr.)

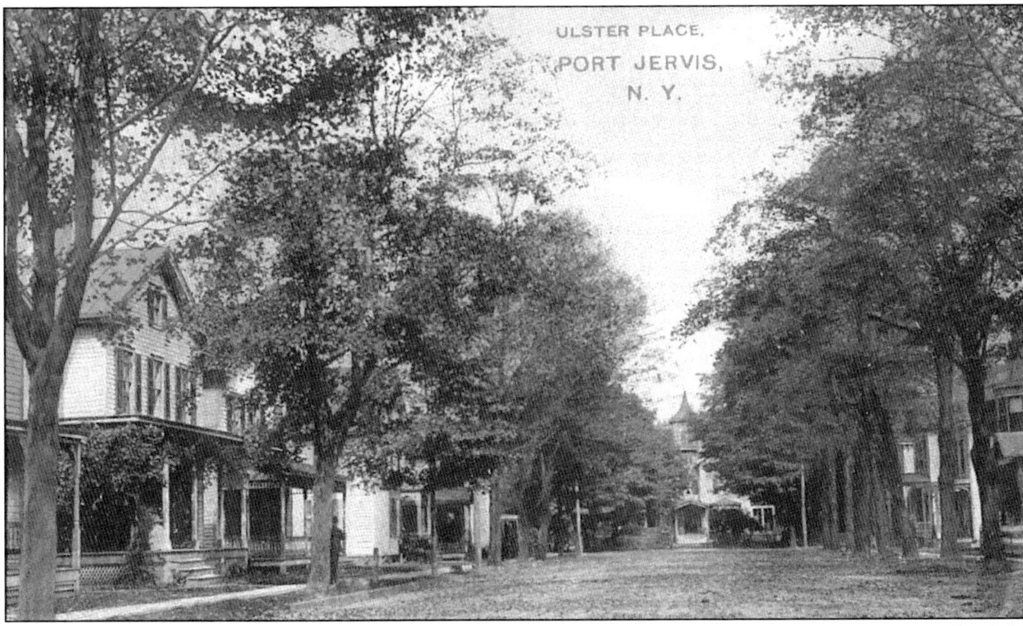

This is the ultimate picture of Ulster Place with the stately Farnum House at the end of the street. (Courtesy of Matt and Carol Osterberg.)

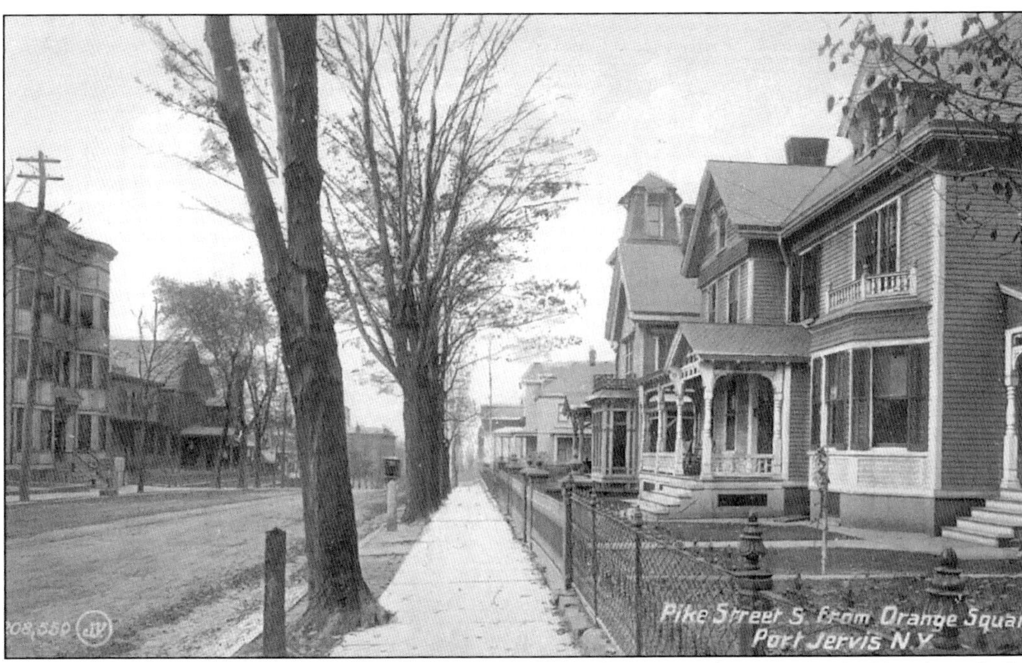

In 1909, these handsome homes lined Pike Street between the Minisink Hotel and the Port Jervis Library. (Courtesy of Ed Nikles Jr.)

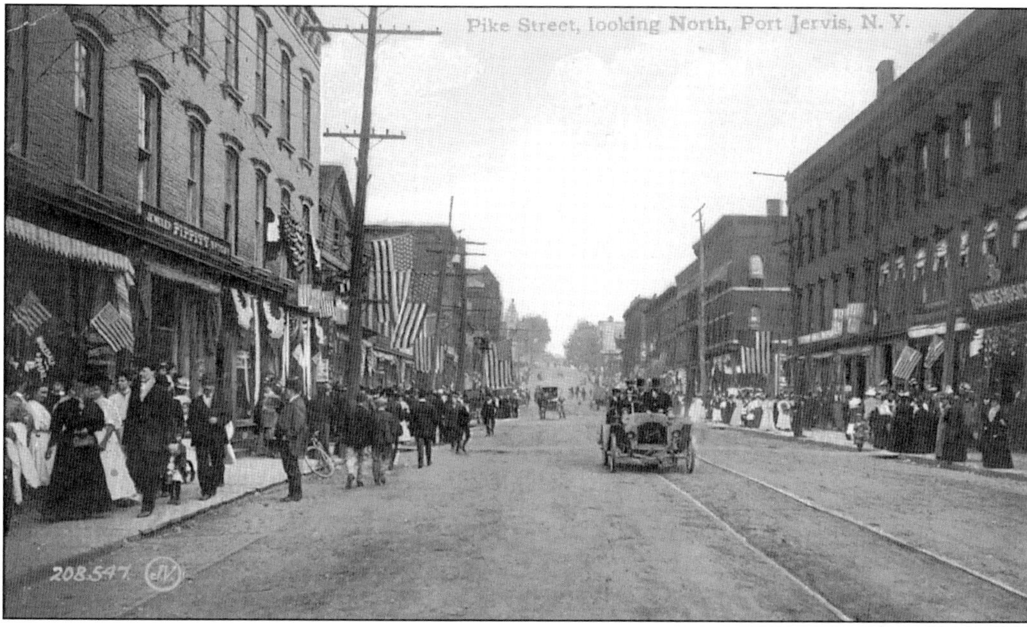

A picturesque postcard of Pike Street dates from the first decade of the 20th century. (Courtesy of Matt and Carol Osterberg.)

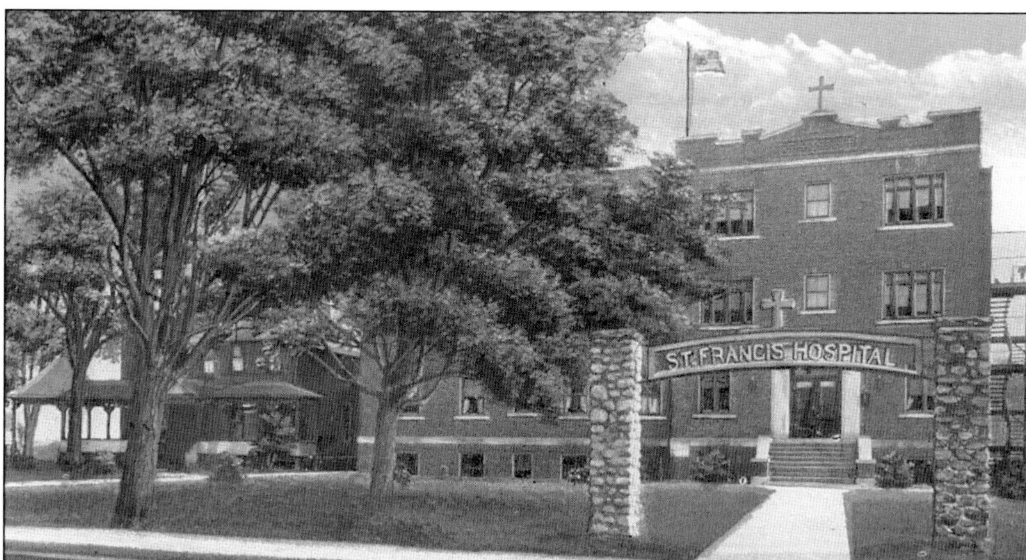

In 1923, the Sisters of St. Francis purchased the Howell estate on East Main Street. This is where the hospital was erected. The hospital had 56 beds and support services to care for the sick and the needy of the surrounding communities. In 1956, the Sisters of Mercy of the Province of New York took over the management of the hospital. After extensive building programs throughout the years, Mercy Hospital is now owned by the organization of Bon Secours. (Courtesy of Matt and Carol Osterberg.)

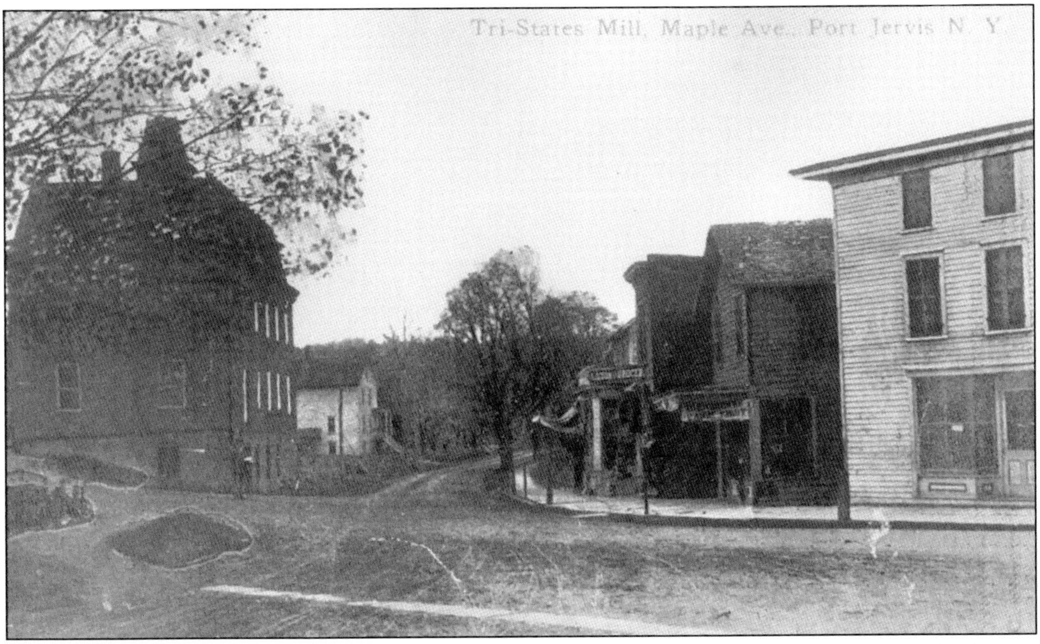

The Old Mine Road entered Port Jervis at Tri-States. This road, one of the oldest highways in the United States, led to Kingston, New York. In earlier years, this area was known as Carpenter's Point. It did not become part of Port Jervis until 1890. (Collection of the Minisink Valley Historical Society.)

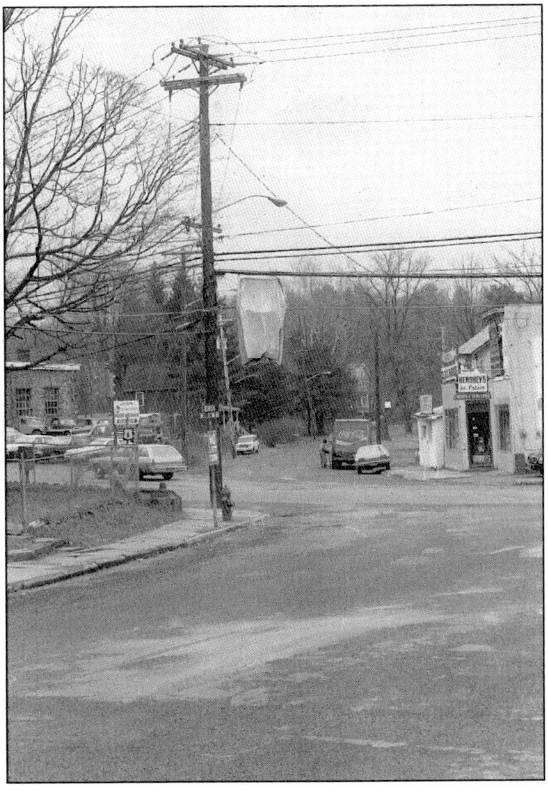

This is a later view of the Tri-States area. By the 1970s, when this picture was taken, many of the original buildings had disappeared. (Collection of the Minisink Valley Historical Society.)

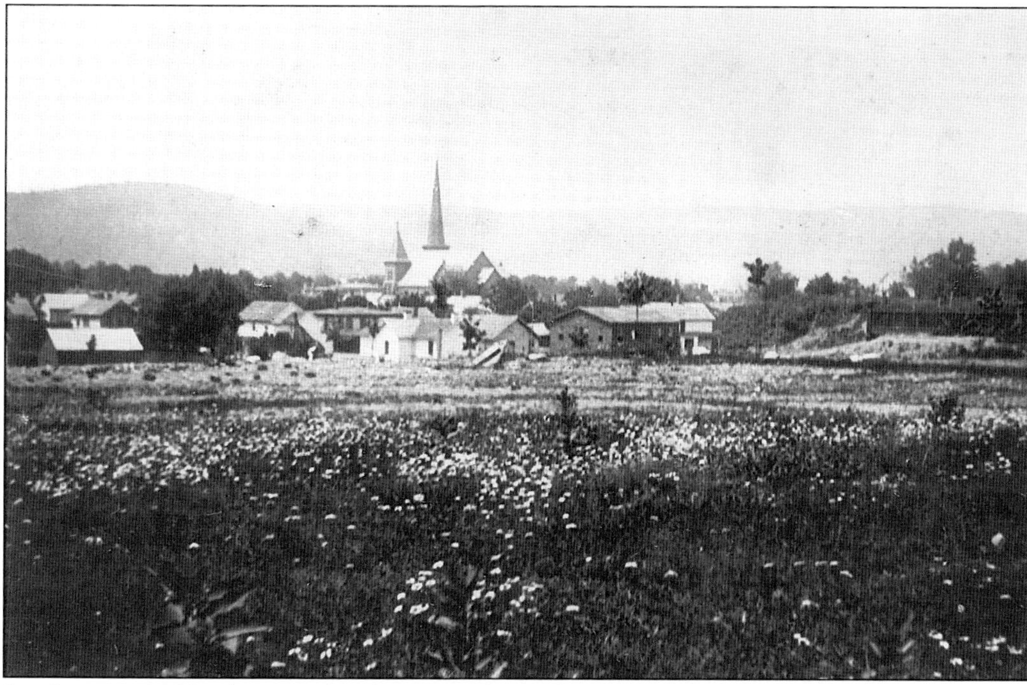

In this pre-1888 photograph, the second ward section of Port Jervis was not heavily populated. Viewed in the distance is St. Mary's Church. (Collection of the Minisink Valley Historical Society.)

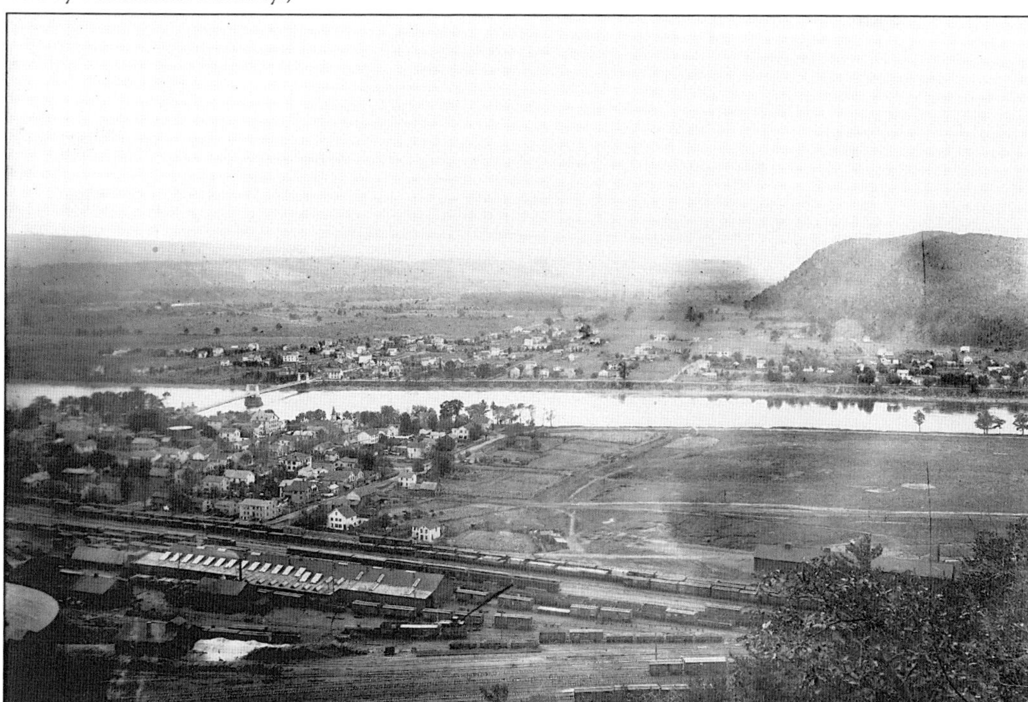

The Acre and almost all of Matamoras, Pennsylvania, are visible in this pre-1892 photograph. (Courtesy of Robbie Smith.)

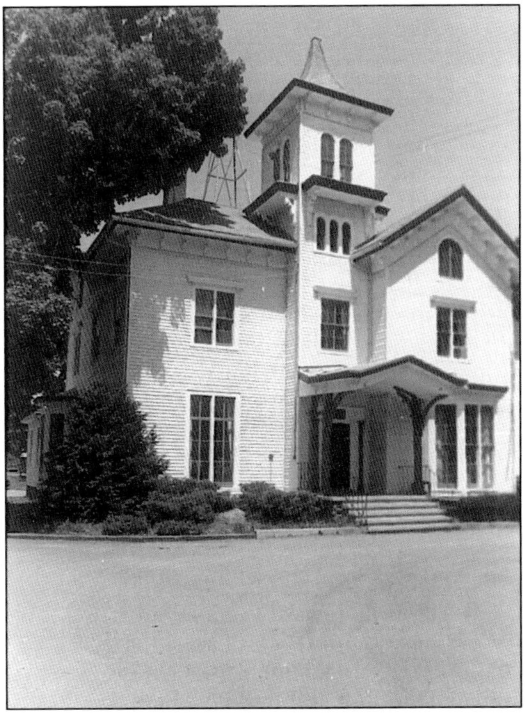

Another of the city's most important parks, the Samuel Farnum homestead was built in the late 1850s and was donated to the city of Port Jervis in December 1936. The Farnums were active in the D & H Canal, local business, and community affairs. It still graces the city at the end of Ulster Place. (Collection of the Minisink Valley Historical Society.)

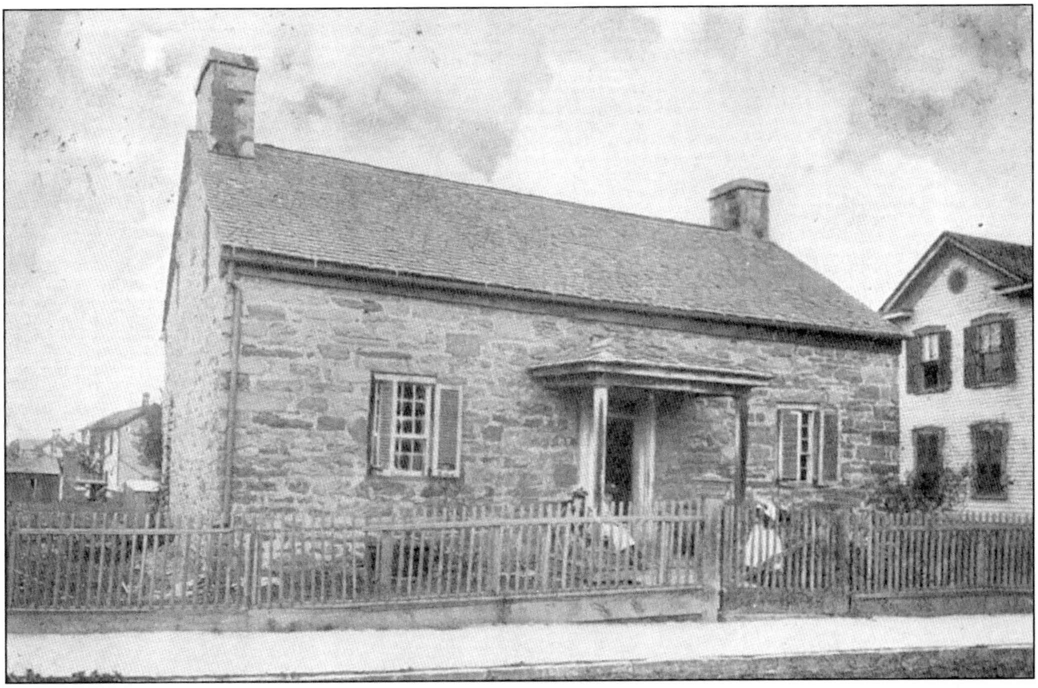

The old Decker Stone House, also known as Fort Decker, was built prior to 1760. In its history, it has been a military post, a trading store, and the headquarters of John B. Jervis while he oversaw the construction of the D & H Canal. Joseph Brandt once attacked it during the Battle of Minisink. The building, at 127 West Main Street, is the home of the Minisink Valley Historical Society. (Collection of the Minisink Valley Historical Society.)

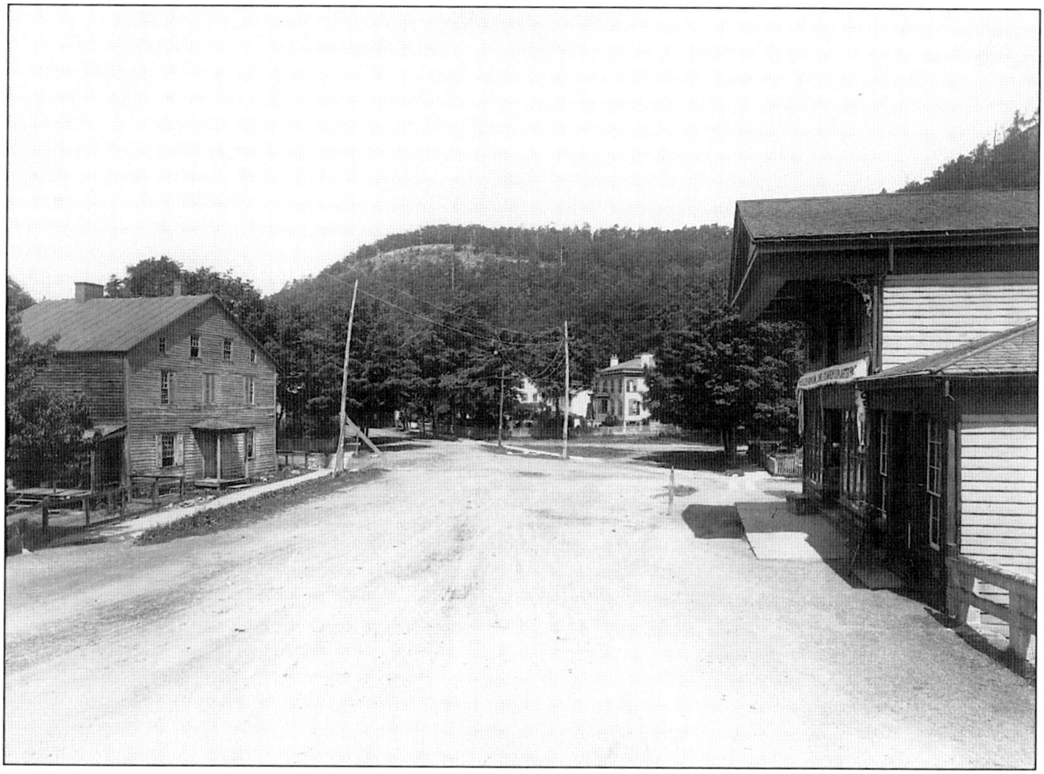

This is an early-20th-century photograph of the corner of West Main, Hudson, and Delaware Streets. (Collection of the Minisink Valley Historical Society.)

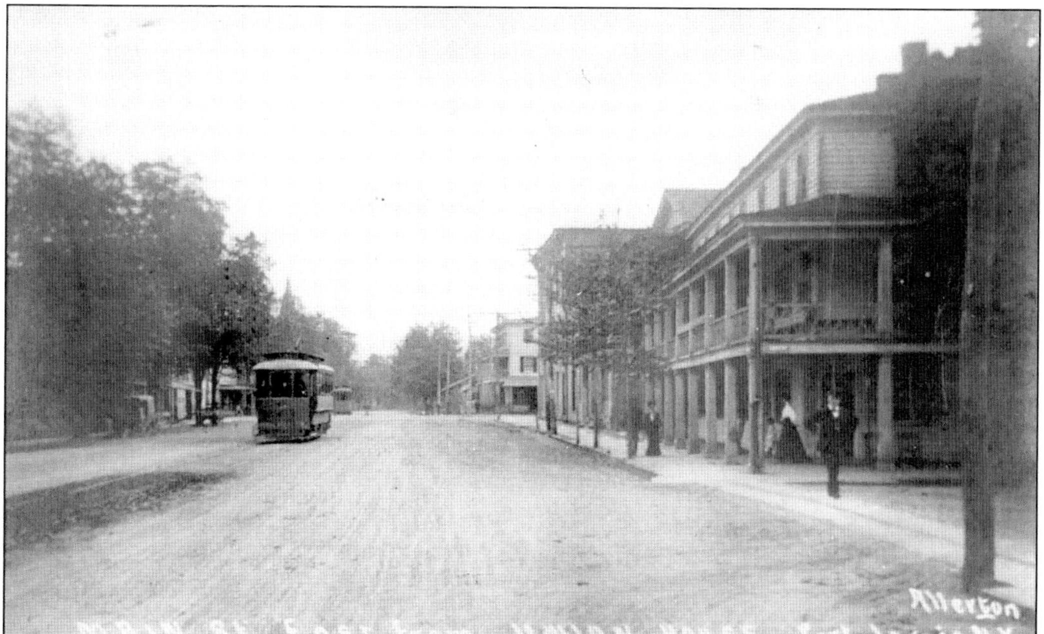

West Main Street, shown in a view looking east in the early 1900s, was home to the Union House Hotel. (Collection of the Minisink Valley Historical Society.)

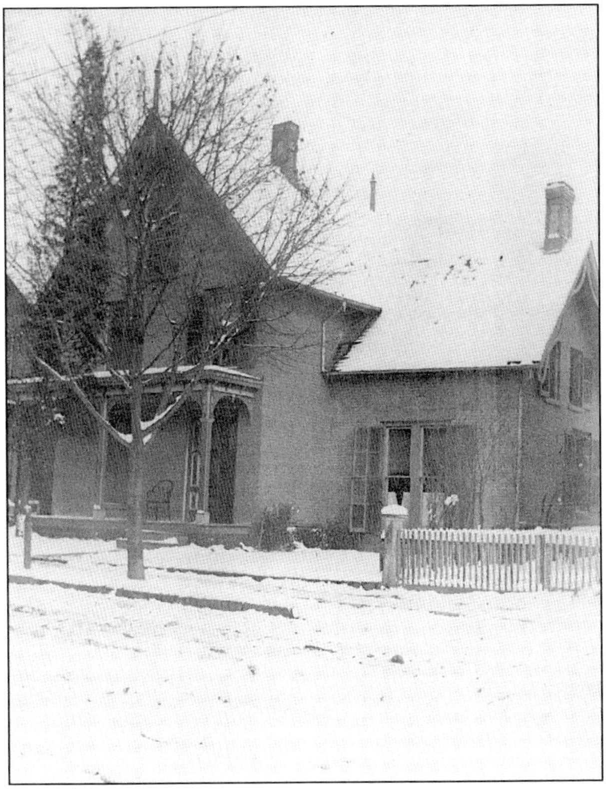

This stately home, built in July 1852 in Port Jervis, can still be seen at 70 Ball Street. Today it is the residence of Paul and Jane Connelly. (Collection of the Minisink Valley Historical Society.)

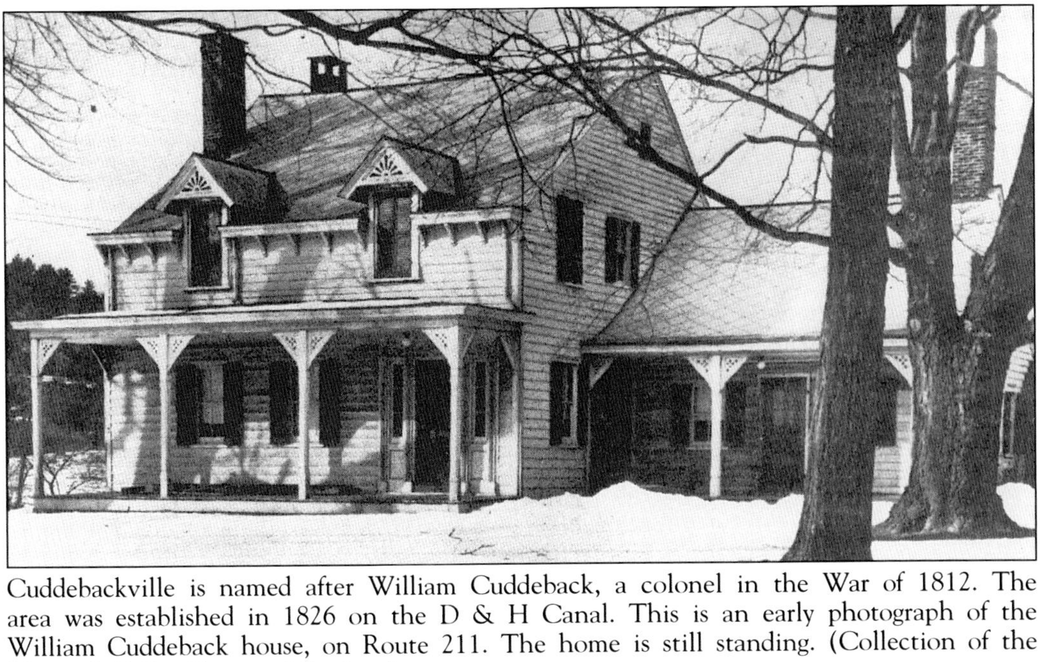

Cuddebackville is named after William Cuddeback, a colonel in the War of 1812. The area was established in 1826 on the D & H Canal. This is an early photograph of the William Cuddeback house, on Route 211. The home is still standing. (Collection of the Minisink Valley Historical Society.)

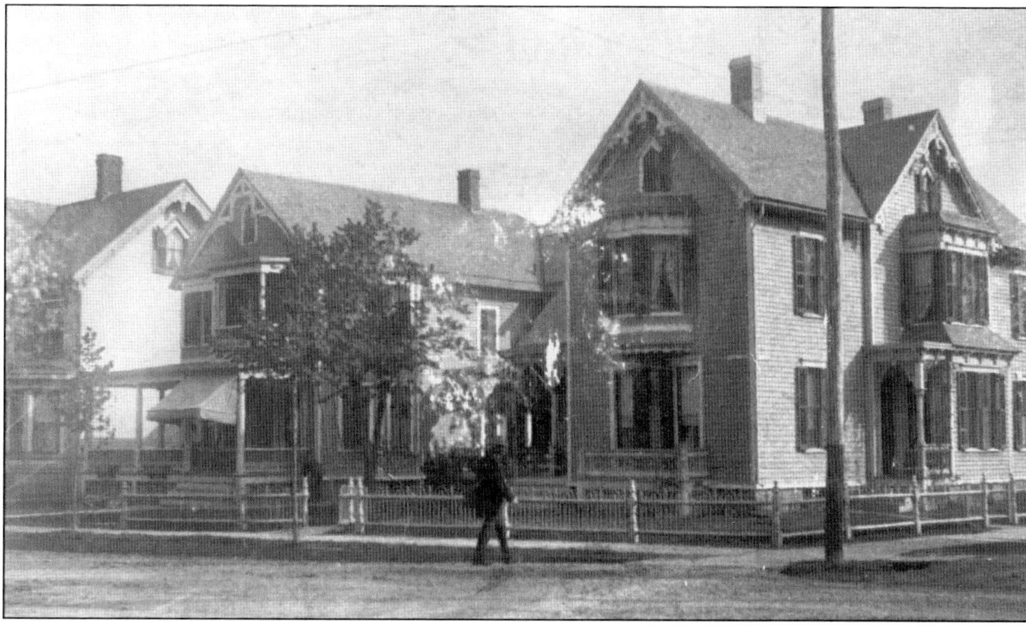

Three elegant houses stand on East Main Street near Sussex Street. The house on the left is the law firm of Cuddeback and Onofry, established in 1873. In the middle is a doctor's office, and on the corner is an apartment building. (Collection of the Minisink Valley Historical Society.)

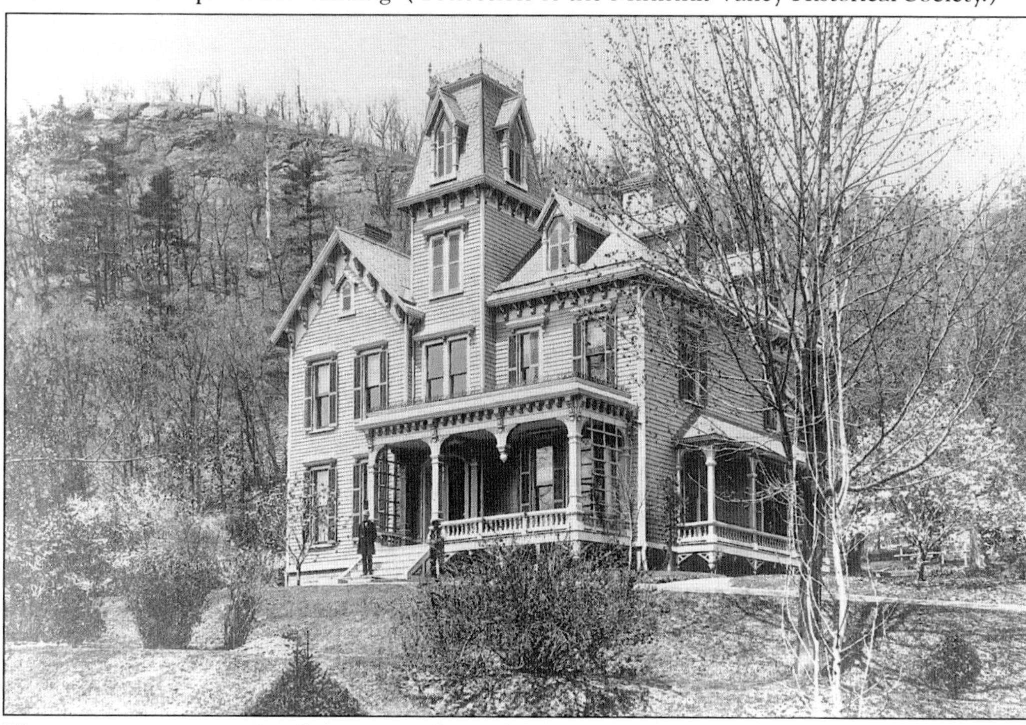

This is a great example of the magnificent homes that dot the landscape throughout Port Jervis. Built in 1865 on West Main Street, this home was owned by one of the members of the Cuddeback family until the late 20th century and is still standing just below Point Peter. (Courtesy of Robbie Smith.)

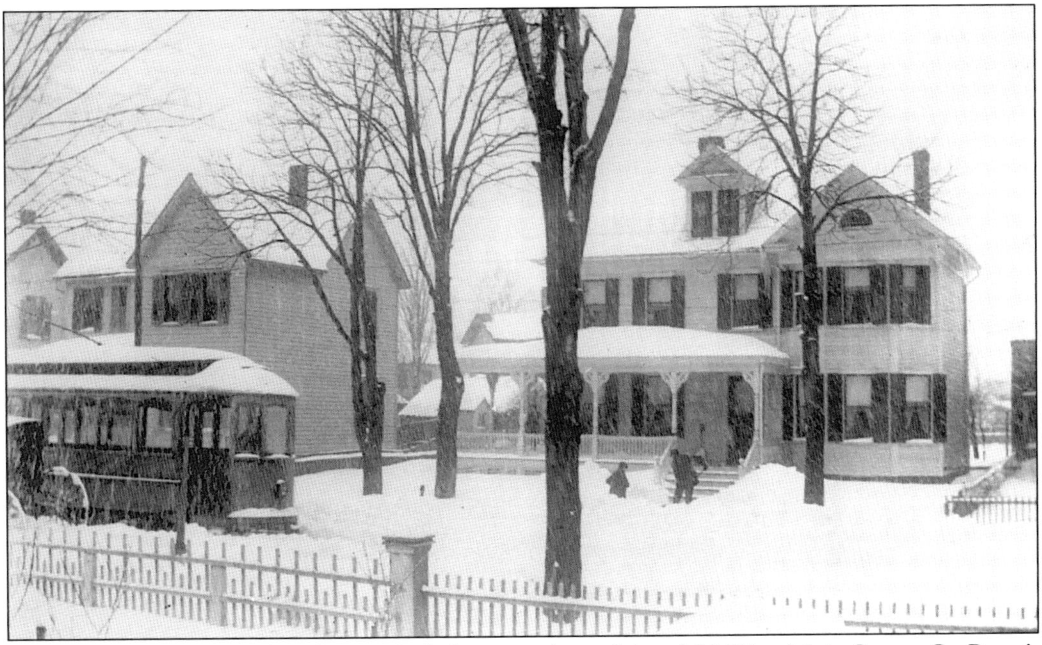

The two houses depicted in this *c.* 1915 photograph are 34 and 36 West Main Street. St. Peter's Lutheran Church is across the street. (Collection of the Minisink Valley Historical Society.)

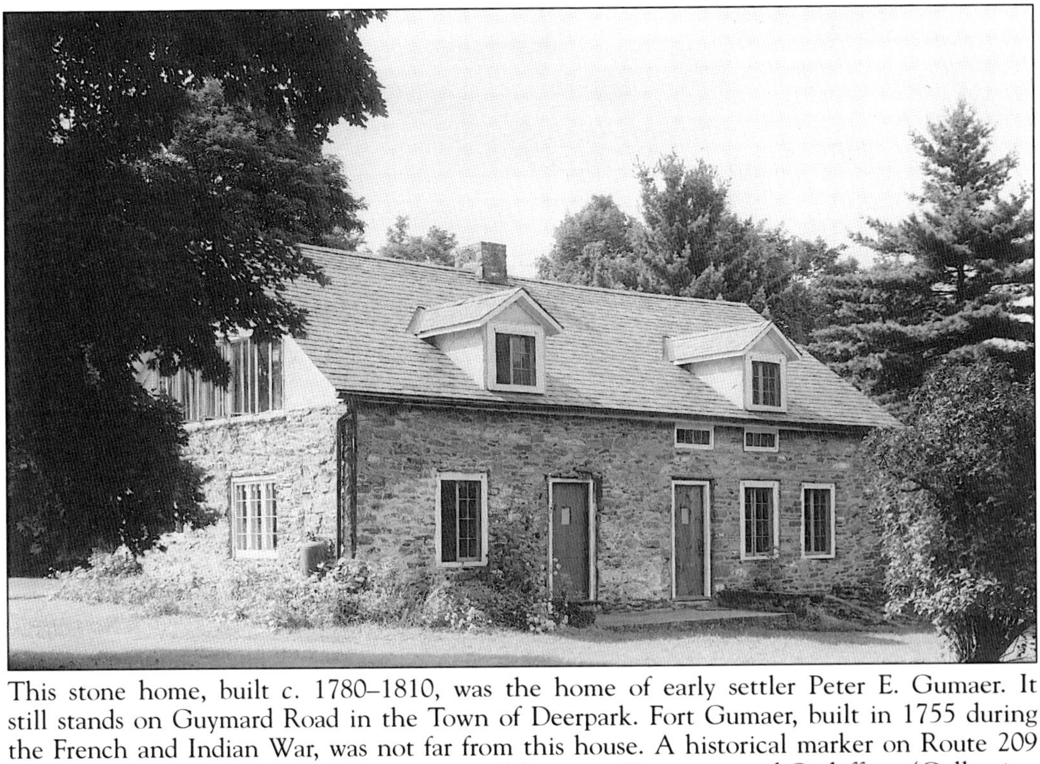

This stone home, built *c.* 1780–1810, was the home of early settler Peter E. Gumaer. It still stands on Guymard Road in the Town of Deerpark. Fort Gumaer, built in 1755 during the French and Indian War, was not far from this house. A historical marker on Route 209 commands the spot where the fort once stood, between Huguenot and Godeffroy. (Collection of the Minisink Valley Historical Society.)

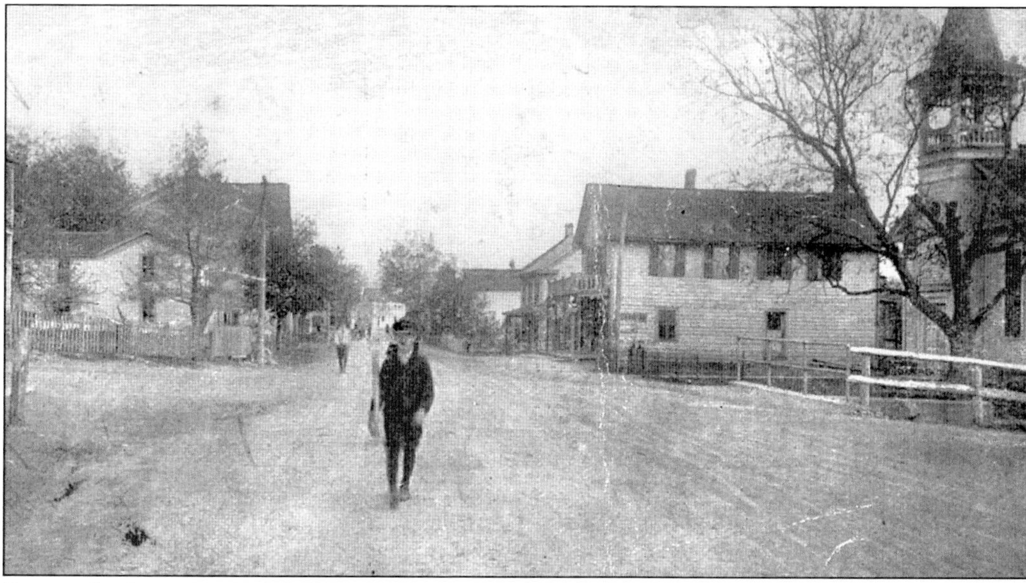

Sparrowbush was named for H.L. Sparrow, a timber dealer who rafted his goods down Delaware River to the Philadelphia shipyards in the early 1800s. The building on the right is the Sparrowbush Methodist Church. Gamo's Country Store is on the left. The view down Main Street looks toward Port Jervis. (Collection of the Minisink Valley Historical Society.)

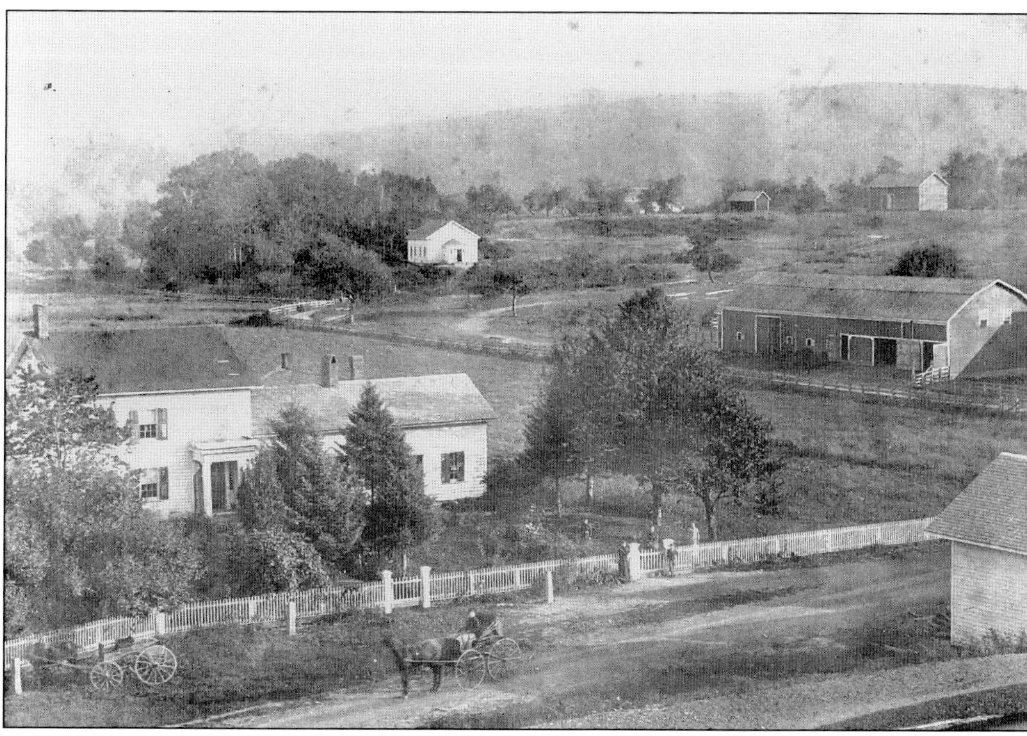

The house on the left in this photograph of Myers Grove in Godeffroy is still standing at 8 Canal Drive. The former Godeffroy School is the small white building in the center of this photograph. (Collection of the Minisink Valley Historical Society.)

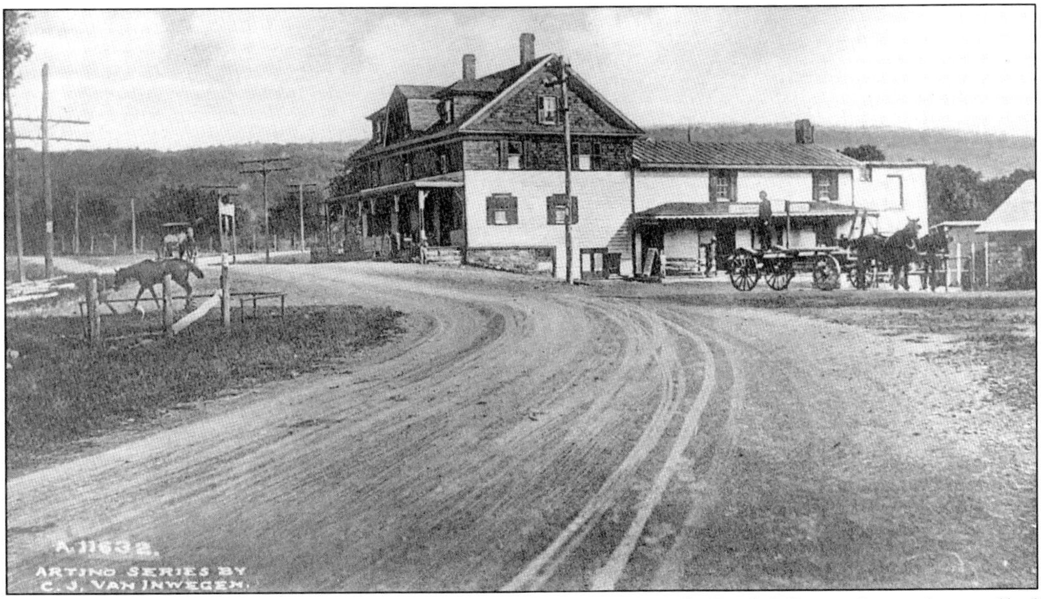

The Huguenot Store and Post Office was located on Peenpack Trail. The early settlers called this area Peenpack, a name derived from the early Protestant refugees of France who settled this area c. 1698. Two of the original families were the Cuddebacks and the Gumaers. (Collection of the Minisink Valley Historical Society.)

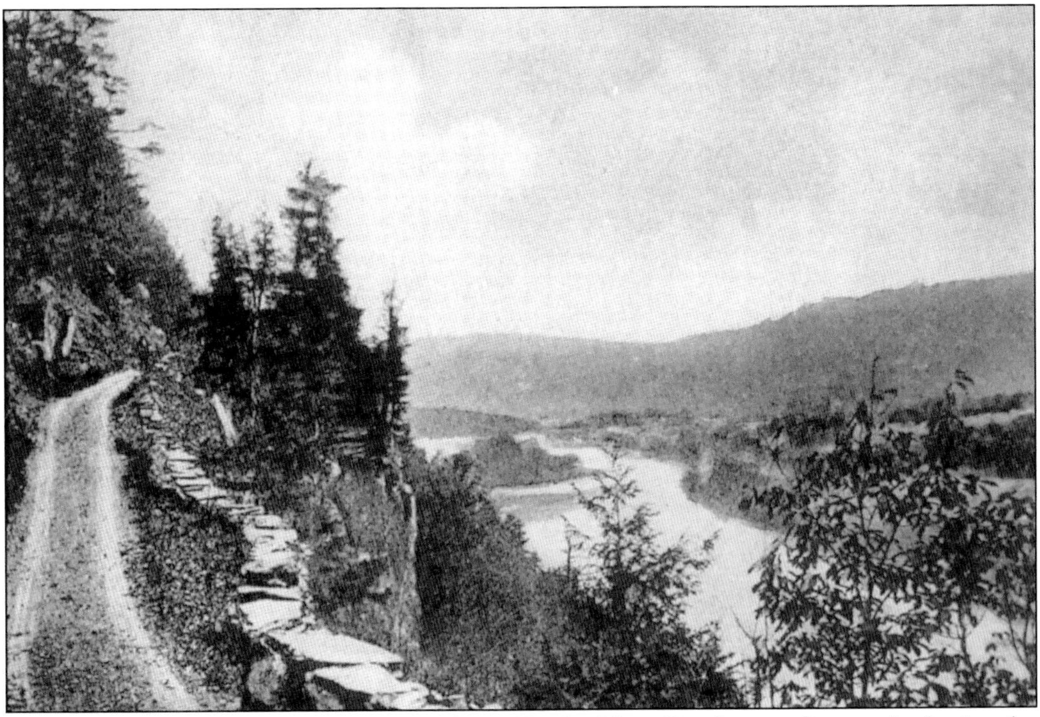

This view looks south to Port Jervis from Hawks Nest Road near Sparrowbush. In the early 1900s, the road was not much more than a towpath. (Collection of the Minisink Valley Historical Society.)

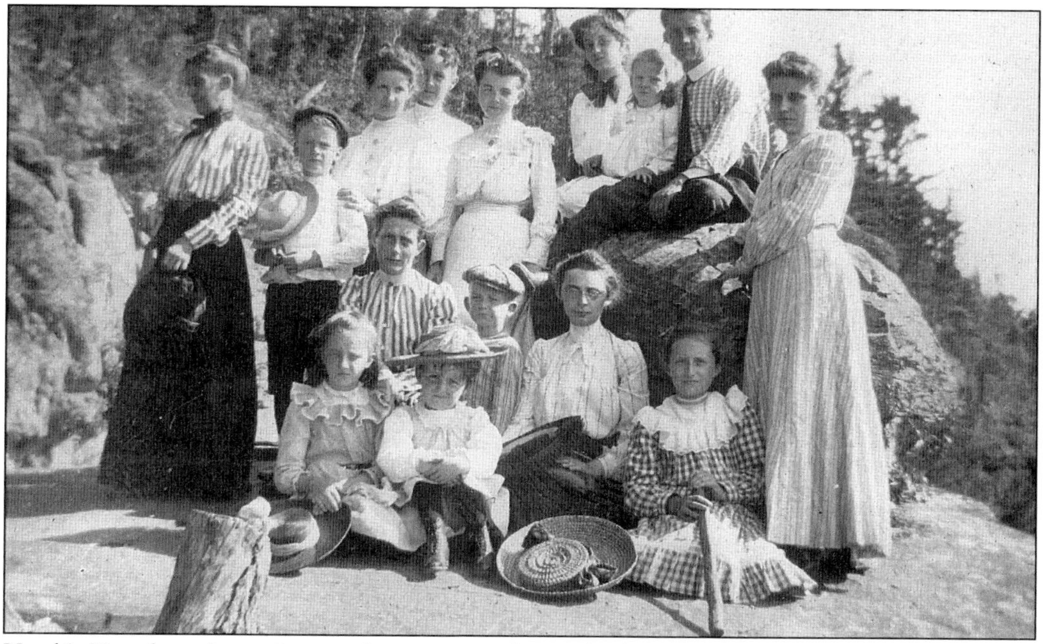

Hawk's Nest has always been a favorite area from which to view the scenic Delaware River. The Peck family enjoys an outing on a summer day. Mary Peck purchased one of the first automobiles from Peter Rutan's Buick Company in 1900. (Collection of the Minisink Valley Historical Society.)

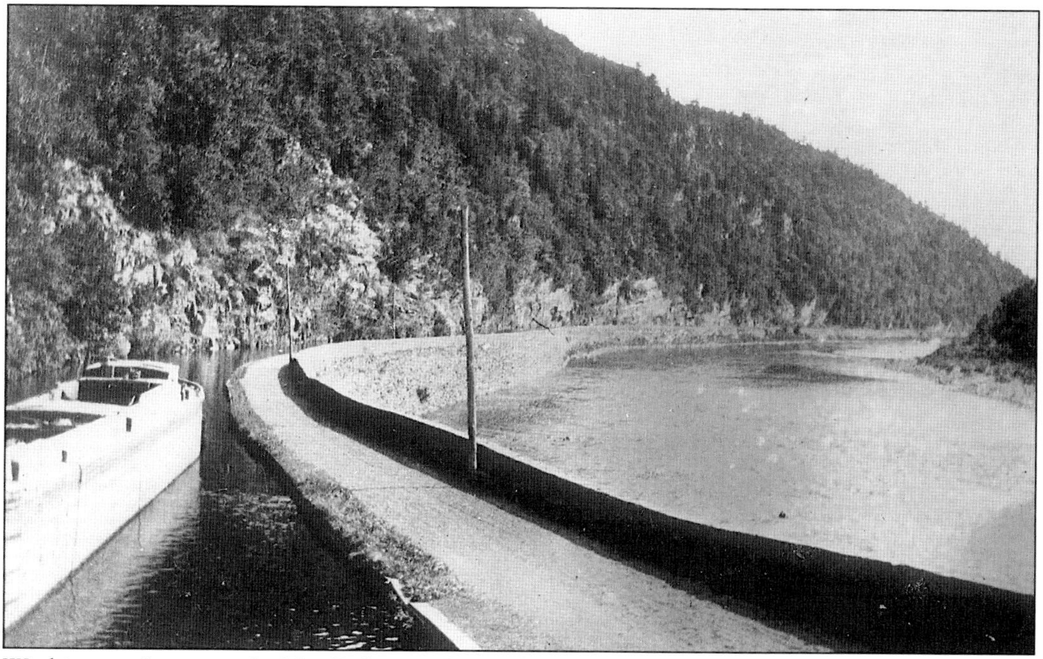

Washington Irving said of the Delaware River, the D & H Canal, and the majestic Hawks Nest, shown in this early photograph, "It would have been famous had it been Europe." (Courtesy of Robbie Smith.)

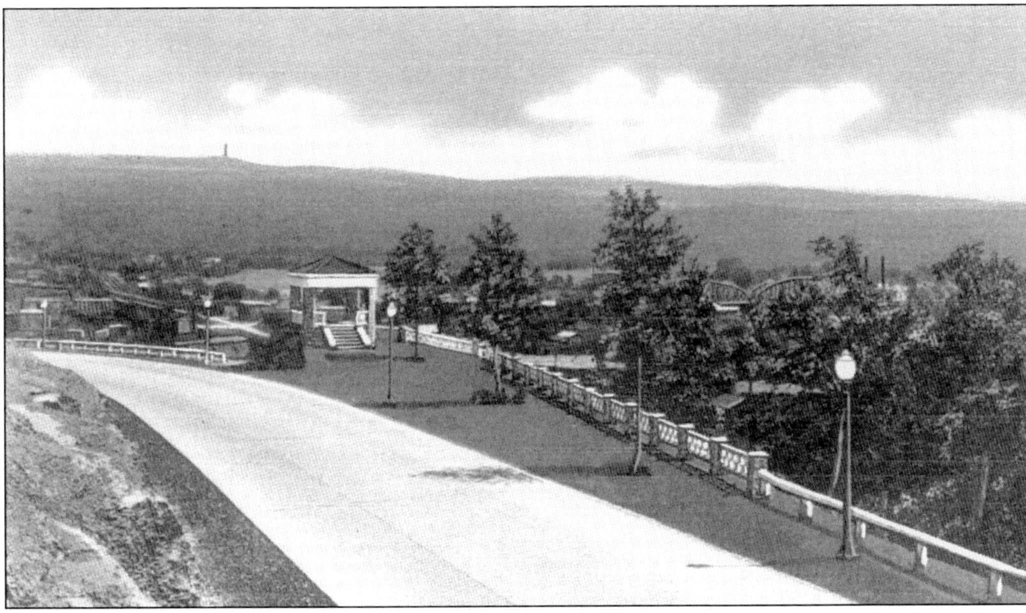

The Route 97 observatory on Park Avenue, erected in the 1930s, gives visitors a scenic view of Port Jervis from its northernmost point. (Courtesy of Matt and Carol Osterberg.)

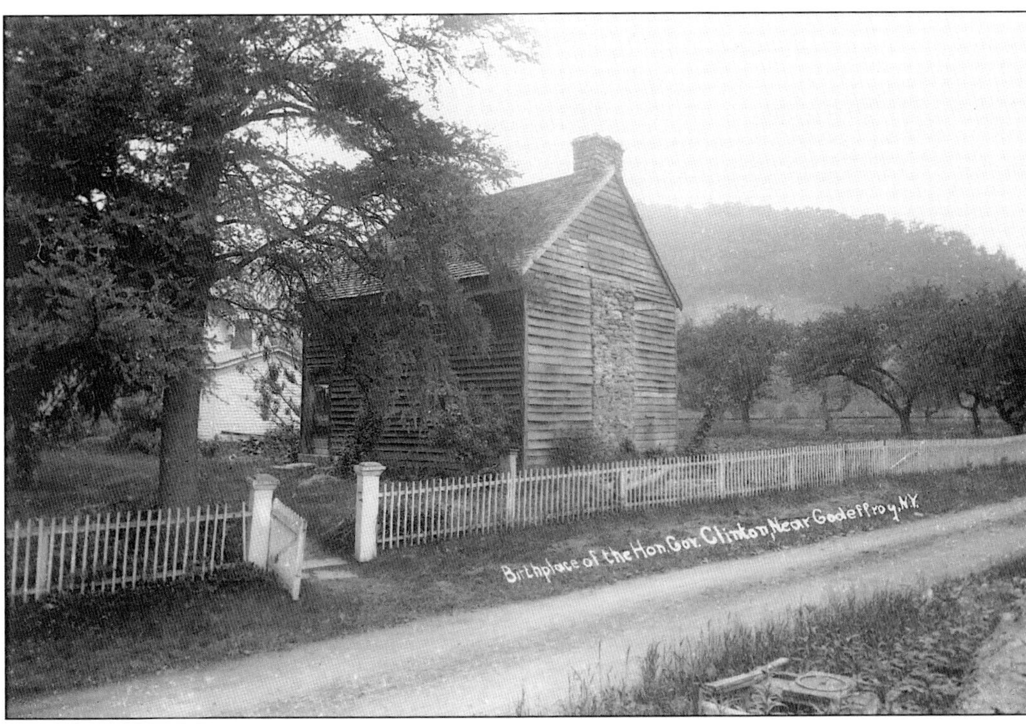

This building on Prospect Hill Road is said to be one of the reputed birthplaces of DeWitt Clinton, once governor of New York and known as the Father of the Erie Canal. He was also instrumental in getting the D & H Canal built in Western Orange County. (Collection of the Minisink Valley Historical Society.)

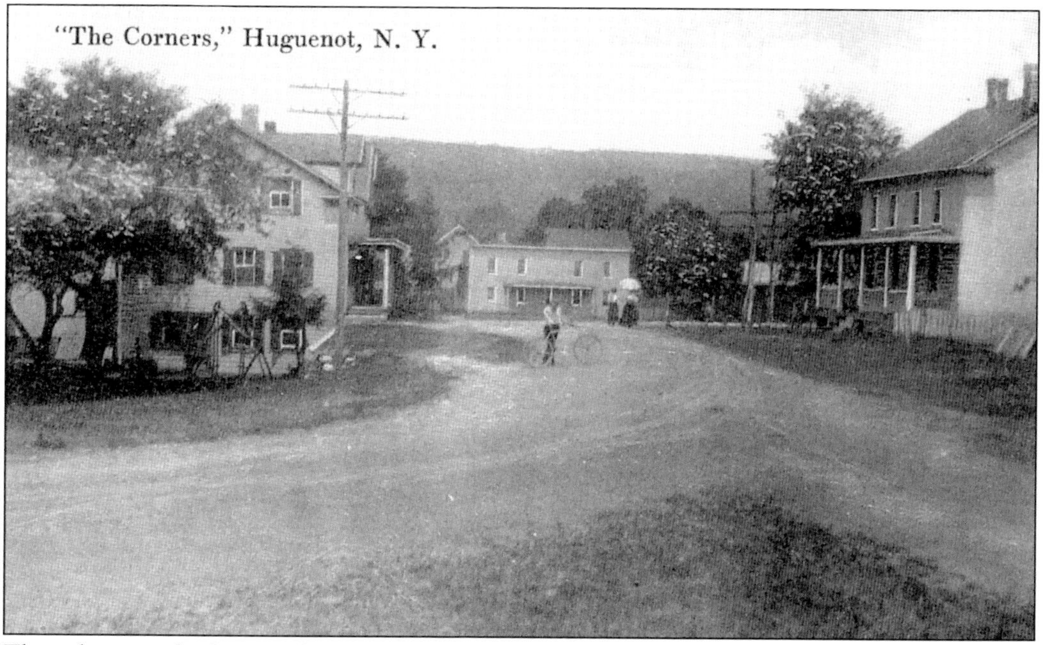

This photograph shows "the Corners" of Huguenot on present-day Route 209. Huguenot was the largest village in the Town of Deerpark for many years. After the construction of the Erie Railroad and the D & H Canal, Port Jervis had a much larger population. (Collection of the Minisink Valley Historical Society.)

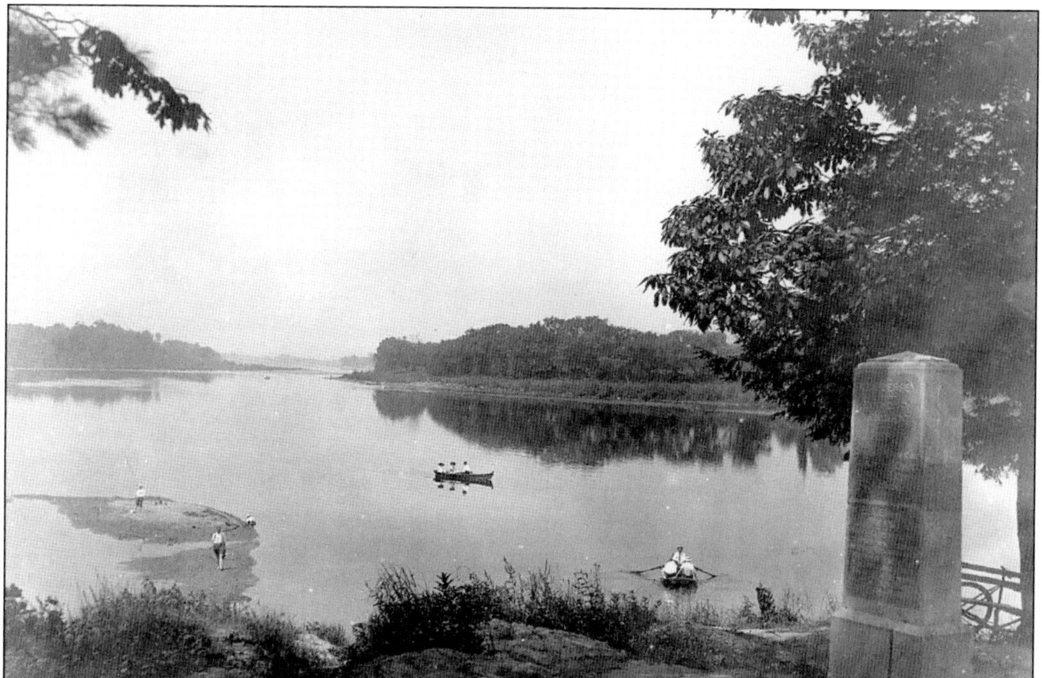

Tri-States Rock sits at the intersection of the Delaware and Neversink Rivers, with boundary lines in New York, New Jersey, and Pennsylvania. (Collection of the Minisink Valley Historical Society.)

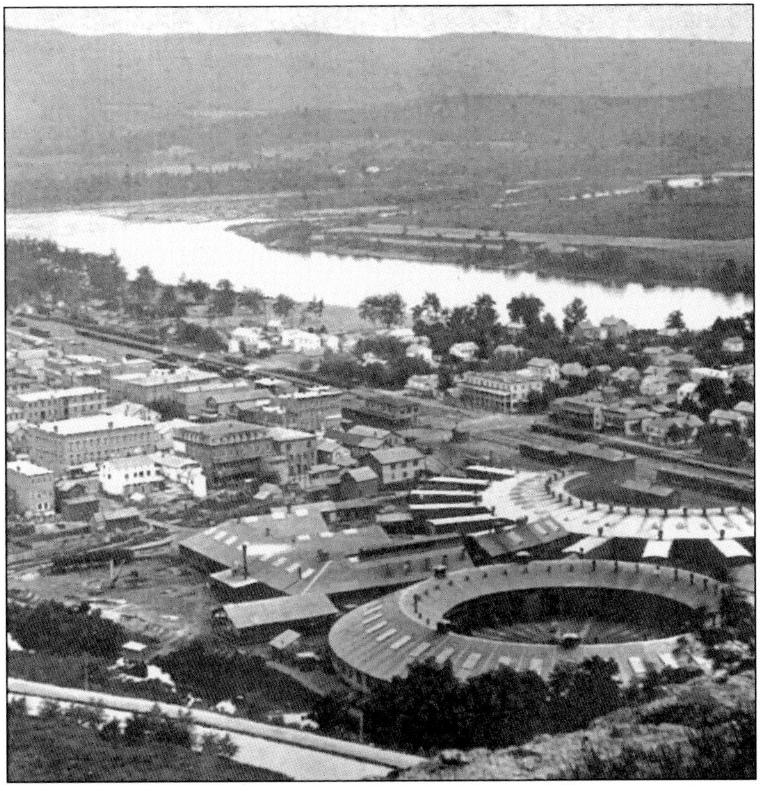

This c. 1880s photograph shows the steam train, roundhouse, and the second turntable, where Burger King is today. One turntable is still used when steam engine excursions come into Port Jervis and is one of the largest operating turntables in the country. (Collection of the Minisink Valley Historical Society.)

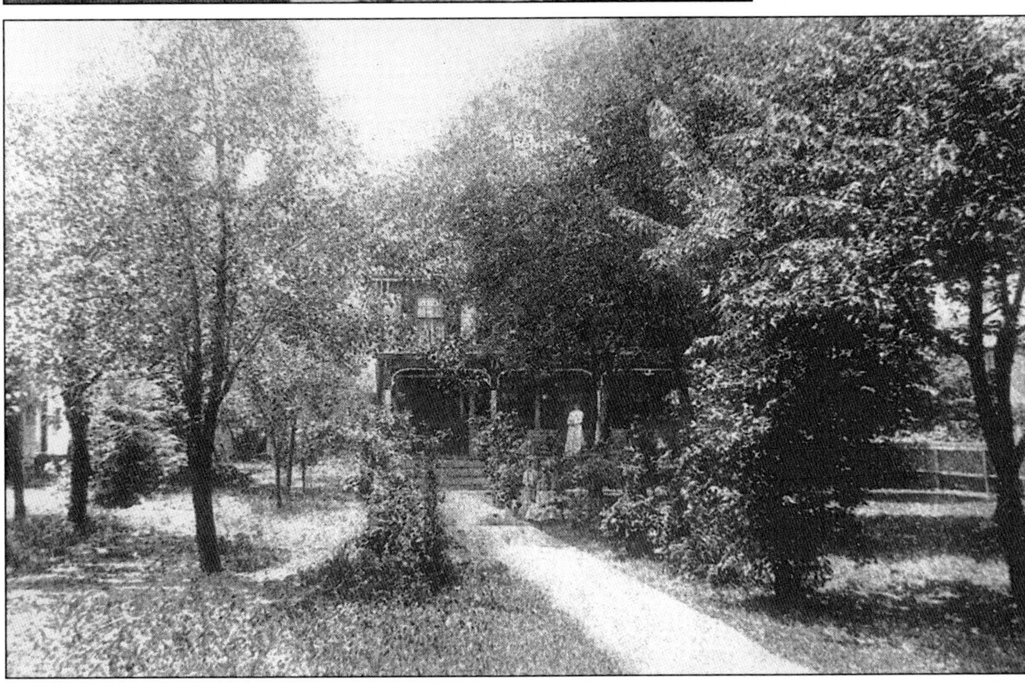

This home on East Main Street was the homestead of Judge William Crane from 1890 to 1901. His brother, author Stephen Crane, visited here from 1891 to 1896. (Collection of the Minisink Valley Historical Society.)

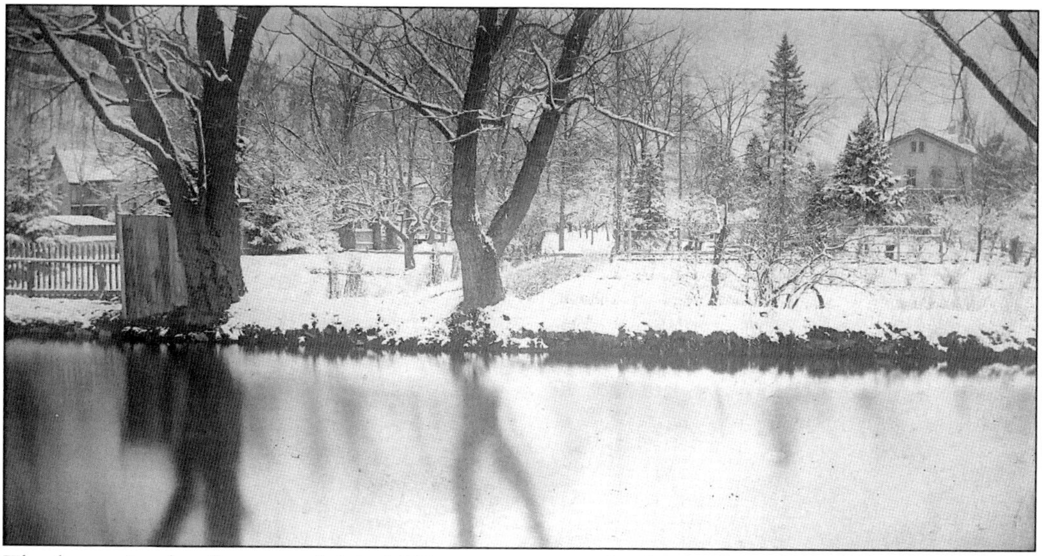

The home in the distance of this 1890s winter scene, looking across the D & H Canal, is at 34 Brooklyn Street. (Courtesy of Robbie Smith.)

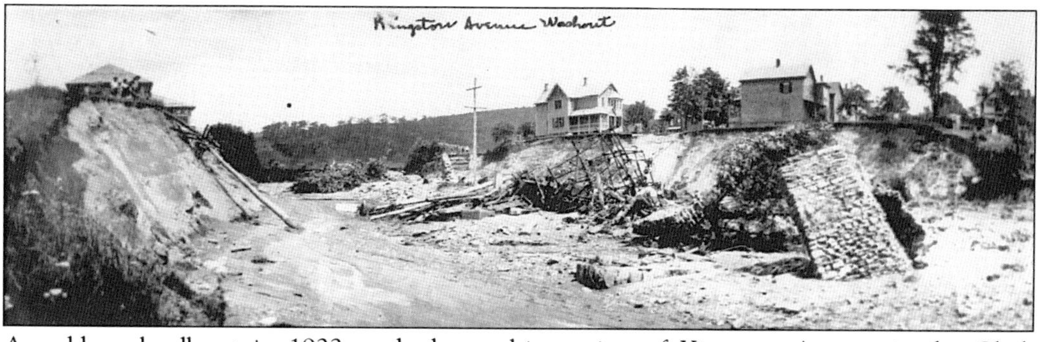

A sudden cloudburst in 1922 washed out this section of Kingston Avenue in the Clark Motors area. The two buildings in this picture are still standing. (Collection of the Minisink Valley Historical Society.)

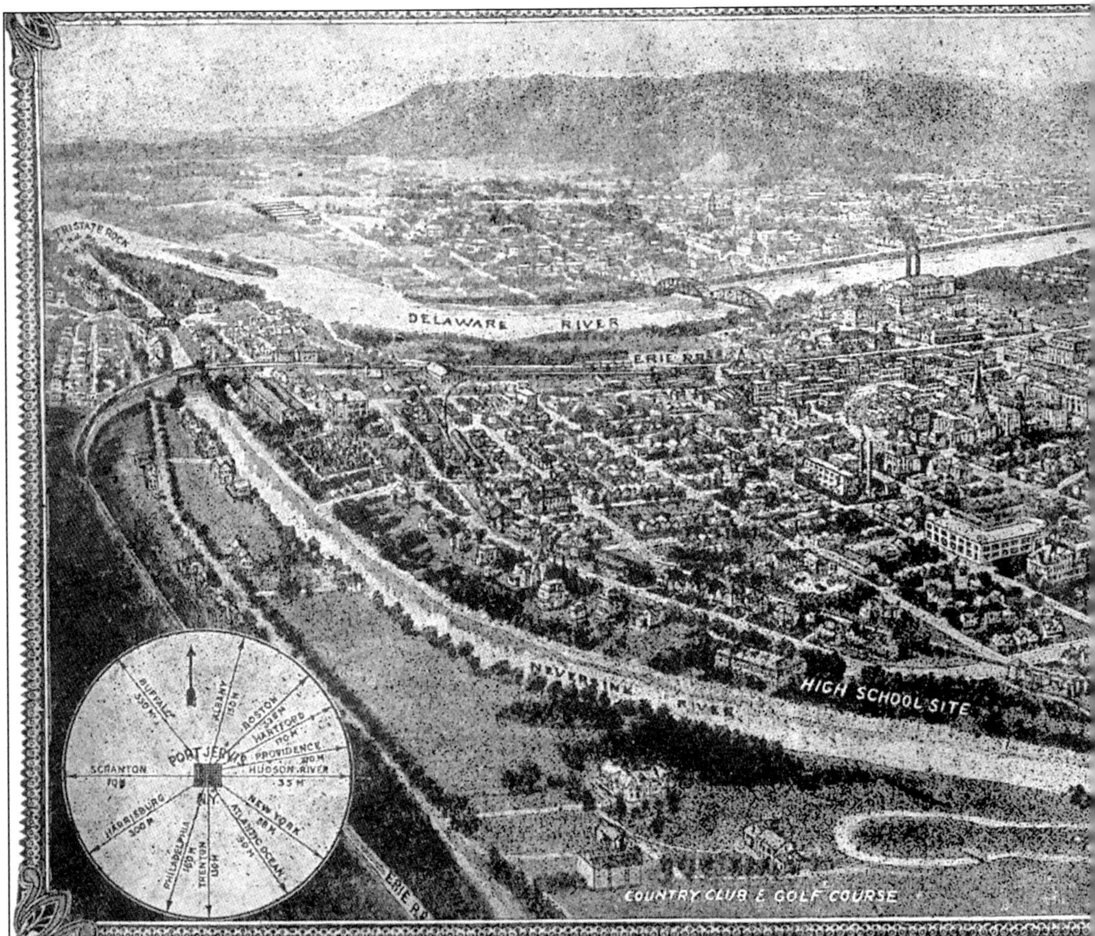

PORT JERVIS,

PORT JERVIS, the picturesque, prosperous and healthful city, is situated at the junction of three states, New York, Pennsylvania and New Jersey. It is also at the confluence of the Delaware and Neversink rivers, where three valleys meet, and these, with Mountain, Lake and Forest Scenery, present a variety of attractions of surpassing interest and beauty, and the recently built "Sky-line Drive" along Point Peter, Mt. William and beyond, affords a succession of splendid panoramic views of the city and its environs.

On the Erie and the N. Y. O. and W. R. Rs., easily accessible to the larger cities, and long known as a R. R. center of importance and activity.

Population 10,000, enterprising and progressive citizens, alive to its civic interests and advancement, educational advantages of the highest order and excellence.

A Modern High School Buildin and equipped for widest range fraternal and religious organiz represented.

Efficient Fire and Police protection.

Light, Heat and Power, W supply fullest and best utilities f

Well managed banks with facility.

Daily and Weekly Newsp with wide circulation.

Many excellent Hotels cate and trading public.

The City is famed as a Su earned popularity is sustained by air and water, superior roads

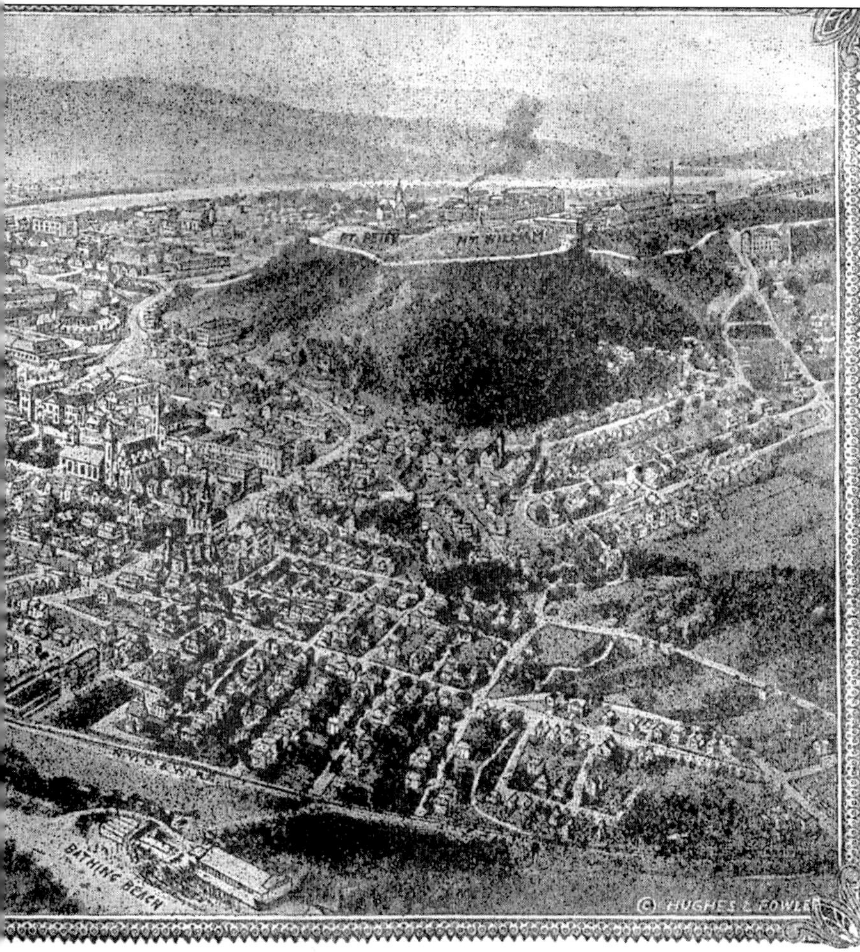

YORK

: constructed
on. Social,
ve and well

ts render safe

as Companies
d public use.
tal and every

onducted and

erous tourists

t and its well
enery, purest
hotels, parks,

bathing beaches, boating, fishing, golf course and country club.

Mercantile houses carry large stocks of newest and best goods in all lines.

Port Jervis is a city of extensive and diversified manufacturing industries, including the Knickerbocker Silver Co., Gillender Bros.—Glass Mfrs., Kattermann & Mitchell Co.—Silk Mills, Mayer Bros.—Cut Glass, Swinton & Co.—Stoves, W. B. Chant & Son—Silk and Fabric Gloves, Chas. Chant—Shirts, Gloves and Ladies' Waists, McCathie Co.—Women's Muslin Underwear, Am. Ignition Co., Marford Silk Co., Inc., Delaware Silk Co., Inc., Hugo S. Adam Co.—Ladies' Undergarments, Sonnenberg Silk Co., Dimex Malt Extract Co., Raymond Gen'l Utility Auto Bodies.

See Port Jervis and share in its countless benefits, advantages and its development.

This is an advertisement from the early 1920s. (Courtesy of Brian Lewis.)

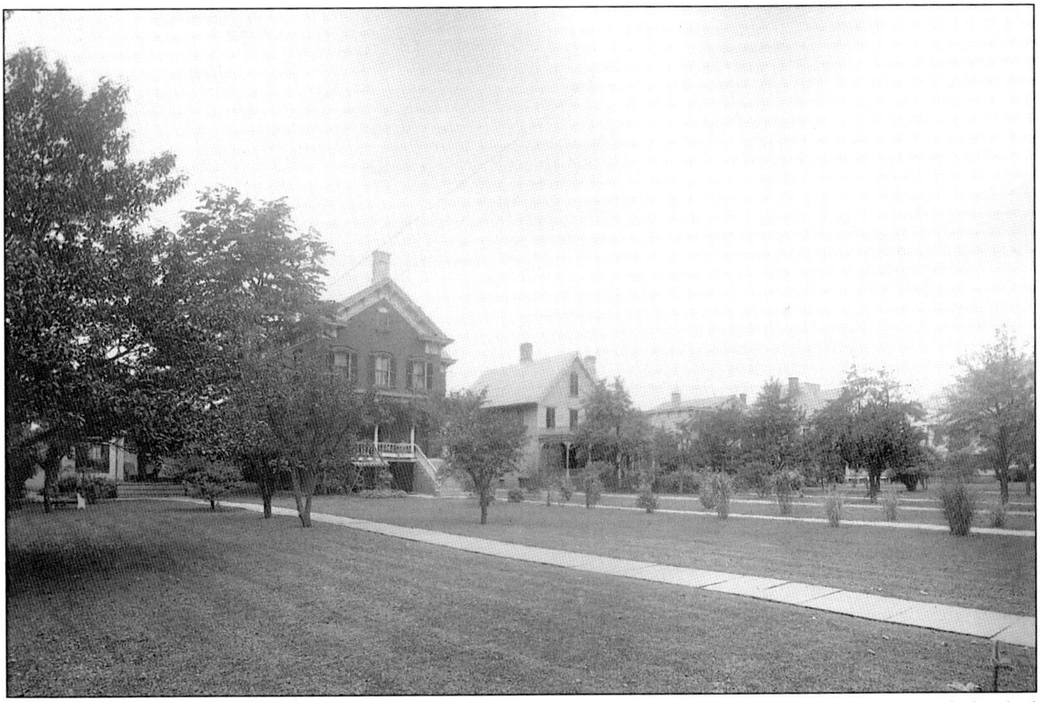

This elegant view of East Main Street shows the beautifully manicured front lawns and shaded trees. (Collection of the Minisink Valley Historical Society.)

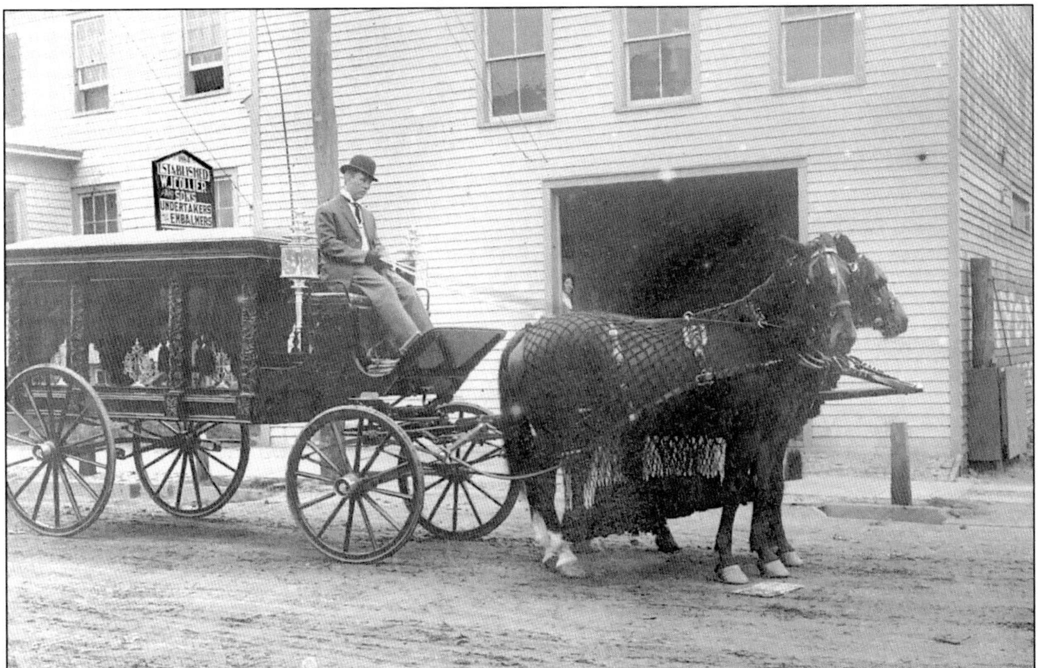

A grand, glass-sided hearse owned by the Collier Funeral Home, which operated in the Acre, was drawn by black horses. The hearse brought many fine citizens to their final resting place. This photograph dates from *c.* 1900. (Courtesy of Dan Dwyer.)